Chronology of World Terrorism, 1901–2001

Chronology of World Terrorism, 1901–2001

HENRY E. MATTOX

McFarland & Company, Inc., Publishers

Jefferson, North Carolina, and London

Library of Congress Cataloguing-in-Publication Data

Mattox, Henry E., 1930–
Chronology of world terrorism, 1901–2001 / Henry E. Mattox.
p.   cm.
Includes bibliographical references and index.

ISBN 0-7864-1992-X (illustrated case binding : 50# alkaline paper) ∞

1. Terrorism — History — Chronology.   I. Title.
HV6431.M379   2004   303.6'25'0904 — dc22   2004012138

British Library cataloguing data are available

Cover art © 2004 Brand X Images

Manufactured in the United States of America

*McFarland & Company, Inc., Publishers
Box 611, Jefferson, North Carolina 28640
www.mcfarlandpub.com*

To the members, past and present,
of the Foreign Service of the United States.
It was an honor to serve with them.

Contents

Preface

This book provides an account of terrorist actions, incidents, outrages, victories, and defeats over a century of recent history, ending for purposes of this narrative on September 11, 2001. The phenomenon of terror as a political tactic to sow fear and dismay in an enemy is nothing new, but it has come to be at this writing not only a known factor in political and national rivalries but a fact of daily life for much of the world's population. Terrorism on increasingly lethal levels has become almost commonplace to many, many people, if not at first hand, then certainly as a featured item of daily information in the news media and at least occasional worry on a personal level. This may be particularly true in the United States. In the first year after the September 11, 2001, attack on New York and Washington, the U. S. government spent the astonishing total of $37 billion on counterterrorism measures. Clearly the danger caught the attention of Americans and their governmental leaders in a fashion never previously experienced.

As a U. S. Foreign Service officer from 1957 to retirement in 1980, with the great majority of those years spent abroad, I had occasion fairly often to be concerned about terrorist dangers. Several brushes with that unpleasant fact of modern-day life came my way. None was very close, fortunately for me, but that exposure in retrospect nonetheless has served to give focus for my undertaking this study.

I have set out to track down a year-by-year accounting of terrorist incidents, beginning with September 1901— the assassination of an American president — and concluding with September 2001— 9/11, the suicide attack on the Twin Towers in New York and on the Pentagon in Washington, D.C. The chronology covers on a necessarily selective basis the well-known incidents and tragedies, very many of which occurred in the last three decades or so of the century. But it addresses obscure or forgotten incidents, as well, so long as the occurrence meets a reasonable denotation of what constituted a terrorist action and illustrates to some extent the norms for the dread phenomenon as the years and decades went by.

It is on the unstable, disputed ground of definitions that the study begins. Then comes the extended twentieth-century chronology of terroristic incidents. A complete listing of every known terrorist incident no matter how obscure or relatively insignificant today simply is not possible — or at least not feasible, given the truly enormous number of such occurrences during the 1900s. Even a reasonably complete listing of every terrorist attack would require hundreds upon hundreds of pages, and very small type at that. This is so not only for the last third of the century, when the number of hijackings and bombings, including those effected by terrorists intent upon suicide, rose exponentially to astonishing figures. The enormity of the numbers involved is almost equally true for earlier assassination attempts by, for example, Russian revolutionaries and European and American anarchists, as well as for the ravages of extensive state-sponsored terrorism, especially in the Soviet Union and Nazi Germany.

Although the forms that terrorism took and their perpetrators changed through the years, the numbers of incidents involved were enormous. The following examples illustrate that fact:

— In the period 1901 to 1909, in Russia alone, at least 1,500 Tsarist government officials fell to assassins.
— With its accession to power in Russia in 1918, the Communist party set forth on campaigns of state terrorism that led to the deaths of millions of people.
— In 1921, one typical weekly summary report of violence in Ireland prepared in London chronicled twenty-six attacks on Crown forces, resulting in eighteen dead and ten wounded.
— In one night in November 1938, the infamous *Kristallnacht, the* Nazis in Germany and Austria destroyed 7,500 Jewish-owned shops and torched 190 synagogues.
— Palestine and the area that soon was to be Israel, beginning in 1948 saw violence become rampant. Deadly incidents took place almost every day, both of the two sides furthering the violence.
— An official 1954 annual Kenyan police report noted that Mau Mau murders of tribesmen thought loyal to Britain took place virtually every day.

And the immediately above partial, limited account of some of the fright spread by terrorism over the past 100 years only brings the litany about half way through the twentieth century, to the 1950's. The world had another fifty years to go of ever-increasing violence, destruction, and death. The compendium herein therefore is necessarily limited in numbers, chosen on a selective basis as representative, decade by decade, of the terrorist threat.

The study ends with an account of nineteen Islamic suicide hijackers taking over four commercial airliners and their success in crashing into three of four intended targets in the United States, killing more than 2,800 persons in one day. It was the worst single terrorist act — given the definition of terrorism set forth herein — ever, anywhere.

Following the above sections, the heart of the study, comes a discussion of how effective the terrorist movements of one sort and another have been over the past century. There I touch upon apparent trends in methods and weapons and reach a judgment about the efficacy of terrorist tactics in light of the 100-year record in these pages. Then this study pulls together for the interested reader an English-language bibliography of sources in the field, including many of those on the ubiquitous, frequently changing World Wide Web.

In the first appendix, the reader will find a long but far-from-exhaustive list of terrorist groups operating during the period under review, along with their dates of inception and the areas in which they were (or are) active. Finally, I include the texts of international agreements and a timely United Nations resolution bearing on the subject of terrorism.

Chapel Hill, N.C., USA
Summer 2004

Defining Terrorism

How do we define "terrorism" as we use the word in the modern-day sense?

On one level the answer is simple. Everyone familiar with the English language knows that the word "terror" signifies dread, extreme fear or apprehension, horror, shock. Terrorism, then, is the state of inducing or being subjected to conditions of fear and dread. There are, of course, words with parallel meanings in other languages, many of which are spelled and pronounced in a fashion similar to the English. The concept is the same and word is spelled the same in Latin. *Terreur* in French is another example, as is *terror* in Spanish. The German word for terror is *Schrecken*, but the word in that language for terrorism is *Terrorismus*. Persians long used the word *terorizm* (or *irhab*).

Paradoxically, it does not follow that "terror" and "terrorism" in the most commonly used sense are equally well conceptualized or understood, at least not in research or academic terms. The meaning in the twentieth century terms addressed in this study perhaps somewhat surprisingly is debatable among different observers and experts.

Terrorism has been defined by the noted scholar Walter Laqueur[1] as the substate application of violence or threatened violence intended to sow panic in a society, to weaken or even overthrow the incumbents, and to bring about political change.

The FBI in the United States holds that terrorism is the unlawful use of force or violence against persons or property to intimidate or coerce a government or the civilian population in furtherance of political or social objectives.

Another way to approach the definition is to note that terrorism is the application of extraordinary violence for the above purposes, that is, by violating the rules of war designed to distinguish combatants—soldiers and policemen—from non-combatants—civilians.

We can also approach an understanding of the term by noting that terrorism is neither wholly political nor criminal, but rather the criminal implementation of political ideals. Even more precisely, terrorism can be called the use of criminal means to influence political programs.

Virtually all efforts at definition of the word on the international scene, however, involve conceptual difficulties, as well as problems of syntax. As an almost startling illustration of how diversely the word is defined, a voluminous 1983 study (revised in 1988) by Alex P. Schmid and Albert J. Jongman cites more than 100 different meanings of terrorism.[2] This multitude of meanings they obtained from surveys of academic specialists in the field. (Several of these will be set forth below.) From the mass of information they collected we can begin to arrive at some commonalities in definitions, as varied as they are in detail.

Schmid and Jongman isolate *three elements* that appear in a majority of those various 100-plus formulations of terrorism. These are:

1) violence and force,
2) political aims, and
3) an emphasis on engendering fear.

They identify no fewer than nineteen additional factors somewhat less significant than those above in this set of definitions. Among these lesser factors are the conveyance of a threat, psychological effects, victim-target differentiation, and the purposive nature of the action.

Schmid in the cited work sets forth his own long, comprehensive definition of terrorism, one that runs to more than 200 words. He apparently intends for it to include the maximum number of pertinent concepts as a means to test theories and language in the academic community. But clearly Schmid's definition is too cumbersome to impart much general understanding, certainly not in a practical research and policy-making setting.[3]

For most nonacademic, operational purposes, it repays an attempt to address the question more concisely and less theoretically than Schmid: Is it the "deliberate and systematic use (or threatened use) of unsanctioned violence to further political objectives through intimidation or coercion of target groups that normally extend beyond the immediate victims."?[4] Or does the "use of organized intimidation"[5] serve equally well to define the phenomenon? Another of the significant factors suggested — that terrorism is no more than a tactical combat method — raises the highly debatable concept of a justified means to an end in a revolutionary struggle.

These various questions and varied efforts at definition raise valid points that might well need to be addressed. But one point seems clear: terrorism has no generally accepted, all-encompassing definition. What different observers term "terrorism" falls within different conventions, and none of these concepts are set in stone by facts or precedents. As one commentator in the field notes, "[Terrorism] is not something that is automatically 'given' by facts or by history."[6] No single circumstance causes or explains terrorism to the satisfaction of those who study the phenomenon. The definitions essayed above are examples of the range, from long to fairly short, of senses that attach to the word and idea.

There is a good reason for this lack of precision. Partly it is due to changing terrorist methods over time, especially in terms of targets, but to a considerable extent terrorism often lies in the eye of the beholder. One man's terrorism can be another's revolutionary violence and yet another's tactical move in a war of national liberation; there are some who would view the same lethal act as no less than murder. To some, terrorists fill the role of freedom fighters, exemplifying the belief that the end justifies the means. Observers sometimes equate guerrilla warfare with terrorism, as they do hijackings, kidnappings, assassinations, riots, military revolts, civil wars, and virtually all other instances of more or less focused destructiveness.

Political violence and terrorism have historical antecedents dating at least to Biblical times. The records of those who have gone before us frequently recount the assassination of tyrants and the not-so tyrannical. As early as the time of Christ, Jewish extremists called the *Sicarii* actively carried out assassinations. A Muslim sect in the eleventh century, the Order of the Assassins, killed numerous enemies, both Muslim and Christian. The Thugees in India followed their macabre practices for ceremonial reasons.

It was not until the latter part of the eighteenth century that terrorism as a concept generally recognized in modern times came to the fore. The French Revolution of 1789 degenerated within a few years into a Reign of Terror in which the revolutionary government under Robespierre ruled France largely by fear. Thousands of citizens, chosen in many instances almost arbitrarily, lost their lives under the heavy blade of the guillotine. The aim: intimidation by the state of the governed, so as to rule more firmly. The revolutionary regime's policy of terrorism reached a peak in 1793 and continued thereafter for some sixteen months, at the end of which time Robespierre himself went to his death by the uniquely French killing machine. The madness had run its course. Ever since that time, "terror" in a political context has been understood not as a remote historical idea or a valueless concept, but as a fearful fact of modern-day life.

Acts of violence do not always equate with generally accepted meanings of terrorism, depending on circumstances. All-encompassing or broad definitions of terrorism thus in many instances describe much but clarify little. They are complex, as indicated above, and even then not fully accurate for general purposes. The literature on terrorism abounds with definitions that render complicated the meaning of these attempts historically undertaken to destroy so as, presumably, to build. Still searching for a workable definition, two clearer-than-average and reasonably focused efforts follow:

The resort to violence for political ends by non-governmental actors in breach of accepted codes of behavior regarding the expression of dissatisfaction with, dissent from, or opposition to political goals endorsed by the legitimate government authorities of the state.

Almost all illegal acts of violence committed for political purposes by clandestine groups.[7]

The first of these definitions has the advantage of an apparent comprehensiveness; the second, the usefulness of consolidation and brevity. Nevertheless, neither seems totally adequate for general purposes. Further refinement is needed before the observer can get, finally, a comprehensive grip on what terrorism means, as the word has been used so often, even early in our twenty-first century.

As an aid to reaching some resolution on the meaning, among the most authoritative and reasoned definitions of terrorism may well be the one set forth by the U. S. Department of State. Employed by the U. S. government since 1983 for statistical and analytical purposes, the following is the definition as spelled out in federal law:

> The term "terrorism" means premeditated, politically motivated violence perpetrated against non-combatant targets by subnational groups or clandestine agents, usually intended to influence an audience [Title 22 of the USC, Sect. 2656f(d)].[8]

Certain of the key concepts are included: The violence, mounted secretly, is premeditated and intended for political gain; it is directed against secondary targets—civilians, that is; and the media implicitly has considerable importance to the terrorists.

(Note: The U. S. government interprets the word "noncombatant" to include unarmed military personnel not on duty at the time of the terrorist incident.)

In few if any definitions encountered in the literature, including the one immediately above, does an organized armed attack of civilians on the on-duty military forces of a nation fall into the terrorism category. Rather, that kind of destructiveness would logically come under the rubric of guerrilla warfare, which requires yet another category of meanings. An example would be Fidel Castro's campaign in Cuba leading to the collapse of the Batista government at the end of 1958: not terrorism, but rather guerrilla warfare. A variation on that distinction — the 1916 Easter Rebellion in Ireland — could, however, be equated with terrorism, especially in light of the historical record, in that the Rebellion was the beginning and foundation of decades of terrorist violence to follow involving civilians. Revolts, especially by the military, and the overthrow of national leadership typically are not terrorism. A clear example of this type of violence was the murder arranged by Abdullah al-Wazir in 1948 of the ruler of Yemen, who in turn was overthrown himself four weeks later and hanged: revolution and deadly palace politics, but not terrorism.

Patently an assault — even under conditions contrary to the usual usages of intercourse between nations — of regular armed forces on the military establishment of another nation would fall outside the meaning of terrorism. An example is the attack without benefit of a declaration of war by Japanese carrier planes on the U. S. naval base at Pearl Harbor in December 1941: surprise attack and the launching of a major war, but not terrorism.

Arguably (and there are those who so argue), wartime bombing or shelling of essentially civilian targets falls into a grouping of terrorism. Examples cited are the Japanese army's massacres in Nanking, China, at the end of 1937. Others are the intensive German bombing raids on Rotterdam and then London during the Second World War, followed by mass British and American air raids on numerous cities in Germany. The ultimate in such attacks was the American use in 1945 of atomic bombs against two cities in Japan. There is a difference, however, between these military actions and terrorism as usually defined: These military powers intended their ac-

tions partly to instill terror among the civilian populace, but the actions basically were undertaken as means to affect a military outcome in situations of all-out war. Even such horrific episodes as the Allied firebomb raids in Germany and American firebombing of Tokyo were designed to defeat militarily a dangerous, armed enemy and to bring on the end the state of war between nation states. They were not an effort to instill terror and thereby effect political change. "War is hell," in Gen. W. T. Sherman's words, and "a continuation of political relations … by other means," according to Karl von Clausewitz. Waging war is not carrying out terrorism, however.

A variety of terrorism that does bear upon political relations is that which is sponsored or backed by a state. This kind of terrorist activity takes two general forms. If the terror-inspiring actions are mounted openly or as a result of official decisions or policies, they equate in a general sense with the French Reign of Terror of the late eighteenth century. Measures of this sort based on official sanction are intended to cow (above all, civilian) subjects of a political system into submission. Prime examples of this kind of twentieth century state terrorism are the actions of the Soviet regime's court and police system in Russia in the 1920's and 1930's and those of Nazi Germany during the latter decade.

Additionally, state terrorism can take the form of surreptitious measures carrying secret official sanction. This type is not too difficult to define, but poses a knotty problem to deal with in research terms. Repressive measures involving violence undertaken by a given government do not always or automatically qualify as terrorism, and in any event they often defy proof. An official agency will mount abuses against a regime's enemies, foreign and domestic, at a remove from official chains of command — this often in mysterious circumstances of behind-the-scenes machinations. Thus, evidence of official involvement at any level often is hard to come by, even many years later. An example of state terrorism almost certainly is the 1914 assassination of Archduke Franz Ferdinand by an agent with no official capacity, an expendable young zealot who was recruited by a secret Serbian organization with police or intelligence officials as members. The whole incident, fraught with significance, was deniable by Serbian authorities and the assassin kept his mouth shut. In order to give an accounting of such happenings and to put them in historical perspective, it seems preferable, at least in this survey, to treat these circumstances not as some separate category of officially sponsored terrorist activity, but rather to focus on the happening at the agent level, where information is more likely to be available. Reliable other data often simply are not to be found.

This study will not address a category of terroristic tactics with yet another meaning, one based on racial or ethnic hatreds. The campaigns of intimidation carried out by the Ku Klux Klan in the southern part of the United States from the latter part of the nineteenth century well into the twentieth without doubt qualify as frightful actions. Those actions lack, at least in the twentieth century, however, the central element of political motivation. Essentially such actions did not have either a political rationale or a supposed justification based on ideas of reform. Similarly, the repressive policies of the South African government during most of the 1900's were lamentable but were founded on social and ethnic antagonisms. Aside from being state sponsored, South Africa's policies cannot be shown to have been based essentially on political grounds, and therefore not terrorism in the sense used here.

One further special case of a form of terror must be mentioned here: Nazi Ger-many from the early 1930's to the mid-1940's experienced itself and inflicted upon Europe a system of mass annihilation of human beings that approached national madness. Germany under Hitler, aided all too often by its minions and allies, launched an organized program of sadistic mass murder that almost defies belief in this modern era. Almost, but not quite. A special kind of extreme wholesale horror taken to its ultimate — the "Final Solution" — resulted in the deliberate killing of six million European Jews and hundreds upon hundreds of thousands of Eastern European civilians: the Holocaust. The prime motivations for this secret policy and these actions were what has come in later years to be called "ethnic cleansing" and a move at least partially motivated to, in effect, empty out Eastern Europe for German colonization. These two factors, then, were a combination of "racial" hatred and a basically economic rationale. "Terrorism" by definition here does not encompass such pointless— in political terms— horror.

Finally, the actions of a lone extremist or an extremist acting alone and out to make a name for himself or herself, or motivated by unfathomable impulses, do not logically belong in an account of international terrorism. Two failed attempts in California during February 1975 on the life of U. S. President Gerald Ford are cases in point. A Manson murder cultist, Lynette "Squeaky" Fromm, and a counter-culture leftist (and sometime FBI informant) named Sara Jane Moore, in unrelated incidents, tried to shoot the president. Fromm did not get a shot off, due to the alertness of a Secret Service agent, and Moore missed because a bystander grabbed her arm. One person was wounded. After trials, each was sentenced to life in a federal prison.

Neither of President Ford's assailants was considered to have a rational motivation for killing him. The incidents thus, while bearing a resemblance to historical acts of politically inspired terrorism, fall short of meeting the definition in the several senses explored here.

The Department of State definition of terrorism above, while slightly wordy in the manner of bureaucratic language, nevertheless pointedly includes violence (of course), political aims, and the planned nature of the use of force. Additionally, it incorporates the usual discrepancy between targeted victims and the actual perceived enemy. A considerably lengthier definition, one that tries to include a range of modern terror tactics, is set forth in a work by Stephen E. Atkins.[9] Terrorism (using slightly abbreviated language here) seeks to:

1. Instill fear in the population.
2. Polarize public opinion.
3. Gain publicity by interviews and manifestos.
4. Provoke government overreaction.
5. Spread false information to put opponents on the defensive.
6. Attract converts and support.
7. Coerce the media through assaults.
8. Divert public attention by bombing their way onto the front page.
9. Use the media to excite public opinion against the government and to communicate with comrades in other countries.
10. Bolster group morale through dynamic acts.
11. Gain a Robin Hood image.
12. Obtain information on counterterrorist strategies and future targets.
13. Exploit the media to build an image of being above the law.

This imposing list serves the special purpose of pointing up as a final essential element of terrorism how very important the news media and public opinion were to most twentieth century terrorists, especially in the latter part of the century. Clearly media coverage of terrorist campaigns can make or break such activities—or alternatively, the political system under attack. Publicity for their cause constitutes a basic, necessary element of the majority of terrorists' purposes in the twentieth century. This definitional element therefore buttresses the argument that certain horrific instances of the use of terror tactics—the Holocaust being an example—must be ruled out of consideration generally in this context.

Curiously, we do not often find the factor of fanaticism explicitly included in definitions as one would logically expect in a full development of the concept. Perhaps it is subsumed in virtually all developments of the concept of terrorism. But Walter Laqueur exceptionally discusses the topic at length in his 2001 study, *The New Terrorism*; this valuable work has as its subtitle, *Fanaticism and the Arms of Mass Destruction*.[10] At the active levels of involvement, extreme devotion to a cause, whatever that cause might be, clearly constitutes a precondition to the deadly and dangerous actions, routinely involving killing fellow human beings and entailing property destruction, that terrorists undertake. Committing terrorist acts is not for the faint of heart nor is it suitable for those only mildly convinced of their movement's righteousness.

One definition from an official source stands out for its conciseness, if nothing else. In testimony before the Congress a Department of State official presented what comes close to being a model of brevity for the ages (other than the special case of a dictionary entry) by defining terrorism as "*politically motivated attacks on non-combatant targets.*" [11] That short, to-the-point statement serves well as a bare-bones defining concept of international terrorism, with a very few modifications introduced as needed during our consideration of the phenomenon in this study. Note that it appropriately does not include guerrilla warfare, nor wars of national liberation, nor armed insurrections. Nor does it usually include criminal acts such as bank robberies even though emerging terrorist groups sometimes have undertaken such depredations. Slightly amplified for this study, this brief definition would, however, include politically motivated assassinations and assassination attempts, beginning in the following pages with the shooting in 1901 of a U. S. president as a political statement by a reputed anarchist. It also includes hijackings, notably with the first wave of such airline incidents in the 1960s, continuing with ship hijackings, and ending for the purposes herein with the horrendous suicide airline hijacking assault on New York's World Trade Center in September 2001.

Picking and choosing from and building upon these various meanings, some set forth at length, and benefiting from the brevity of the formulation immediately above, we can state our working definition of twentieth century terrorism as:

Politically motivated attacks, including assassinations and hijackings, usually inflicted on civilian targets.

We can note well here that the expression encountered on occasion in the literature — "political terrorism" — seems clearly to be a redundant phrase: Modern terrorism is by its very nature politically moti-vated, even in instances, as in recent years, where a religious impulse can be ascribed partially to a terrorist act. Fundamentally, the political aims of a terrorist group predominate in every instance yet known in the literature on the subject since the 1789 era.

NOTES

(Full citations to books below and noted in following chapters may be found in the bibliography.)

1. See Walter Laqueur, "Postmodern Terrorism: New Rules for an Old Game," *Foreign Affairs,* September/October 1996; *A History of Terrorism* (2001).
2. Schmid and Jongman, *Political Terrorism* ; and Boaz Ganor, "Defining Terrorism," www.ict. org.il/articles/definition.htm/.
3. See Schmid and Jongman, *Political Terrorism,* 1-2.
4. Kenneth A. Duncan, "Terrorism," *Encyclopedia of U. S. Foreign Policy,* vol. 4 (Oxford, Oxford Univ. Press, 1997), 186.
5. *The Oxford Essential Dictionary* (New York, Berkley Books, 1998), 618.
6. See Fred Halliday, *Islam and the Myth of Confrontation.*
7. Sobel, *Political Terrorism,* 3.
8. Cited in Ganor, "Defining Terrorism."
9. Atkins, *Terrorism: A Reference Handbook,* 19-20.
10. Laqueur, *A History of Terrorism,* 85.
11. The official concerned was Ned Walker, a senior career diplomat with long experience in the Middle East. His testimony may be found in the "Report of the Committee on Foreign Affairs," House of Representatives, 101st Cong., 1st sess., p. 66.
See also the formulation by columnist Charles Krauthammer, cited in Anzovin, ed., *Terrorism,* 98.

1901–1909

Russia's Social Revolutionaries were the dominant source of terrorism early in the new century, not being brought under control by the Tsarist police for several years.

1901

Sep. 6. Buffalo, NY, USA. President William McKinley, while standing in a receiving line at the Pan American Exhibition, shortly after 4:00 p.m. was shot twice at close range by an avowed Anarchist, Leon Czolgosz. The conservative leader of the Republican Party died eight days later; his office passed to Vice President Theodore Roosevelt. The assassin was convicted in a speedy trial and sentenced to death. On October 29, 1901, he went unrepentant to the electric chair. (In 1890, that means of execution had replaced hanging in New York state.)

It was not clear that Czolgosz, a twenty-eight-year-old U. S.-born sometime factory worker, was affiliated with any Anarchist group, but he read widely in the movement's literature. An Anarchist's assassination of King Umberto I of Italy the previous year made a deep impression on him. (That assassin, Gaetano Bresci, may have had ties with Italian Anarchists based in New Jersey in the United State.) He was inspired also by the rhetoric of the American Anarchist, Emma Goldman, with whom he met briefly twice in 1901. (She bore no responsibility for the assassination, but was jailed on suspicion for a time and in 1919 deported to Russia.) Czolgosz proclaimed he killed the president because he was "an enemy of the working people."

The U. S. Secret Service, originally an anti-counterfeiting agency, assumed full-time protection of American presidents in 1902.

Thus began, in 1901 in the United States, a century of terror worldwide .

1902

Jan. 1. Albany, NY, USA. Governor Benjamin B. Odell, having received three separate death threats by letter, and in light of the recent assassination of President McKinley, was placed under protection by the police at his New Year's Day reception. Detectives took up vigil in the reception hall and anyone entering who was not well known received thorough scrutiny. Nothing untoward took place.

From 1902 to the beginning of World War I, in Russia alone at least 1,500— estimate give totals as high as 4,500— government officials of all ranks from exalted to low fell to assassins. The following segment includes a sampling of senior victims.

Anarchist Leon Czolgosz shoots U.S. President William McKinley with a concealed revolver at the Pan-American Exposition, Buffalo, N.Y., September 6, 1901. Wash drawing by T. Dart Walker. Published 1905. Library of Congress LC-USZ62-13856.

April 1, 5, 7. Moscow, Russia. The police prefect of Moscow, Gen. Dimitri F. Trepoff, survived no fewer than seven assassination attempts dating back to a sensational case in 1897. On the first of the dates listed in 1902, a woman named Allart shoved a loaded pistol into his chest and pulled the trigger, only to have the weapon misfire. Four days later, a would-be killer drew a dagger in Trepoff's outer office, attempted to force his way into the prefect's presence, and was disarmed in the ensuing struggle. Finally, on April 7, a person believed to be a student jumped onto his open carriage with the intent of stabbing Trepoff, but managed only to wound an accompanying police officer. The assailant was captured.

The incidents cited were connected with student unrest at Moscow University, among other locations such as St. Petersburg, Kiev, and Odessa. More than 30,000

Russian university students had been out on strike since February. The Czarist government tried and convicted 567 Russian students for "political disaffection;" ninety-five were sent to Siberia in March. Schools in the Polish provinces were shut down by students to protest Russian rule.

The hated Trepoff died of a heart attack in September 1906.

April 15. St. Petersburg, Russia. A Socialist Revolutionary stude⁻ ⁻rom Kiev University named S. P. Balmashev assassinated notoriously reactionary Minister of Interior Dimitri S. Sipyengin. The authorities seized the assassin on the spot; he was soon executed. The equally repressive Wencelas (or Vyacheslav) K. von Plehve succeeded as minister.

At Sipyengin's funeral, a Socialist Revolutionary made an unsuccessful attempt on the life of Chief Procurator of the

Holy Synod Konsantin P. Pobedonostsev, a noted conservative statesman. The seventy-five-year-old Pobedonostsev lived on until 1907.

May 17. Vilna, Russia. Provincial governor Lt. Gen. von Wohl was attacked by one Hirsch Lekert late at night upon leaving the circus. The assailant fired three times, wounding von Wohl slightly in the hand and foot. Bystanders wrestled Lekert to the ground and police arrested him.

Von Wohl had been dismissed previously by the Czar from his position as police prefect at St. Petersburg, quite remarkably due to his reputation for fomenting student riots so as to be able to put them down. At Vilna, he ordered the wholesale flogging of political prisoners regardless of social standing, for which, however, in this instance the Czar commended him. Lekert was hanged on June 20.

May 26. Tsarskoe-Selo, Russia. Police arrested a young woman outside the Czar's summer residence carrying a bomb concealed in a scarf.

Belgian King Leopold II, who escaped an assassination attempt in late 1902.

June 25. Finland and Russia. The Social Revolutionary organization, a merger of radical groups underway since the founding of the party in Kharkov in 1900, issued in Finland its first proclamation, a call by the leadership for terrorist action by the peasantry. This group they saw as the only true agents of Russian revolution. Led initially by Grigorii A. Gershuni, a pharmacist from Minsk turned professional revolutionary, the political assembly had finally coalesced after the demise of its predecessor terrorist organs of twenty years earlier.

Aug. 10, Kharkov, Russia. Prince Ivan Obolensky, governor of Poltava and Kharkov, underwent two attacks, one in late May in which a shot was fired at him to no effect, and another, more serious attempt on his life in August. On the latter occasion, Obolensky was attending a theater production in the Tivoli Gardens. A worker not identified by name shot at him four times, wounding slightly both Obolensky and Chief of Police Bossonoff. A woman standing nearby grabbed the attacker's arm, throwing off his aim. The Prince wore an armored waistcoat.

The following month, the assailant smuggled out a letter published in Paris and London newspapers in which he wrote, "The peasants ... know that this cruel enemy of the people deserved death.... [W]e are struggling for the welfare of the people."

Nov. 15. Brussels, Belgium. An Italian Anarchist, Gennaro Rubino, failed in an attempt on the life of King Leopold II. The would-be assassin fired three shots at the monarch as he and his party left a church service in memory of Queen Henriette. No one was injured. When questioned in custody, Rubino said he did not regret his act because "monarchs are tyrants who cause the misery of their peoples." The following

February he was tried and convicted of attempted regicide.

1903

April 13. Monastir, Macedonia. Reports circulated that Bulgarians killed 165 men, women, and children. This was cited as an example of the murder, pillage, and atrocities practiced in the region daily by all sides.

April 29. Bulgaria. In support of a coup attempt to overthrow Turkish rule, revolutionaries exploded numerous bombs throughout the country.

June 11. Belgrade, Serbia. In an instance possibly of state terrorism, mutinous Serbian army officers, rumored to be backed by a Czarist-supported group *Omladina* ('Youth'), assassinated Serbian King Alexander Obrenovic and Queen Draga in the palace. Killed also were a number of family members and court officials. (*Omladina*, a predecessor of the Serbian Black Hand, sought an enlarged Slavic state encompassing much of the Balkans.) The highly unpopular, autocratic young king was shot repeatedly and his body dumped in the palace courtyard. Rather than tolerate a rumored naming of Alexander's brother-in-law as the heir, the army then installed Prince Peter Karageorgevitch as King Peter I.

Sep. 8. Belgrade, Serbia. As further indication of the murderous unrest in the Balkans, reports surface that Turkish troops had slaughtered 30,000 people in the Monastir district in the course of putting down the Bulgars' revolt against the Ottoman Empire.

Oct. 3. Barre, VT, USA. A group of fifteen Anarchists, said to be trying to break up a meeting of fifty or more Socialists at the town's Labor Hall, ran into armed resistance. In the scuffle, Socialist Alexander Garrett fatally shot Anarchist leader Elia Corti and wounded a colleague. It took a large police detail to control the conflict.

Nov. 21. Cripple Creek, Colo., USA. Although Harry Orchard (original name, Albert Horsley) was involved in violence back in 1899, his union "enforcer" career of really began when he blew up the Vindicator mine, killing two men, for a fee of $500. Six months later, he planted a bomb at an Independence, Colorado, train station that exploded, killing thirteen nonunion miners. In 1905, a court found him guilty of the murder of an ex-governor and he was imprisoned (below).

Orchard's mixed motivations included anger at mine operators and nonunion strike breakers, union loyalty, and love of money.

1904

March 18. Liege, Belgium. A bomb exploded outside Police Commissioner Laurent's home, killing an army officer examining the package. Six other persons were wounded, one seriously. The police arrested three Anarchists, who were tried and convicted in May. Two of them, named Lambkin and Gudefin, were sentenced to death and an accomplice, Boutet, received penal servitude for life.

April 12. Barcelona, Spain. A nineteen-year-old Anarchist attempted to assassinate Prime Minister Antonio Maura y Montaner. The assailant, Joaquin Miguel Artao, leaped upon the minister's open carriage with a dagger, crying "Long live anarchism!" But he only managed to wound slightly his intended victim. Maura had a reputation for severity in dealing with student unrest.

April 26. Alicante, Spain. A second attempt on Maura's life was no more successful. A fusilade of shots was fired at the train in which he was returning to Madrid after a trip to the Balearic Islands. Police on the train returned fire. There were no casualties.

June 16. Helsinki, Finland. Socialist Revolutionary (and son of a former Finnish senator) Eugen Schauman assassinated Gov. Gen. Nickolai I. Bobrikov, a fanatic in the cause of "Russianizing" Finland. After shooting Bobrikov as he entered the Senate House, the assassin took his own life. He left a note to the Czar to the effect that he acted to convince the Czar that great injustice prevailed in the Grand Duchy of Finland.

July 28. St. Petersburg, Russia. On orders of the Socialist Revolutionary Party, Egor S. Sazonov carried out the assassination of Interior Minister W. K. von Plehve, viewed widely as an unswerving reactionary. Sazanov threw a powerful bomb under the minister's carriage that blew von Plehve and his vehicle into small pieces. The Czar replaced the minister with the more liberal Prince Svyatopolk-Mirsky.

The assailant was imprisoned for life; reportedly he committed suicide in 1910.

1905

In the period 1905-07, the Socialist Revolutionary Party in Russia was at its peak of power and deadly activities. During that time its members carried out more than 200 major assassination attempts on senior officials of the Czarist government. Due to the government's countermeasures, includ-

ing the use of double agents, the party's effectiveness rapidly declined thereafter. For a period, terrorists with Anarchist leanings had returned to the scene, only to be largely vanquished in turn.

Jan. 22. St. Petersburg, Russia. The event that sparked the Revolution of 1905, called "Bloody Sunday," began as a peaceful, if very large, march of petitioners with their families to present their grievances to Czar Nicolas II at the Winter Palace (who was not actually there). Troops drawn up in front of the Palace opened fire on the huge crowd led by Father Georgiy Gapon, killing and wounding hundreds. Resulting disturbances forced the Czar to accept a constitutional monarchy, with the national legislature, the Duma, established in August. The massacre, along with Russia's defeat by Japan the same year, began years of highly unsettled politics that led to revolution in 1917.

The following year, Socialist Revolutionaries abducted Father Gapon when an informant revealed that he was a long-time Okranka (secret police) agent; they hanged him in Finland on March 28, 1906.

Feb. 6. Helsinki, Finland. An terrorist dressed as an army officer gained entry into the home of provincial Procurator General Eliel Soisalon-Soininen. There in the study the intruder fired a pistol at close range, killing the official. The latter's seventeen-year-old son dashed in at that point and shot the assassin three times; the latter's wounds did not prove to be fatal, however.

Feb. 17. Moscow, Russia. Grand Duke Sergei Aleksandrovich, uncle of the Czar, died when Ivan Kalayev threw a grenade into his open carriage as it entered the Kremlin gates. The Social Revolutionaries had placed the duke, the governor general of Moscow, near the top of its assassination

Russia's "Bloody Sunday," January 22, 1905, St. Petersburg, when the Czar's troops killed hundreds in breaking up a demonstration. This illustration was published that year. Library of Congress LOT 3665.

list; given that danger, he had moved to the Kremlin from his mansion a few days earlier. A detective assigned to the Grand Duke's party soon arrested Kalayev. He was hanged on May 23, proclaiming his loyalty to the "Peoples' Will" tradition of violent political change, a reference to the nineteenth century revolutionary terrorist group *Narodnaya Volya*.

May 24. Baku, Azerbaijan, Russia. Prince Nadashidze, governor of the province, disdained military protection and appeared in the streets of the city unattended. A bomb thrown by persons said to be Armenian revolutionaries severely wounded the prince — it landed short or he would have died instantly — and killed three other nearby persons.

June 28. Moscow, Russia. Socialist Revolutionaries killed the military governor of Moscow, Count Pavel P. Shuvalov. This took place two weeks after the crew of the battleship *Potemkin* had mutinied in St. Petersburg, thus exacerbating an already tense situation.

Oct. 18. Russia. A week-long pogrom began. Hundreds of Jews were murdered in riots which spread to dozens of towns and villages throughout the country. It was adjudged one of the bloodiest brief periods in the country's history.

Nov. 28. Dublin, Ireland. At a convention at the Rotunda, with the inspiration of an editor, Arthur Griffith, Sinn Fein's leadership declared the Catholic-oriented nationalist educational movement founded in 1893 a political party.

Dec. 30. Caldwell, Idaho, USA. Ex-governor Frank Steunenberg opened the front gate at his home and died soon after the explosion of a dynamite bomb rigged thereto. In 1899, Steunenberg, a populist, as governor had called in federal troops to put down rioting in Idaho mines. Mine union militant Harry Orchard confessed;

after trial he was sentenced to death, but his sentence was commuted to life in an Idaho prison. He died there in 1954, tending chickens as a trusty. (In 1907, International Workmen of the World labor leaders, who immediately came under strong suspicion, were tried and cleared of complicity in the crime.)

Dec. 30. Moscow, Russia. Governor General Doubashoff reported to the Czar that troops had closed in on some 3,000 workers gathering at the Prokharoff cotton mills, a revolutionary stronghold. The army opened fire and with an artillery bombardment buried hundreds of workers in the rubble.

Dec. 30. Barcelona, Spain. Reports circulated about the prevalent fear of Anarchists and how they hampered the city's night life. Bomb outrages took place, it was said, at regular intervals.

1906

April 28. Argenteuil, France. Revolutionaries attempted to blow up the railroad bridge at this small town fifteen miles northwest of Paris.

May 31. Madrid, Spain. Opposition to the marriage of King Alfonso XIII and Victoria Ena surfaced on religious grounds, but a failed assassination attempt at the wedding was ascribed to an Anarchist. Publishing company employee Matteo Morral threw a bomb at the young couple—the king was only twenty—as they left the cathedral after the ceremony. It missed them, but the explosion and subsequent panic caused the deaths of thirty-one persons. The new Spanish queen gained popularity by appearing the next day at a bull fight.

King Alfonso XIII and Queen Victoria Ena of Spain on their honeymoon in 1906 shortly after a failed attempt on their lives. Library of Congress LOT 11148(F).

Morrall escaped from Madrid by train two days later, but was challenged by a station guard only fifteen miles from the capital. After shooting the guard, he then turned the gun on himself, committing suicide.

July. Barcelona, Spain. A sudden call-up of military reserves causing hardship among workers was used by trade unions and other leftists as a reason for a general strike that mushroomed into what was remembered as "the Tragic Week"—*la Semana Trágica*—of July 1909. Barricades went up in many parts of the city; one-third of the religious buildings were damaged or wholly destroyed and more than 100 people killed. In the aftermath, the government executed four men. One of these was Francisco Ferrer Guardia, a well-known anarchist, shot by a firing squad on October 13, 1909; he had been suspected of fomenting the attempted assassination in May 1906 of King Alphonso XIII (above) and arrested, but eventually released after a year in prison for lack of proof.

Aug. 25. St. Petersburg, Russia. Two Socialist Revolutionaries disguised as police officers brought a powerful dynamite bomb hidden in a large, ornate vase into the villa of newly appointed Prime Minister Pytor A. Stolypin, where a reception was underway. Stolypin luckily escaped serious harm. His fifteen-year-old daughter and some thirty-two other persons, including the two bombers, died, however, and Stolypin's three-year-old son was among the more than thirty injured. Two accomplices of the bombers waiting in a carriage outside the front door (one of whom was injured in the blast) were immediately taken to the dreaded St. Peter and St. Paul Fortress.

Oct. Russia. In that one month, reports had it that revolutionaries carried out more than 360 "expropriations" to fund their activities. Twenty banks were robbed, netting a million rubles.

Nov. 17. Naples, Italy. An Anarchist named Saverio Lagana stabbed and killed Professor Giovanni Rossi of the University of Naples. Recently returned from contacts with Anarchists in New Jersey, USA, the assassin said he killed the zoologist because of a public speech Rossi made condemning the Anarchist movement for its barbarity.

Nov. 18. Rome, Italy. On a Sunday, a bomb exploded in St. Peter's Church with a loud roar, accompanied by much dense smoke. No one in the large crowd was injured, but mass confusion and terror reigned. Only four days previously, a bomb exploded in front of the Café Aragno in Rome, again with no deaths or injuries. Both incidents were blamed on Anarchist terrorists. The police saw the bomb at St. Peter's as a challenge to society in general, not particularly a protest against the Papacy.

1907

March 11. Sofia, Bulgaria. Prime Minister Dimitur Petkoff fell to an assassin's three bullets while walking with other members of the cabinet in the Boris Garden. Also head of the Stambuloff Party, an anti-Russian group, he was the third senior party official to be murdered since it's founding less than a decade earlier. Given that Prince Ferdinand, a rival for power, held pro-Russian views, there was speculation that the court and Russian interests arranged the assassination.

June 25. Tiflis, Georgia, Russia. In an "expropriation" organized by a then-minor functionary called Josef Stalin, Bolsheviks led by an Armenian named Petroyan (also known as "Kamo") pulled off a robbery of at least 250,000 rubles. Kamo tossed a dynamite bomb at a State Bank carriage transporting the funds, killing as many as thirty people, and then fled with the money to be used for revolutionary purposes.

1908

Jan. 19. Rio de Janeiro, Brazil. Police announced they had stymied an Anarchist plot to blow up one or more U. S. Navy ships then on a visit in the Rio harbor. It was noted as the first Anarchist conspiracy ever in Brazil. *The New York Times*, however, termed the affair "comic opera."

Feb. 1. Lisbon, Portugal. King Carlos I and his elder son were killed by gunfire in an open carriage in the Praça de Comêrcio on its way to the Necessidades Palace. The two assassins, disgruntled republicans, thus brought to the throne the eighteen-year-old Prince Manoel, himself wounded in the attack. (Queen Amelie, also in the carriage, tried unsuccessfully to shield in turn the king and her son Manoel, but was unhurt in the attack.) Two years later, as a result of an uprising by the military, Manoel II and the royal family fled to England. The revolutionaries proclaimed a republic, with author Teófilio Braga as provisional president. The Portuguese monarchy was no more.

Feb. 20. Guatemala City, Guatemala. In a reprise of an assassination plot the previous February, an unsuccessful attempt was made on the life of President Manuel Estrada Cabrera. Students reportedly fired on the president as he was on his way to give an audience to the newly arrived American ambassador. Troops immediately surrounded the students. The Estrada Cabrera government reacted with a show of force that can only be termed state terrorism. Authorities executed almost immediately eighteen prisoners held since the previous year, including two women. The president promised more to come. A Honduran official was implicated but escaped. Reports circulated three months later in Mexico that the attempt on the president's life was faked in order for him to rid himself of political opponents.

Feb. 28. Tehran, Persia. The aged Shah Mohammed Ali Mirza escaped unscathed from an assassination attempt in a narrow street of the capital. The would-be killer or killers threw a bomb at his automobile, which was empty (the Shah, as a safety measure, was in a carriage farther back in the procession). The errant bomb killed more than a score of people, and the royal cavalry escort's protective rifle fire in all directions wounded at least twelve bystanders. The authorities found no culprits.

Shah Mohammed Ali Mirza of Persia, who escaped an assassination attempt in February 1908. Photograph taken late the previous year. Library of Congress LOT 11148(F).

May 3. Calcutta, India. Police unearthed a plot to murder Europeans with bombs. An indicated target was Lord Kitchener, commander of the British forces in India, along with other high officials. None of the devices, believed to be early versions of letter bombs, had yet been successfully employed. A month later, the Viceregal Council adopted a measure known as the Explosives Bill, providing "stern measures" to be used against bomb attacks.

Dec. 13. Chicago, USA. Unknown parties exploded a large bomb at an annex to the Chicago Coliseum, causing minor injuries but considerable damage. The action evidently was taken by reformers in an effort — unsuccessful — to thwart the plans of local ward bosses to raise funds by hosting an annual ball. Policed said it was the work of "fanatics."

1909

July 1. London, England. At the end of an evening "at home" for students of the Imperial Institute, an Indian youth, Madarlal Dhinagri, shot and killed Lt. Col. Sir William H. C. Wyllie and, probably accidentally, a bystander, Dr. Cawas Lacaca. The assailant was immediately seized and held. Wyllie had served many years in India; since 1901 he had been an aide to the secretary of state for India. Less than three weeks after the incident, a court sentenced Dhinagri to death for the double murder; at the trial, he claimed his was an act of patriotism. He was hanged on August 17.

The previous February an Indian student had assaulted Sir William Lee Warner in the streets of London.

Oct. 26. Harbin, Manchuria. On a visit to the area, Japanese elder statesman Prince Ito Hirobumi was assassinated by a Korean nationalist named An Chung-gun. Ironically, Ito was known as a compromiser on the question of Japan's formal acquisition of Korea. Dying, realizing he had been shot for political reasons related to Korean autonomy, Ito said of his assassin, "He is a fool!" His killer was executed in Japan on March 26, 1910. Japan formally annexed Korea that same year.

Nov. 14. Buenos Aires, Argentina. Anarchist Simón Radowitsky threw a bomb into the carriage of Police Chief Ramón Falcón, killing him and an aide. The action came at a time of labor unrest and police repression. Radowitsky was sentenced to death, but his youth — he was eighteen — brought him a prison term instead. Released in 1930, he eventually fought in the Spanish Civil War and took asylum in Mexico when the Franco forces won. Radowitsky died there in 1956, a renowned hero of the Anarchist movement.

1910–1919

Sarajevo, 1914 — the most fateful assassination of the twentieth century.

1910

Feb. 20. Cairo, Egypt. Premier Boutros Ghali Pasha, the first native-born prime minister, was shot three times by a young Swiss-trained pharmacologist, Ibrahim al-Wardani, recently returned from Europe. The Coptic Christian former foreign minister and justice minister (and grandfather of the later secretary general of the UN) died the next morning. Boutros Ghali was viewed by nationalists as far too closely associated with Egypt's British overlords, especially in that he had just acceded to a British demand for extension of the Suez Canal Company concession.

May 10. Yokohama, Japan. Police arrested four Anarchists after discovering them with bomb-making equipment. Even though no attacks had been mounted, hundreds of suspects were taken into custody. Twenty-six of these were tried and convicted of a plot to assassinate the emperor; twelve eventually were executed. Included (on Jan. 24, 1911) was a leader named Kôtoku Shûsui, who had become a convert to Anarchism during a stay in the United States. Anarchism thus was effectively stymied in Japan.

Oct. 1. Los Angeles, USA. Shortly after midnight, dynamite exploded at the plant of the *Los Angeles Times*, killing twenty persons. Brothers John and James McNamara, represented by famed attorney Clarence Darrow, eventually pled guilty. They said the act, taken during a strike to unionize, was a protest against the newspaper's adamant anti-labor stand. Both were connected with the AFL Bridge & Structural Iron Workers Union. James received a life sentence and John, fifteen years, of which he served ten.

Dec. 10. London, England. A half-dozen men led by a Russian Anarchist named Peter Platkow were interrupted by police in the act of robbing a jewelry store in the East End section of Houndsditch. The ensuing shootout resulted in three policemen killed and the Anarchists escaping.

1911

Jan. 24. Tokyo, Japan. Following a trial in December 1910, radical Socialist Kôtoku Shûsui, who was influenced by the ideas of the Industrial Workers of the World in the United States, along with eleven other persons, was hanged for plotting to assassinate the emperor. None had actually attempted to carry out such a con-

20

spiracy. The government thus demonstrated a clear example of officially sanctioned terror.

Sep. 14. Kiev, Russia. A revolutionary-cum-police informer shot and fatally wounded Prime Minister Pyotr A. Stolypin during intermission at the opera, with Czar Nicholas II and two of his daughters also in the audience. Stolypin, who had been the object of an assassination attempt in 1906 (above) died five days later. A strict disciplinarian, he nevertheless was noted for sometimes bold reform measures. The motives of the assassin, Dmitri Bogroff, are not clear, given his dual capacity and the fact that he made no attempt on the life of the nearby Czar. A week later a military tribunal found him guilty and he was soon hanged.

In Czarist Russia during 1908-9, 3,862 people were executed and 4,517 sentenced to hard labor for political crimes; the gallows had been nicknamed "Stolypin's neckties."

Nov. 11. Santo Domingo, Dominican Republic. Pres. Ramón Cáceres, who had been in office since 1905, was assassinated. He had made progress toward stability and economic progress, but his death led to civil war and eventual control (in 1916) by the United States.

Dec. 12. Paris, France. A gang headed by an Anarchist named Jules Bonnot shot and robbed a bank messenger for the Societé Général of half a million francs ($200,000).

1912

Jan. 12. Peking, China. Opponents of a move to force child emperor Henry Pu-Yi's abdication had the leader of the Man-

chu court, Liang-pi, killed. The hired assassin who fired the shots was named P'eng Cia-chen.

March 25, Chicago, USA. In incidents among the first that can be categorized as involving a letter or parcel bomb, the newly organized Secret Service found three parcels that contained a spring device and powder intended to blind the recipient upon opening. One reached the Chicago chief of the U. S. Department of Justice, but caused no harm; the other two were disarmed. An accompanying note indicated that the sender was an Anarchist.

April 28. Choisy-le-Roi, France. Police tracked down and killed Jules Bonnot, Anarchist leader of *"la bande tragique,"* as it was called, that had committed five robberies in Paris the previous four months (above). All thefts supposedly were to fund political activities, but critics said they kept ninety percent of the loot. Two victims lost their lives. After trial, three members were sentenced to death and guillotined on April 13, almost exactly a year after Bonnot had died. The authorities arrested or killed the rest of the gang in 1913.

July 3. Hong Kong. A former hospital employee shot at but missed the newly appointed British governor, Sir Henry May. The would-be killer viewed an action taken by the colonial government on the circulation of coins as directed politically against China.

Oct. 14. Milwaukee, USA. In a case only marginally appropriate for inclusion in a compendium of terrorist acts, John Schrank shot at close range and wounded Progressive Party presidential candidate Theodore Roosevelt as the latter left the Hotel Gilpatrick on his way to deliver a campaign speech. Schrank admitted guilt and proclaimed, "Any man looking for a third term ought to be shot." (Roosevelt had previously served as president from McKinley's death in 1901 to 1909.) Although hurt and bleeding, Roosevelt refused medical aid until he had delivered most of the speech. His overcoat, plus the thickly folded pages of the written speech in his inner coat pocket, had saved him from a more serious wound.

The motivation for his action as expressed in his statement could be termed political, but Schrank was adjudged insane by a panel of psychiatrists and confined to a mental hospital until his death in 1943.

Nov. 12. Madrid, Spain. An Anarchist named Manuel Pardinas killed Prime Minister José Canalejas y Mendez with one shot as the latter entered the Ministry of Interior building. The assassin immediately committed suicide. Various groups of revolutionary foes of the government had agreed on eliminating Canalejas as their chief foe, whom they viewed as extremely repressive, even more so than King Alfonso XIII. In actuality, he was a liberal who had undertaken a number of reforms.

Dec. 23. Delhi, India. Riding on an elephant for a formal entry into the capital, the British viceroy of India, Lord Hardinge, was wounded slightly by a bomb thrown from the rooftop of a house near the procession. His wife, who was seated on the back of the same elephant, was uninjured; the blast killed one Indian attendant and seriously wounded another. Several persons fleeing the scene were caught and arrested. Officials suggested that Indian "Anarchists" were responsible.

1913

The widespread availability of dynamite is indicated by the fact that a reported thirty-two bombs were set off in New York City alone in 1913.

Feb. 18. Walton-on-the-Hill, England. Seeking equal rights for women, the Women's Socialist and Political Union fire bombed and partially destroyed a house being built for David Lloyd George, chancellor of the exchequer. The suffragette movement, founded in 1903 by Emmeline Pankhurst, had come to use increasingly violent tactics, including an occasional fire bombing, and active resistance in prison (by 1914 some 1,000 members had been jailed). Pankhurst and the WSPU abandoned these tactics upon the outbreak of World War I.

March 18. Salonika, Greece. The popular King George I, walking near the harbor and the White Tower with a solitary aide, was shot in the back and died almost instantly. His assailant, a Greek named Aleko Schinas, a confirmed Anarchist said to be well educated, had worked at one time in New York. His principal grievance evidently was the closure by the government of a school of Anarchism he had established in Greece.

Serbia's Black Hand reportedly planned the king's assassination two years previously, but there is no evidence it was involved in this attack. Schinas committed suicide while awaiting trial. Constantine I, the late king's son, succeeded to the throne.

April 28. Hanoi, Indochina. A bomb thrown into a group of Europeans killed two French officers.

June 11. Istanbul, Turkey. The assassination of Mahmud Sevket Pasha, former head of the revolutionary "Army of Deliverance," in office as grand vizier for less than five months, accentuated the nation's unsettled political situation.

Sep. 15. Los Angeles, USA. The suspicions of a servant prevented harm to Gen. Harrison G. Otis, owner of *The Los Angeles Times*, from a parcel bomb. The package delivered by mail to his home contained a high-powered explosive that police set off in a safe place with a great roar. Press accounts quoted police officials as saying the package contained sufficient dynamite to kill half a regiment.

Three years previously, two labor agitators had dynamited the *Times*'s printing plant, with twenty people losing their lives (above). Speculation for the current attack centered on opponents of Otis' anti-union stand.

1914

Jan. 10. Salt Lake City, USA. Two storekeepers named John and Arlind Morrison died in a shoot-out with two would-be robbers. Police soon arrested Joe Hill (born Joel Haggland in Sweden), a well-known organizer and activist for the radical Industrial Workers of the World (IWW). The circumstantial evidence against him was overwhelming, even though he proclaimed his innocence. Found guilty, Hill died facing a firing squad on November 19, 1915.

June 28. Sarajevo, Bosnia, Austria-Hungary. In the most fateful assassination of the twentieth century, Gavrilo Princip, one of a small group of terrorists recruited by the Serbian nationalist Black Hand organization, fired two pistol shots at close range and killed a member of one of the ruling empires of Europe. Archduke Franz Ferdinand, heir to the Austro-Hungarian throne, and his wife, Sophie, both died almost immediately. (There is a lack of clarity on whether or not the Black Hand had actually ordered that particular assassina-

tion at that particularly unsettled time.) The archduke was on his way out of the city in an open automobile after an inspection trip designed to show the empire's interest in Sarajevo. A short while beforehand, another of the terrorist group named Gabrinovic, seventeen years old, had tossed a bomb at the royal party's car, but failed to injure them (bystanders were wounded). Immediately upon firing his automatic, Princip was set upon, beaten by guards, and taken prisoner.

At his trial Princip defied the court. Due to his youth — he was presumed to be just under twenty years old — he received twenty years in prison for the double murder rather than a capital sentence. He died four years later of tuberculosis, thus lending credence to stories that Serbia's Black Hand had recruited potential assassins for the job who were ill and not far from dying anyway.

The story of the aftermath is all too familiar. The confrontation that followed between Austria-Hungary and Serbia and their allies set the wheels of world war in motion. It was to be the deadliest conflict in history to that point, one precipitated by a high-profile assassination by Slavic nationalist forces opposed to the hegemony of Austria-Hungary. When the war ended in 1918, Austria-Hungary had disappeared from the map of Europe, the German Empire was decisively defeated, and Tsarist Russia was no more, while Britain and France had suffered grievous losses.

July 31. Paris, France. On the eve of the Great War, which he opposed, Socialist intellectual Jean Jaurès fell victim to a fanatical rightist named Raoul Villain, who shot and killed him at a café. Villain claimed he had no accomplices and was thought perhaps to be demented. Jaurès, a noted author, editor, and member of the Chamber of Deputies, was known to represent a voice for peace, crying out in vain at a time when war with Germany was at hand. The cabinet attended his funeral.

Jaurès' seventeen-year-old son was killed only weeks later, fighting the invading German army north of Paris. In 1919, a French jury failed to find Villain guilty of murder, in effect by determining that his crime was "political." He lived on until the beginning of the Spanish Civil War in 1936, when he was killed in Spain.

1915

April 24. Istanbul, Turkey. Authorities of the nationalistic Committee of Union and Progress (CUP), installed in power in 1908, rounded up and murdered about 600 Armenian intellectuals and other notables. That action led to mass deportations and massacres that left an estimated 1.5 million Armenians dead by 1917. They were seen as a potentially traitorous "fifth column." Eastern Anatolia — the historical land of the Armenians — was effectively "cleansed."

Turkish officials denied the accusations of genocide, claiming that the loss of life was associated with general unrest during the final years of the Ottoman Empire. But a CUP spokesman in a February 1915 closed party leadership meeting, commenting on the Armenian question, is quoted as saying that "if [a] purge is not general and final, it will inevitably lead to problems. Therefore it is absolutely necessary to eliminate the Armenian people in its entirety."[1]

Armenians since that time have marked April 24 internationally as Genocide Memorial Day.

Aug. 21. Beirut, Lebanon. Jamal Pasha, Ottoman military governor, caused to be executed the first group of activists in the Arab nationalist movement. The following year in May, he had twenty-one Arab leaders and intellectuals hanged in Beirut and Damascus.

1916

Feb. 10. Chicago, USA. Anarchist Jean Crones, assistant chef at the University Club, poisoned some 250 guests at a banquet held to honor newly appointed Archbishop George W. Mundelein. Crones laced the soup liberally with arsenic. None of the guests died, however; he had used too much poison, causing the victims to have an immediate physical reaction, with predictable results. The police arrested numerous Anarchist friends and acquaintances of Crones, but he had left town that same night. During the following days, in New York he wrote three letters to *The New York Times*, railing against the failures of society — and especially the Catholic Church — to provide for the poor.

The poisoner was not apprehended, but within two weeks of his near-deadly attack on the banqueters, Crones shot and killed himself in Camden, New Jersey.

April 24–29. Dublin, Ireland. The Easter Rising took place, led by Patrick Pearse, who proclaimed the "Irish Republic." Focused at the time on the war effort against Germany, Britain was taken by surprise, but by the second day London had sent troops that soon put down the major uprising. Civilian casualties were numerous. The courts sentenced the Irish leaders to death, with the sentences later commuted in many instances.

Michael Collins soon thereafter established the Irish Republican Army (IRA), which became the military arm of the Sinn Fein party.

May. Beirut, Lebanon, and Damascus, Syria. Military Governor Jamal Pasha hanged twenty-one Arab separatist leaders and intellectuals.

July 22. San Francisco, USA. The explosion of a bomb concealed in a suitcase at a huge patriotic Preparedness Day parade killed ten and wounded forty. Two known labor agitators, Thomas Mooney and Warren Billings, were hastily tried and convicted on evidence that few found convincing. President Woodrow Wilson facilitated the commutation of Mooney's death sentence to life in prison, the punishment that Billings received. In 1939 both received pardons.

Oct. 21. Vienna, Austria. Well-known intellectual and secretary of the Austrian Socialist Democratic Party, Dr. Fritz Adler, shot and killed Count Karl von Sturgkh, prime minister and virtual dictator of Austria. The assassin shouted as he pulled the trigger, "We want peace!" The son of Victor Adler, leader of the same party, he served only two years in prison before the war ended and he was amnestied. He lived on until 1960.

1917

Dec. 20. Petrograd, Russia. Vladimir Lenin established the secret police agency Cheka under the notorious Felix Dzerzhinsky as an instrument of official terror. It had as a principal aim the destruction of the Russian bourgeoisie.

1918

June 20. Petrograd, Russia. A Socialist Revolutionary killed Bolshevik commissar Moisei Goldshtein-Volodsky.

Felix Dzerzhinsky, first head of Russia's Cheka, the feared secret police of the Bolshevik government, appointed by Lenin in late 1917.

July 6. Moscow, Russia. Upon the signing of the Treaty of Brest-Litovsk that ended the war between Russia and Germany, Berlin sent Count Wilhelm von Mirbach to Moscow as ambassador. Russia's Socialist Revolutionaries, out of power since the Bolshevik October Revolution the previous year, decided to assassinate Mirbach to provoke renewed war with Germany. (There is some indication of a plot within a plot: The Leninists may have become aware of the planned attack, but failed to warn the German embassy, viewing the development as an opening to crush the Socialist Revolutionaries.) A teenager named Jacob Blyumkin gained access to the ambassador, murdered him, and escaped. No renewed war erupted, and Moscow easily put down Social Revolutionary-inspired uprisings.

Years later Blyumkin was shot by the Stalin regime on charges of Trotskyism.

July 16. Ekaterinburg, Russia. As the Russian White forces approached, Bolshe-

Russian Czar Nicholas II (front, left of center), family, and officials at St. Petersburg, ca. 1912. He and all of his family were murdered in 1918. Library of Congress LC-USZ62-46347.

vik revolutionaries executed Nicholas II, until the previous year the all-powerful Czar of the Russian Empire. He was shot, along with six members of his Romanoff family and a number of personal retainers, in the cellar of the house in which they were being held. Their firing-squad executioners were acting on the orders of regional Bolshevik officials in a deed ultimately laid at the doorstep of Vladimir Lenin. They then hauled the bodies to nearby mine shafts. The bodies were not recovered and identified until the end of the twentieth century.

Leon Trotsky, later to fall victim to an assassin himself, justified the murder of the Romanoffs on the need to horrify and frighten the enemy — and to urge on his own Bolshevik army, then engaged in civil war. Certainly the murders removed a potential player or possible embarrassment, the Czar, from the political board.

Aug. 30. Moscow, Russia. News reached Moscow that Moisei Uritisky, head of St. Petersburg's Bolshevik secret police (Cheka), had been assassinated by a young student. Lenin spoke at a workers' meeting that evening, using unusually violent language. As he left the building, Dora (Fanya) Kaplan, a veteran Socialist Revolutionary who had served eleven years at hard labor in Siberia in Czarist days, shot him twice, seriously wounding the Bolshevik leader. Kaplan was promptly captured. In a statement she made to the secret police that night, she termed Lenin an enemy of the people for closing the Constituent Assembly. On September 3, in an execution organized by a Cheka officer named Yakov Sverdlov, Kaplan was shot and her body then obliterated. (Sverdlov died of influenza six months later.)

Lenin never fully recovered. The attacks on him and on Uritisky led immediately into a program that came to be called the "Red Terror." During the following year, the Cheka executed without trial at least 6,300 hostages and prisoners all over the nation.

From 1918, with the party's accession to power, the Russian Communist party began the all-out use of state terror tactics to intimidate its foes and to solidify its political position — this despite sometimes ambivalent statements by Lenin on the need for and efficacy of terrorism. Millions of their own people were to die in the Soviet Union during coming decades under Lenin and, later, Stalin. As Lenin quite unambiguously observed: "If for the sake of Communism it is necessary for us to destroy nine-tenths of the people, we must not hesitate."[2]

Oct. 31. Budapest, Hungary. Blaming him for the nation's losing effort in the war, Communists assassinated former premier István Tisza de Boros-Jeno. He had already been ousted from power in May 1917.

Dec. 15. Lisbon, Portugal. Gen. Sidónio Paes, who was elected president in May during an era of political instability, fell to an assassin, said to be a radical leftist. The president was fatally wounded as he entered Rossio Station only weeks after surviving a previous assassination attempt.

1919

Jan. 7. Buenos Aires, Argentina. In the confrontation between Anarchists and their supporters and the government, another *"Semana Trágica"* as in Barcelona ten years earlier, began when police moved on the striking Vasena metallurgical plant workers. The strike was brutally put down by a locally infamous Colonel Hector Varela; numerous fatalities resulted. In retaliation, Anarchists and Syndicalists supported a general strike called for January 10 and 11. The wave of strikes soon subsided, but government repression worsened. The police, army, and right-wing civilians launched an assault on the workers' quarter in a central zone of the city, Villa Crespo. According to the press, the "Tragic Week" left a toll of 700 to 800 dead and 4,000 injured. The police made 52,000 arrests. Anarchism at that point began a steady decline in influence in Argentina.

Four years later, on January 27, 1923, in Patagonia, a German-born Anarchist, Kurt Wilckens, wounded Col. Varela with a bomb he threw and then ended Varela's life with revolver shots. Wilckens, sentenced to seventeen years in prison, was soon murdered in his cell.

Jan. 15. Berlin, Germany. In a notorious example of state terrorism, German leftists Rosa Luxemburg and Karl Liebkneckt were taken into custody separately by the German military, beaten half to death, and then each shot in the head. Luxemburg's body was thrown into a canal and not recovered for four months. Their transgression: As leaders of the radical post-World War I Spartacus movement, with their communist and socialist followers engaged in a general strike, they had plans to set up a soviet republic led by the newly established Communist Party of Germany. This the provisional government and army leadership would not permit. With the murders of the two leaders, the political left's plans collapsed. After a long cover-up, the army lieutenant and soldier who killed Luxemburg received two-year prison terms.

Feb. 8. Barcelona, Spain. A strike begun after a layoff of workers by the anarchosyndicalist *Confederación Nacional del Trabajo* (CNT) against the electrical company called *"la Canadienne,"* expanded into a city-wide general strike lasting forty-four days. It ended with victory for the CNT. The union's leaders then attempted another general strike to win the release of imprisoned comrades. That brought a crackdown against the CNT, which responded by forming squads of gunmen to murder employers, foremen, policemen, and dissident workers. Employers and the police responded in kind and a circle of violence spiraled upward that lasted into the following year.

Feb. 19. Paris, France. Georges Clemenceau, premier of France since 1917, was attacked and wounded on his way to the Hotel Crillon to meet with the American peace delegation. The venerable statesman (he was close to eighty years old) recovered and lived on until 1929. Clemenceau's would-be assassin, a young man named Emile Cottin, had uncertain motives. Less than a month later, a court condemned him to death, but eventually his life was spared.

Feb. 20. Kollagosh, Afghanistan. An unknown assailant shot and killed Emir Habibullah Khan, ruler of Pakistan since 1901. The circumstances were not clear, but the motive for the assassination lay at least partially in nationalist opposition to Habibullah's cooperation with Britain. His son and successor, Amanullah Khan, soon engaged Britain in war.

Feb. 21. Munich, Germany. Socialist Prime Minister Kurt Eisner, who had seized power in the closing days of World War I, was shot and killed by a right-wing student. Eisner was on his way to hand in his resignation to the Bavarian parliament. The murder led to a Communist take-over attempt that was suppressed by the army.

April 13. Amritsar, India. Disturbances on April 10 resulting in several Indians being killed by British army rifle fire led to an enraged Indian mob rioting, killing several Englishmen, and burning British banks. Exacting retribution, three days later Gen. R. E. H. Dyer marched fifty troops to the entrance of an enclosed park area in which some 10,000 unarmed civilians were mounting a protest meeting. Upon orders, the troops opened fire and continued shooting for about ten minutes, expending 1,650 rounds of ammunition into the panic-stricken crowd. About 400 civilians died and over 1,000 were wounded.

Gen. Dyer was relieved of command and returned to England, a hero to many there. But the massacre turned millions of moderate Indians into nationalists who would never again trust Great Britain.

April 26. New York, USA. Police uncovered a plot involving at least thirty-six bombs mailed from New York to prominent national and regional figures. One of the bombs had detonated, gravely wounding one person. The rest — all of them constructed alike — were defused. The authorities opined that it likely was the work of labor radicals or Bolsheviks and was timed to coincide roughly with May Day.

June 2. Washington, DC, USA. An Italian Anarchist blew himself up when he set off an explosive outside the home of Attorney General A. Mitchell Palmer, a proponent of repressive measures against Communist and other left-wing political elements. Palmer's views during what was called "the Red Scare" were strengthened by the discovery of thirty-eight letter or parcel bombs sent to prominent U. S. politicians (none of which in the event resulted in fatalities).

Oct. 8. Berlin, Germany. Independent Socialist leader Hugo Haase (who was briefly foreign minister after Germany's surrender in 1918) fell seriously wounded on the steps of the Reichstag, shot by a monarchist assassin. Haase died on November 7.

Ironically, less than six months earlier Haase had excused the use of terrorism, telling an interviewer that as practiced by his colleagues, terrorist tactics were only temporary and would be abandoned when Socialist ideals were realized in Germany.

Notes

1. Graber, *Caravans to Oblivion: The Armenian Genocide, 1915*, 87-88. See also http://www.gendercide.org/case_armenia.html.

2. Parry, *Terrorism From Robespierre to Arafat*, 165.

1920–1929

In this decade, organized terror groups mainly took the form of right-wing and ultra-nationalist groups.

1920

Jan. 14. Berlin, Germany. Forty people were killed and 105 injured in riots against the Weimar Republic instigated by rightists. A mob rushed the Reichstag.

Jan. 26. Berlin, Germany. A right-wing fanatic, Oltwig von Hirschfeld, shot Minister of Finance Matthias Erzberger as he left the Criminal Courts Building. Junkers cheered the news when it became known (Erzberger had signed the 1918 Armistice on behalf of Germany). He recovered, only to be assassinated the following year (below). Hirschfeld defended his action because, in his view, the victim was putting his interests above those of the German state.

Feb. 7. Irkutsk, Russia. Admiral Alexesandr V. Kolchak, head of the White forces opposing Lenin's Bolsheviks, fell into enemy hands at the end of 1919, was turned over to the Reds in January 1920, interrogated, and on the above date, summarily executed.

March 20. Cork, Ireland. Tomas Mac-Curtain, elected lord mayor of Cork and a Sinn Fein notable, died in an attack carried out in his home by disguised gunmen. Accounts differ, but the assassins possibly were members of the Constabulary.

March 26. Dublin, Ireland. As one more instance of the recurring violence in Ireland at this time, gunmen pulled Magistrate Alan Bell from the streetcar in which he was commuting to Dublin Castle and shot him to death. The six armed men escaped; forty Sinn Fein members were rounded up soon thereafter.

June 12. Cairo, Egypt. Premier Tewfik Nessim Pasha, being driven to his office, escaped injury in an assassination attempt that left his chauffeur and two onlookers wounded. An assailant threw a bomb and fired an automatic pistol at police in pursuit, but soon was captured.

Aug. 4. Valencia, Spain. Five men, said by police to be trade unionists, seriously wounded the Count de Salvatierra with a barrage of gunfire as he and his wife and sister-in-law were out in the evening for a carriage ride. Both he and his wife's sister died the following day; his wife eventually recovered. Salvatierra was the former civil governor of Barcelona and a firm opponent of trade unions.

Aug. 12. Paris, France. Greece's Prime Minister Eluetherios Constantine Venizelos was wounded by shots from two disaffected former military officers, George Thyriakis and Apostolos Iserpris, as he walked into a train station. Supporters of former monarch Constantine reportedly were involved.

Aug. 15. Matewan, W. Va. USA. A. C. Hatfield, shot while sitting in front of his hotel, died of his wounds in Kentucky the next day. He was a witness in a court procedure that resulted in indictments of fourteen men for taking part in a bloody labor battle in Matewan three months earlier. Police arrested one Fred Burgraf for the crime.

Sep. 16. New York, USA. At noon a horse-drawn wagon-load of 100 pounds of dynamite exploded before the Stock Exchange at the corner of Broad and Wall streets. Forty people were killed and 300 injured. Property damages totaled $2 million. Several sources attributed the act to Anarchist Mario Buda, who undertook to protest the indictment of Sacco and Vanzetti. Police suspected Anarchists, but they never charged Buda or anyone else.

Oct. 6. Cairo, Egypt. A court convicted twenty-five members of the so-called "Vengeance Gang" of organizing political assassinations. Included in the group was Abdul Rhamen Bey Fahny, former provisional governor.

Oct. 17. Milan, Italy. Following two earlier bomb explosions at the hotel housing the British delegation to a League of Nations conference, police arrested Anarchist newspaper director Enrico Malatesta and four others for the crime. Authorities uncovered bombs and firearms in their search.

Nov. 15. London, England. At mid-month the chief secretary for Ireland made

known in the House of Commons that a total of 115 Royal Irish Constabulary policemen had died and 195 had been wounded in the conflict. On the 24th, he announced to the House that Sinn Fein had prepared detailed plans to blow up the Liverpool docks and the Manchester power and water plants. He appealed for continued support for the police.

Nov. 21. Dublin, Ireland. In one morning IRA gunmen mounted a coordinated attack on nineteen officials who had been active in prosecuting cases against the organization. Fifteen of the victims died. Four members of several Irish nationalist groups were captured. That afternoon, police surrounded Croke Park, where a hockey match was scheduled. Firing broke out; ten Sinn Fein adherents were killed and "many" wounded, along with two persons killed in the ensuing crowd stampede. The day came to be widely known as "Bloody Sunday."

Dec. 17. Dublin, Ireland. Masked men shot and killed Royal Constabulary Inspector O'Sullivan in front of the general post office. The police later raided the business district. That same day in London the Houses of Commons and Lords reached agreement on amendments to the Irish Home Rule Bill.

Dec. 23. London, England. The "Government of Ireland Act" became law, partitioning Ireland into the south and the north, the latter with its six counties. Sinn Fein rejected the move and continued its support of the IRA in its campaign for a united Irish Republic.

Dec. 24. Budapest, Hungary. Djelal Munif Bey, former Turkish consul general in New York, was murdered. Armenian terrorists were suspected. While assigned in New York several years previously, he had publicly denied Turkish complicity in any massacre of Armenians.

1921

Feb. 18. Tokyo, Japan. Korean nationalists assassinated Bingen Shoku, a Korean advocate of assimilation with Japan, at his hotel. He was on a visit to Japan to seek enfranchisement of his countrymen.

Feb. 28. Dublin, Ireland. In retribution for the execution by firing squad of six Sinn Fein activists, gunmen killed five British soldiers and wounded eleven others in the streets of Cork.

March 8. Madrid, Spain. Gunmen used a motorcycle with sidecar in killing conservative Premier Eduardo Dato y Iradier as he was being driven home in the evening from the Senate Chambers. When his vehicle reached Plaza Independencia, the motorcyclists pulled even with his car and fired twenty-one bullets at the passenger. They then sped off. Dato died shortly thereafter.

The assassins were later identified as three Anarchists named Mateu, Casanellas, and Nicolau.

March 15. Berlin, Germany. Mehmed Talat Pasha, former grand vizier of the Ottoman Empire, died at the hands of a lone assassin, an Armenian named Saro Melikian. Because of Talat's role in the wholesale deportation and massacre of Armenians from eastern Turkey during World War I, a German court declined to convict his killer.

April 1. Dublin, Ireland. Crown forces reported eighteen killed in their ranks, with twenty-eight wounded. The Sinn Fein was said to have carried out nine assassinations.

May 12. Dublin, Ireland. A bomb thrown at a government lorry resulted in the injury of fourteen people. The weekly summary chronicled twenty-six attacks on Crown forces, resulting in eighteen dead and ten wounded.

The above entries pertaining to the long-standing and continuing strife in Ireland indicate the extent of death and destruction. Numerous similar notations of casualties among both civilians and the military or police could be made.

July 21. Belgrade, Serbia. Interior Minister Milorad Drashkovics was assassinated. reportedly by a Bosnian. The authorities subsequently made more than 600 arrests.

Aug. 26. Baden, Germany. Former army officers Heinrich Shulz and Heinrich Tolleson accosted Matthias Erzberger, on holiday in the Black Forest, and shot him repeatedly at close range. He died almost instantly. The former minister of finance had advocated a negotiated settlement of World War I and in 1920 had survived an assassination attempt. The same band, identified as the Ferme Group, a spiritual forerunner of the Nazis, killed Foreign Minister Rathenau the following year (below).

Oct. 19. Lisbon, Portugal. In the continuing post-war political turmoil, with the military in control behind the scenes, the Liberal Party's Antonio Joaquim Granjo assumed the post of prime minister, not for the first time. A new revolt broke out that same day. Men not known to be with the military seized Granjo and killed him in front of the Navy Arsenal.

Nov. 4. Moscow, Russia. Two shots were fired at Russian Foreign Minister Georgi V. Chicherin in his reception room, but without effect. The authorities reportedly rounded up 3,000 people on suspicion.

Nov. 4. Tokyo, Japan. A nineteen-year-old youth stabbed to death Premier Takashi Hara, the first commoner to hold the office, on a railway station platform. The assassin, Ryichi Nakoka, had obscure but far right-wing political motives for the deed. (A May 1920 plot to kill Hara came to light earlier; police had arrested the would-be assassin and seized his explosives.)

Nov. 21. Kovno, Lithuania. Senior minister Ernestas Galvanauskas suffered severe wounds from a large bomb thrown into his residence early in the morning. The political issue in dispute was believed to be his acceptance of League of Nations plans for Vilna.

Nov. 26. San Juan, Argentina. In a political power play, two rifle-bearing brothers named Cantoni assassinated Gov. Amable Jones of San Juan Province and fired on provincial supreme court president Luis Colombo as the two officials stepped from an auto.

1922

Jan. 15. Dublin, Ireland. With the signing of a treaty between London and Sinn Fein leaders, the Irish Free State came into legal existence, consisting of the island except for the Protestant North. Many Irish objected to the exclusion of Ulster; a state of virtual civil war ensued.

Feb. 14. Helsinki, Finland. Two-time Minister of Home Affairs Heikki Ritavuori was killed by an assassin's bullet at the front door of his home.

June. Moscow, Soviet Union. The new Soviet government tried thirty-four Social Revolutionary leaders for high crimes against the state. All were found guilty, although international pressure led to the commutation of the death penalty. (Years later Stalin had all but two of the defendants executed.)

June 22. London, England. Two IRA gunmen shot to death Field Marshal Henry Hughes Wilson, a retired officer from a landed, Protestant Irish family who held a seat in the House of Commons from Ulster. He was a military advisor to the government in Northern Ireland. The murder took place just in front of Wilson's Eaton Place home. The police chased on foot through the streets and caught James Connolly and James O'Brien, reportedly recently arrived from Ireland. After trial, they were hanged on August 10.

June 24. Berlin, Germany. Anti-semitic ultranationalists murdered Walter Rathenau, Weimar Republic foreign minister (and a Jew), in the street as he walked to work. Rathenau was brought down in a hail of bullets, plus a hurled grenade. Police reportedly killed two of the assailants as they attempted to flee the country. Four days later, the police revealed the names of three of the assassins—Tchow, Fischer, and Knauer; at least two others, von Salomon and Kern, later were implicated.

Although members allegedly of a monarchist organization. their essential nihilism was demonstrated by their response to police questions: When asked what they wanted, von Salomon replied,

"We did not act according to plans and well-defined aims." Kern answered, "Oh God, how little does it matter."*

Aug. 22. County Cork, Ireland. In a blow to prospects for stability on the Irish scene, a force reportedly of anti-Free State irregulars ambushed Michael Collins, traveling with a small motorized group of soldiers, and cut him down with rifle fire. The charismatic and controversial thirty-one-year-old Collins was head of the new Irish Free State and its nascent army. Precisely who or which group was responsible for the killing has never been made clear.

Nov. 18. Valetta, Malta. The former head of the Ottoman Empire, Sultan Mohammed VI, arrived hurriedly from Constantinople in great fear for his life and took up residency under armed British protection. He and his followers believe his assassination has been decreed because of his support for Britain's role in the Middle East.

Dec. 6. Leipzig, Germany. The state supreme court passed sentences of ten years at hard labor for two assailants who

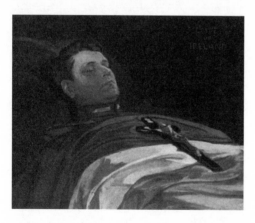

IRA leader Michael Collins, lying in state in 1922 following his somewhat mysterious death in County Cork, Ireland.

*Laqueur, A History of Terrorism, p. 165.

threw acid in the face of Philip Scheidemann, Socialist leader and former foreign affairs secretary. He survived the attack, which took place near Wilhemshohe in early June.

Dec. 7. Dublin, Ireland. IRA gunmen attacked two Irish Free State deputies, Seán Hales and Pádrag Ó Máille. Hales died,; his colleague survived. In retaliation, early the next day the Free State government executed by firing squad four IRA members held in the Mountjoy Jail — Mellows, O'-Connor, McKelvey, and Barrett.

Dec. 16. Warsaw, Poland. After two days in office, the nation's surprise choice as its first elected president, center-leftist Gabriel Narutowicz, fell to an assassin's gun. A middle-aged rightist artist named Niewiedomski shot him in the back three times at an art exhibit, killing him almost instantaneously. Two weeks later a court martial sentenced the gunman to death.

1923

Jan. 23. Paris, France. Twenty-year-old Germaine Berton, an avowed Anarchist, shot to death militant Monarchist Marius Plateau. Almost a year later in a Paris trial, a jury quickly declined to find her guilty due to the "political" nature of her crime.

May 10. Lausanne, Switzerland. Vaslav Vorosky, the unofficial Soviet delegate (the USSR was not invited) to an international conference, was shot and killed at a restaurant. Two aides were wounded. The police arrested Maurice Conradi, a Swiss subject, and Paul Polonnine, a former Czarist official. Moscow's redoubled its protests about the lack of protection for its representative when in November 1923 a Swiss jury's split decision in the trial of the two assailants acquitted both. Not until 1927 did the Swiss and Soviet governments settle their differences over the incident; the Swiss finally apologized and provided compensation for Vorovsky's family.

June 4. Zaragoza, Spain. Juan Cardinal Soldevilla y Romero, who was reputed to be extremely wealthy and an opponent of the labor movement, fell victim to the guns of two young Anarchist assassins, Buenaventura Durruti and Francisco Ascaso. Both escaped to Argentina, later to return to Europe, serve short prison terms, continue terrorist activities, and to die early in the Spanish Civil War fighting for the Republic.

June 8. Sofia, Bulgaria. Reacting against what was seen as a burgeoning agrarian-based dictatorship, a combination of army officers, right-wing intellectuals, and Macedonian nationalists rebelled against reformist Prime Minister Alexander Stamboliski, in power since 1919, and took over the capital. Six days later, after fierce resistance Stamboliski was captured by the military in his home village; he was executed under what was described as exceptionally barbarous conditions, either by a leader of the Internal Macedonian Revolutionary Organization (IMRO) or the military (accounts differ). A right-wing government came to power, ending agrarian reform.

June 27. Belgrade, Serbia. The aging Premier Nikola Pachitch, who had ruled Serbia for two decades and who opposed the formation of Yugoslavia, was wounded by Croat attackers in an assassination attempt. He lived on until the end of 1926.

Sep. 1. Tokyo and Yokohama, *Japan.* A major earthquake hit the Kanto region, devastating both of the area's major cities. Some 100,000 people died with an additional 40,000 missing. Hundreds of thousands were left homeless. Unprepared to cope with or account for such a disaster, the government of Crown Prince and Regent Hirohito circulated rumors that the earthquake was somehow caused by the Korean populace and that they were setting fires and poisoning wells in the aftermath of the quake.

On September 3, anti-Korean riots erupted in Tokyo and other major cities. Some 800 Korean students were killed by the police and over 100,000 Koreans were mobbed and expelled from Japan. The secret Black Dragon Society rounded up more than 4,000 Koreans from the Tokyo slums and beheaded them in the streets. Other radicals met their deaths at the hands of the authorities and vigilante groups.

Dec. 27. Tokyo, Japan. In the what is known as the "Toranomon Incident," a would-be assassin named Daisaku Namba shot at Emperor Hirohito as he rode in the imperial limousine, narrowly missing him. The gunman was arrested on the spot and eventually beheaded. The entire Yamamoto cabinet resigned the next day; the chief of the Tokyo police, Shoriki Matsutaro, was forced to retire in disgrace.

1924

Jan. 5. Tokyo, Japan. A Korean nationalist failed in an attempt to dynamite the Imperial Palace.

Jan. 18. Itzehoe, Germany. Near Hamburg, unidentified assailants threw a bomb at a torchlight procession being held in defiance of Weimar authorities to commemorate the founding of the Reich. Fourteen persons were wounded.

March 12. Athens, Greece. Two diplomatic missions were the targets of unknown terrorists. Dynamite went off not long after midnight outside the British legation, causing considerable damage, but no casualties. Police discovered and disarmed explosives on the front steps of the Rumanian legation. Speculation as to a motive centered on an effort to embarrass the government.

June 1. Vienna, Austria. Chancellor Ignaz Seipel was shot and wounded, supposedly by an opposition Social Democratic activist. The party denied responsibility. Monsignor Seipel recovered, only to resign October 1st. He returned to power in 1926.

June 10. Rome, Italy. Socialist leader Giacomo Matteotti, after denouncing in the Chamber of Deputies the recently installed regime of Benito Mussolini, then predicted to his fellow deputies that he was soon going to his death. He was right. A Fascist Black Shirt terror squad kidnapped and murdered him. Those responsible were not brought to account until after the Second World War.

Three months later, a Fascist deputy, Amando Casalini, was killed in Rome, reportedly in revenge for Matteotti's death. Doubts arose, however, centered on the suspicion that dictator Benito Mussolini's forces might have arranged the murder to show that it faced a threat from the left.

Aug. 22. Rio de Janeiro, Brazil. A bomb exploded at the front of the Argentine embassy just as Ambassador Mora y Araujo was entering the building. He escaped unhurt, however. The Brazilian press kept the incident quiet, as it did five other bomb explosions that same night, one at the Italian embassy. The purpose of the attacks seemed to have been to make international difficulties for the current government.

Aug. 31. Pirin Mountain, Bulgaria. A noted leader of the Macedonian terrorist organization IMRO, Todor Alexandrov, met his death along with a companion at the hands of two killers designated to carry out the sentence of a grouping of military officers, IMRO rivals, and Comintern activists. A small party made its way on foot toward talks between Alexandrov and political foes. In the early afternoon, while all paused for a rest, Shteryu Vlahov and Dincho Vretenarov suddenly shot their victims repeatedly in the back with rifles and escaped the remote scene. At question had been, among other issues, the role that the Soviet Union would play in utilizing IMRO for its own purposes.

Nov. 19. Cairo, Egypt. Nationalists shot and fatally wounded Sir Oliver Stack, British governor general of Sudan and Egyptian army commander, on his way by auto to his Zemalek Island headquarters. He died the following day. His driver and an aide were wounded. The assassination was one of a series of killings of British officials that had begun in 1920. This murder of Stack led directly to heightened British control over Egypt for years to come.

In June 1925, a court handed down guilty verdicts on nine men for the murder, including a lawyer, Shafik Mansur, and a former legislative deputy, Mahmud Ismail; the two were said to be the leaders. The police also found the latter to have kept a supply of bombs in the house of a friend.

1925

April 16. Sofia, Bulgaria. A bomb blast outside the Sveta Nedelya church in which a funeral was underway killed as many as 150 persons and wounded scores more. Two government ministers were in-

The funeral procession of Italian Socialist deputy Giacomo Matteoti, murdered by Fascist Black Shirts in June 1924.

jured, including Premier Alexander Tsankoff. Communists had been ousted from power in 1923 and clearly were responsible; indeed, the funeral was being held for a general assassinated earlier by Communists to bring together a high-level group of mourners. The general chaos led within months to the ouster from office of Prof. Tsankoff.

King Boris III, who was in attendance, survived unhurt, as he had the previous day when a would-be assassin failed in an attempt to kill him. And less than a month later, on May 2, he survived yet another attempt on his life. Boris III lived until 1943, when he died under mysterious circumstances after a strained interview with Hitler (below).

May 8, Vienna, Austria. The last of the Federalist Macedonian leaders, Todor Panizza, died at the hands of a female assassin named Anna Karlinciu, who was possibly a Bulgarian agent. Both Bulgaria and Yugoslavia had long opposed the political aims of Panizza and his colleagues, virtually all of whom had been eliminated by assassination. The murderer, who had recently befriended Panizza and his wife, shot and killed him at the climax of a performance of Ibsen's "Peer Gynt." She also wounded the three other members of his party, even though all were armed. Karlinciu was seized on the spot.

July 17. Vienna, Austria. Members of an anti-Semitic group attacked Vienna's Stuttgart Casino and wrecked several Jewish coffee houses, causing about $4,000,000 in damage. They were demanding cancellation of a Zionist World Congress scheduled for Vienna on August 16th.

1926

June. Izmir, Turkey. During the course of the month, a conspirator revealed an assassination plot against

Mustafa Kemal (Atatürk), "the father of the Turkish Republic," headed by a former follower, Ziya Hurshid. Fifteen of the plotters were rounded up, tried, convicted, and executed.

April 23. Geneva, Switzerland. Theodore Aubert, a lawyer who defended Conradi in the 1923 slaying of Soviet delegate Vorovsky (above) and a known anti-Bolshevik, narrowly escaped death. A gunman gained entrance to his home, fired a pistol at Aubert point-blank but somehow missed him. He escaped on a bicycle. Police concluded that it was an attack in revenge for Vorovsky's assassination.

1927

July 10. Dublin, Ireland. Opponents of the unpopular Irish Free State minister of home affairs, Kevin O'Higgins, shot and killed him as he walked unaccompanied to Sunday Mass at Booterstown Church.

Aug. 6. New York, USA. Bombs exploded in two Manhattan subway locations, one in the 28th Street IRT (Lex Line) station and the other in the 28th Street (Broadway) BMT station. Several persons were injured, two seriously, but there were no fatalities. The authorities put 14,000 policemen on special duty and made several arrests. It remained obscure, however, what had motivated the attack; speculation touched upon Anarchists, Communists or protesters exercised over the current Sacco-Vanzeti case.

1928

March 27. Buenos Aires, Argentina. In the midst of a widespread strike calling

for the release of an Anarchist, Simon Radowitsky, jailed back in 1909 (above), a bomb exploded on the railroad tracks as a passenger train passed over. A guard was slightly injured, the only casualty. A youth found other explosive materials in the underground railway and police were able to neutralize the bomb. Authorities believed the violence was aimed at forcing the rail operators to join in the strike.

May 16. Pontiac, Mich., USA. In a nonpolitical harbinger of things to come, one Clarence Frechette hired an airplane and, once aloft, attacked the pilot, attempting to hijack and crash the aircraft to commit suicide. The pilot, Harry Anderson, managed to stave off the attack and land safely despite being injured. The would-be hijacker, reportedly disappointed in love, was taken away for a mental examination.

June 28. Belgrade, Serbia. In a session of the parliament, a radical Serbian named Punisa Racic opened fire with a revolver, killing two Croatian deputies, Pavle Radic and Djuro Basariceck, and seriously wounded Stjepan Radic, leader of the outlawed Croatian Peasant Party, along with two other deputies. Widespread violence broke out as a result. Radic died from his wounds six weeks later, on August 8. The Serbian secret police were believed to have orchestrated the assassinations.

Oct. 7. Bombay, India. An explosion on a train killed four people on the eve of the arrival of the Simon Commission, a wholly British body charged with deciding the future of India. Possibly the bombs were intended for use against the Commission but exploded prematurely.

Dec. 11. Buenos Aires, Argentina. The police stymied an attempt on the life of newly elected U. S. President Herbert

Hoover. Details are lacking, but it came during his seven-week goodwill visit to Central and South America.

Dec. 17. Lahore, India. Three assailants shot and killed a British police constable named J. P. Saunders, this in retaliation for the loss of a nationalist leader, Lala Lajpat Rai, who had died as a result of the beating he received in a demonstration against the Simon Commission (above). The three, Baghat Singh, Rajguru, and Azad, joined forces to kill Saunders, whom they took (erroneously) to be the officer responsible.

An organization called the Hindustan Socialist Republican Army the next day issued a manifesto stating, *inter alia*, "Sorry for the bloodshed of a human being; but the sacrifice of individuals at the altar of the Revolution that will bring freedom to all and make the exploitation of man by main impossible, is inevitable."

In 1928, Hassan al-Banna, an Egyptian teacher, founded the Muslim Brotherhood as a youth association. The Brotherhood was gradually politicized in the 1930's. In 1939 it evolved into a political group. Many members engaged in terrorist actions inside Egypt.

1929

April 8. Delhi, India. Two nationalists, Bhaghat Singh and Batukeswar Datta, each threw a grenade into the Indian Legislative Assembly from the public gallery. The double blast injured five members on the floor; no one was killed. Observers called it the most serious terrorist incident since 1912, when Lord Hardinge was wounded (see above). The two assailants (one a university student), although armed with pistols, gave themselves up without using them.

They, along with three others involved in the plot, were tried and sentenced to death. In court they said they had tried by their action to make the deaf hear. All were hanged in Lahore Central Jail on March 23, 1931.

Dec. 28. New Delhi, India. Unknown terrorists exploded a bomb buried under the track of the train bearing the viceroy, Lord Irwin, and his entourage to the capital. Providentially for the British party, the damage done to the rails and roadbed was not sufficient to derail the many cars that passed over the spot on a thirty-foot-high embankment. The authorities noted that the bombing was the result of careful planning and scientific skill.

1930–1939

1930

Feb. 5. Mexico City, Mexico. Following victory in an arranged election (not an unusual event in the Mexico of the *Partido Revolucionario*), on inauguration day President Pascal Ortiz Rubio was painfully wounded in a failed assassination attempt. His wife, a young niece, and several other persons nearby also were slightly injured by a gunman in his mid-twenties named Daniel Flores. He opened fire as the party was leaving the National Palace in a chauffeured automobile and was immediately subdued by motorcycle police. The new president recovered from his wounds, but apparently never quite got over the traumatic event; increasingly fearful for his life, he resigned from office in 1932.

Flores was suspected of acting for Ortiz Rubio's chief political rival, José Vasconcelos; several of the latter's followers were arrested. Sentenced to twenty years imprisonment, Flores died behind bars in April 1932, of natural causes according to prison officials. He never admitted taking part in a plot or having accomplices.

June 8. Lisbon, Portugal. The German minister to Portugal, Dr. Henry Albert von Baligand, was assassinated.

Nov. 14. Tokyo, Japan. In an incident that formed part of a period in Japan that has been labeled "politics by assassination," a member of the right-wing group called Love of Country Association shot and seriously wounded Premier Yuko Hamaguchi. The attack took place in the same railway station in which Premier Hara was killed in 1921 (above). Hamaguchi's relatively restrained policy in China and "soft" diplomatic measures angered the government's critics. Hamaguchi never fully recovered; he left office and died the following year.

1931

Feb. 18. Zagreb, Yugoslavia. The noted Croatian scholar Dr. Milan Sufflay, returning home on a main street of the Croatian capital, was attacked from behind and beaten very badly with an iron rod. He died the next day. The murderer, Branko Zwerger, was a member of a pan-Serbian organization, *Mlada Yugoslavia* (Young Yugoslavia). The deed reportedly was planned by the military commander of the city, Gen. Belimarkovic.

No less world figures than Albert Einstein and Heinrich Mann appealed to the International League of Human Rights in Paris for the protection of Croats against Serbs. Their letter to the League concludes, "[I]t should not be tolerated that killings be allowed as a means to achieve political goals. We should not allow killers to be promoted as national heroes."

Feb. 21. Vienna, Austria. King Zog I of Albania barely escaped an assassination attempt as he left the Vienna Opera House — one of several such attempts. He survived many years, however, and died in exile in Paris in 1961.

Feb. 21. Piura, Peru. The volatile circumstances of multiple revolts against a provisional government brought the first known instance of skyjacking in a political setting. Three insurrectionists in northern Peru, including a Captain Jaramillo, seized a Faucett Aviation domestic airliner, a Ford Tri-Motor. They forced the pilot (and owner of the airline), Elmer Faucett, to fly them forty miles to Piura. There, troops loyal to the government in Lima promptly captured the three revolutionaries.

Aug. 22. Chicago, USA. In the midst of labor disputes, three movie houses were bombed almost simultaneously. No casualties resulted.

1932

Jan. 8. Tokyo, Japan. A grenade thrown by a young Korean nationalist exploded near Emperor Hirohito's carriage outside the main entrance to the Imperial palace. No one was injured. The attack occasioned anti-Japanese comments in the Chinese press, which sparked the "First Shanghai Incident." That episode resulted in large-scale fighting in China between Chinese and Japanese forces.

Jan. 16. Lisbon, Portugal. By rounding up 200 persons, the police headed off what they said was a plot to assassinate President António Oscar de Fragosa Carmona and Finance Minister António de Oliveira Salazar. Leading the reported plot was a former priest named Fuarec, who had returned clandestinely from exile in the Azores.

In August of that year, Salazar took power and ruled until his death in 1968.

Jan. 22. El Salvador. A peasant and worker uprising broke out that the government of Gen. Maximiliano Hernández Martínez swiftly put down. In following weeks, the new military dictatorship launched a program of reprisals called "*La Matanza*" — "The Slaughter" — another extreme example of official terrorism. During the course of the rebellion itself, some 4,000 people had lost their lives. As punishment for the uprising, acting on orders, the Salvadorian army killed another 20,000 to 30,000, mostly Indian peasants. The two leaders of the insurrection, Farabundo Martí and José Feliciano Ama, were hanged upon capture.

It was the largest single bloodbath ever in the Western Hemisphere.

Jan. 29. Shanghai, China. In perhaps the twentieth century's first deliberate mass terror bombing — the first of innumerable such attacks — the Japanese army and navy shelled and bombed the Chinese quarter of this international city. Thousands of civilians were killed and damage was extensive.

Feb. 9. Tokyo, Japan. Entering a political meeting, former finance minister Junnosuke Inouye was gunned down by Sei Konuma, a member of what was called a "super-patriotic society." Inouye, who opposed the military's 1931 incursion into Manchuria, died within minutes.

April 29. Shanghai, China. A Korean threw a grenade in Hongkew Park that killed one Japanese official and wounded two other persons.

May 7. Paris, France. The president of France, Paul Doumer, was assassinated by a Russian emigre Anarchist, Paul Gorguloff. The fatal shot was fired while Doumer was presiding at the opening of a book fair.

May 15. Tokyo, Japan. Members of a right-wing group called the Young Officers Association burst into the home of elderly Prime Minister Tsuyoshi Inukai, shot him in the head, and wounded two other people. He died a few hours later, just after midnight. Traveling about the capital in autos, the group also threw bombs at several locations, including the government political party headquarters and the home of Count Nobuaki Makina, an adviser to the emperor. Five policemen and a reporter were injured. The police arrested eighteen of the attackers, all wearing military or naval uniforms. The officers eventually were tried and convicted, but served no time. The public trials allowed them to air their ultranationalist views.

The prime minister had opposed Japan's seizure of Manchuria and the growing control of the military.

June 7. Zagreb, Yugoslavia. Three men attacked Dr. Mile Budak with clubs and daggers on Zagreb's main street, near the Italian embassy. Budak, a prominent Croatian nationalist leader and lawyer,

died at the hospital to which he was taken. All three assailants were believed to be members of the pan-Serbian Young Yugoslavia; questions were raised about their affiliation with the Yugoslav secret police in Zagreb.

1933

Feb. 15. Miami, USA. Franklin D. Roosevelt escaped harm in a shooting attack shortly before his first inauguration. An unemployed Italian-born man named Giuseppe Zangora opened fire at close range with a pistol at the conclusion of a short speech at Bayside Park by the president-elect. Roosevelt was untouched, but several people were wounded, including the mayor of Chicago, Anton Cermak, who died two weeks later. Zangora, promptly captured and tried, was first sentenced to eighty years in prison; when Cermak succumbed to his wound, the killer received a death sentence. He was electrocuted at Raiford prison in Florida only thirty-three days after the shooting. Meanwhile, Roosevelt was inaugurated on March 4.

The record remains unclear as to whether Zangora was a unstable Anarchist whose target was Roosevelt, the representative of American capitalism, or perhaps a killer acting for organized crime to do away with the Chicago mayor. Some reports indicate, however, that he went to his death cursing and railing against capitalism to the end.

Feb. 27. Berlin, Germany. The new Nazi government attributed a suspicious fire that gutted the Reichstag building to Communists and other leftists. The Nazis claimed that it signaled an uprising and used the fire as justification for arresting thousands of opponents. A day later, all left-wing newspapers were closed and two decrees issued which permanently annulled basic citizens' rights spelled out in the Weimar constitution.

On January 10, 1934, at Leipzig, the Nazi government executed Marinus van der Lubbe for setting the fire.

March 8. Berlin, Germany. The Nazi minister of the Interior, Wilhelm Frick, announced the establishment of a system of government concentration camps for political prisoners. The first four were Oranienburg, north of Berlin; Esterwegen, near Hamburg; Dachau, northwest of Munich; and Lichtenburg, in Saxony. All of these, with the exception of the infamous Dachau, were gradually dismantled and replaced by 1939 with six additional main camps under the jurisdiction of Hitler's Black Shirts, the SS (*Schutzstaffel*).

April 30. Lima, Peru. President Luis Miguel Sanchez Cerro, departing the reviewing stand after watching troops pass in review, was shot twice by Albert Mendoza, a member of the leftist APRA party (the *Alianza Popular Revolucionaria Americana*). Although rushed to the Italian hospital, the president (and former general) died within fifteen minutes. Guards and police fell upon the assailant, hacking him to pieces as a general melee ensued. That evening the congress elected Gen. Oscar Benevides provisional president.

June 21–26. Germany. The paramilitary SA (*Sturmabteilung*). along with SS troops, reportedly killed ninety-one civilians nationwide, mostly Social Democrats and Communists.

Aug. 11–16. Simele, Iraq. Orchestrated by the Iraqi government, the army, commanded by Bakir Sidqi, massacred an estimated 3,000 Assyrians in the village of Simele and its surrounding area in the north. (Three years later Gen. Sidqi, a Kurd, led the first coup in the modern Arab world.) On September 20, the Catholic Patriarch of the Assyrians in Cyprus issued an appeal to the League of Nations, but without effect.

Oct. 3. Vienna, Austria. Chancellor Engelbert Dollfuss, an opponent of the Nazi party's increasing inroads on Austrian politics, was slightly wounded in an assassination attempt by an Austrian Nazi Party member.

Nov. 8. Kabul, Afghanistan. King Nadir Shah was shot to death by a lone gunman while presiding over a student prize award ceremony. The assassin was a relative of a man executed a year earlier for plotting rebellion. The king's nineteen-year-old son, sitting next to him, unsuccessfully tried to intervene. Ousted in 1973, the latter returned from exile in Rome almost thirty years later, upon the overthrow of the Taliban regime.

Dec. 30. Carpathia, Romania. Three Iron Guard adherents named Nicolae Constantinescu, Doro Belimace, and Ion Caranica shot to death Premier Ion Gheorghe Duca, a relatively liberal political figure in office only six weeks. They immediately surrendered to police. In April 1934, a military court sentenced the three to life in prison at hard labor for the crime. The assassination set off years of violence that led to the rise to power of Ion Antonescu, an ally of Hitler.

1934

Jan. 11. Berlin, Germany. German police raided the homes of dissident clergy.

June 30. Berlin, Germany. Chancellor Adolf Hitler began his purge of poten-

France's Paul Doumer (right), president from May 1931 to his death by assassination a year later.

tial political and military rivals in Germany in the "Night of the Long Knives." Among those shot before firing squads against the walls of Stadelheim prison were Ernst Roehm, leader of the SA and an early supporter of the Nazi party. Other SA leaders such as Edmund Heines and August Schneidhuber died, as well. Hitler sought thus to downgrade the SA, which had had a strength of as many as 400,000 men, and substitute therefore the smaller SS, which followed his orders.

The same day, the Gestapo seized Gregor Strasser, a Socialist and the then-number two figure in the Nazi party, at his Berlin home; they murdered him at Gestapo headquarters with a gunshot to the back of the head. Hitler feared Strasser as a political rival.

Murdered as well—for the same reason—was former chancellor Gen. Kurt von Schleicher, along with his wife and a close friend, Gen. Kurt von Bredow. SS gunmen killed them near Berlin; Hitler thought both the officers were possible opponents.

June 16. Warsaw, Poland. A group described variously as Ukrainian nationalists or anti-semitic assassinated Col. Bronislaw Pieracki, the interior minister. As an ominous foretaste of the future, the government set up a concentration camp for terrorists and other dangerous subversives at Bereza Kartuska.

June 30. Dachau, Germany. Yet another victim at that time of official terror tactics was the elderly Gustav von Kahr, a former Bavarian official. Members of the SS abducted him and left his bullet-riddled body to be found near Dachau. Although far to the right politically, von Kahr had opposed Hitler in the latter's failed 1924 Munich Beer Hall Putsch; the Fuehrer's memory was long.

July 25. Vienna, Austria. Fascist Chancellor Engelbert Dollfuss, resisting takeover by the Austrian Nazi party backed by Hitler, was shot twice by Otto Planetta, an SS leader. Planetta, with 150-odd troops, had managed to invade the chancellery shortly after a handful of Nazi troops had seized Vienna's radio station. Planetta allowed the chancellor to bleed to death before Austrian forces retook the building seven hours later and quashed the coup attempt. Hitler thereupon disowned the rebels.

Six days later the two coup leaders, Planetta and Holzweber, were summarily executed; eleven other participants eventually were hanged.

July 25. Lwow, Poland. Jan Wadij, director of the Ukrainian College, was shot dead leaving his apartment. The assassin, twenty-year-old Jasyl Sawtzuk, a member of the Ukrainian Nationalist organization, was taking retribution for his victim's condemnation of terrorism by the Nationalists.

Oct. 9. Marseilles, France. King Alexander I of Yugoslavia, along with French Foreign Minister Louis Barthou, were assassinated on the orders of a Croatian nationalist movement, apparently for the king's pro-French policies. The killer, Blade Chernozamsky, emptied his pistol into the open car in which the two rode, along with French general Alfonse Georges (who survived). Chernozamsky was shot by a policeman in the ensuing scuffle and died some hours later. Rumor had it that the assassination was furthered secretly by Premier Benito Mussolini of Fascist Italy.

Two cameramen in the king's party filmed moving pictures of the event—a first—which were shown widely on the movie screens of Europe and America. Adolf Hitler ordered the footage bought and used it to organize and instruct his own security detail.

Dec. 1. Smolny, Soviet Union. The secret police, the NKVD, instigated the assassination of Sergei M. Kirov, a promi-

Nazi Germany's Chancellor Adolf Hitler in an early portrait. He unleashed virtually unlimited state terror in the 1930s and '40s.

nent Communist Party leader and Stalin protégé whom Stalin had come to consider a potential rival. A veteran party worker named Leonid Nikolayev gained access to Kirov's office with suspicious ease. There Nikolayev shot and killed him. Investigation over the years has shown fairly conclusively that the killing was arranged on the orders of Stalin himself.

Dec. 5. Leningrad, Soviet Union. In the aftermath of the Kirov assassination, the Soviet authorities decreed the deaths of thirty-nine people; twenty-nine were executed in Moscow.

Dec. 28 and 29. Leningrad, Soviet Union. Kirov's death was followed immediately by the arrest and execution of fourteen persons, including Nikolayev, who in a secret trial had been found to be guilty of the murder. Eventually in the aftermath, a reported 104 alleged foreign agents and terrorists were shot.

The "Great Purge," or "Great Terror," had begun.

1935

In Russia in 1935, after the assassination of Kirov (above) Stalin launched an attack on the party aimed at eliminating potential rivals. Anyone could be denounced for being Trotskyites or counter-revolutionaries. Dozens of old Bolsheviks were executed in the wave of state terror. The number of prisoners in the gulag rose above half a million.

Jan. 15–18. Moscow, Soviet Union. The "Moscow Center" trials resulted in the conviction of party leaders G. E. Zinoviev, L. B. Kamenev, and seventeen others to prison terms for alleged counter-revolutionary activities and complicity in the Kirov assassination.

June 2. Montevideo, Uruguay. Pres. Gabriel Terra escaped an assassination attempt with a scratch to his leg. While at the Maronas race course with visiting Brazilian President Getulio Vargas, the president and his party encountered a former deputy, Bernardo Garcia, who fired point blank at Terra. His aim was deflected by a bystander, however, and he was immediately taken into custody.

July 25. Moscow, Soviet Union. Kamenev, tried again, and thirty-seven co-defendants were tried and found guilty of plotting against Stalin. Two were executed; Kamenev received a sentence of ten years.

Nov. 1. Nanking, China. Premier Wang Ching-wei and three cabinet-level officials, all bearing the onus of appeasing Japan, were wounded in an assassination attempt. The four were shot in a blaze of

King Alexander I of Yugoslavia, who was assassinated in October 1934, along with French Foreign Minister Louis Bartou, before two movie cameras.

gunfire while posing for a group photograph. The assailant, killed shortly afterward, was identified as a member of the central committee of the Kuomintang (Nationalist) Party. The premier recovered and lived until 1944.

1936

Feb. 26. Tokyo, Japan. Led by relatively junior officers (with civilian political backing), troops seized an area around the Imperial Palace and parts of downtown Tokyo. Prime Minister Keisuke Okada escaped unharmed, Grand Chamberlain Kantaro Suzuki was wounded, and former ministers Makato Saitô and Korekiyo Takahashi were killed. The revolt collapsed after the Emperor labeled the leaders rebels; loyal army units and the navy restored control. Most rebels were executed without a public trial. Okada soon resigned and lived on in retirement until 1952.

July 13. Madrid, Spain. Leftists murdered former finance minister José Calvo Sotelo, who had incurred the wrath of the republican government by his verbal attacks in the parliament. His death can be counted as the first of many in the ensuing Spanish Civil War.

In the Soviet Union, 1936 saw the beginning of the Moscow Show Trials. Important Party members were put on public trial, found guilty, and in most cases, executed. A year later a purge of the armed forced began. By 1939 almost every top navy and army commander and about half of all other officers had been executed.

Aug, 9. Granada, Spain. Falangist soldiers dragged leftist poet and playwright Federico Garcia Lorca and three companions into a field in the foothills of the Sierra Nevada Mountains, shot them, and tossed their bodies into unmarked graves. Considered a dangerous intellectual, he was one of the most famous casualties in Spain's civil war.

General Francisco Franco's government tried to obliterate Lorca's memory, but without lasting success: Today he is considered Spain's greatest poet and dramatist of the twentieth century.

Aug. 19-24. Moscow, Soviet Union. The First Show Trial. Zinoviev and Kamenev (both being tried yet again) and fourteen other senior Communist Party officials were found guilty of plotting, with Trotsky (who was in exile), to murder Stalin and other Party leaders. All were shot on August 25. The families of Zinoviev and Kamenev also were executed or exiled.

Soviet leader Joseph Stalin at about the time of the "Moscow Center" trials in 1935.

1937

Jan. 23–30. Moscow, Soviet Union. The Second Show Trial. These proceedings resulted in the conviction of all seventeen defendants accused of sabotage and a plot to overthrow the Soviet government. Of these, thirteen were shot and four received prison terms of eight to ten years.

April 26. Guernica y Luno, Spain. An operation of no military consequence intended as a show of force was carried out by the elite Kondor Legion of the German Luftwaffe for Francisco Franco's Nationalist forces: a saturation bombing of a strategically inconsequential town near Bilbao in northern Spain. Some 800 civilians died. The raid inspired condemnation world wide and resulted in the famous painting *Guernica* by Pablo Picasso, which now hangs in the Museo de Reina Sofia in Madrid.

By 1940, and for the rest of the century, aerial bombardments by all military powers routinely targeted civilian population centers.

June 11. Moscow, Soviet Union. In another of the Stalin regime's tribunals, Marshal Mikhail Tukhachevsky, arrested earlier in the month and charged with conspiracy with Germany, along with seven other top commanders, was found guilty and executed.

Aug. 12. Baghdad, Iraq. A group of army officers, unhappy with Gen. Bakir Sidqi Pasha's left-leaning government, had him assassinated. The Kurdish general had seized power only the year before.

1938

March 2–12. Moscow, Soviet Union. The Third Show Trial. Twenty-one Party luminaries, including Nikolai Bukharin and Alexei Rykov, long-time Communist leaders, were tried for allegedly cooperating with foreign intelligence to wreck the economy, with a view toward overthrowing the USSR.

On Mar. 15 Bukharin and Rykov were shot. All but three of the defendants were executed; those spared received prison sentences of fifteen to twenty-five years.

July 25. San Juan, Puerto Rico. At a parade celebrating the fortieth anniversary of the American acquisition of Puerto Rico, nationalists tried to kill Governor Blanton Winship by firing more than eighty shots at the reviewing stand. As unlikely as it seems, Winship escaped injury,

but his bodyguard was wounded and a nearby official, Lt. Colonel Luis Irizarry, was killed. One of the gunmen was killed on the spot. The following day, in the city of Ponce, thirteen persons were arrested; photos in the slain Antongiorgi's pocket led to the identification of several of these. Among those arrested was Elias Escobar, who had been tried and acquitted of killing a policeman in Ponce the previous year.

Six months later, on January 26, 1939, the trials of the accused ended with six men sentenced to life terms. Three other nationalists who became witnesses for the prosecution were released.

Nov. 9. Germany and Austria. In the infamous *Kristallnacht*, a night of terror, Nazis destroyed some 7,500 Jewish-owned shops, harried Jews in the streets, and torched 190 synagogues. Police arrested 300,000 Jews and others described as opponents of the Hitler regime.

1939

Aug. 25. Coventry, England. The IRA exploded a bomb that killed five people.

Sep. 21. Bucharest, Romania. In his official automobile on a busy downtown street, Prime Minister Armand Calinescu was shot and killed by six pro-Nazi Iron Guard gunmen in an attempt to set off an uprising. They failed in that aim. The same evening, police summarily executed nine men implicated in the attack. The days after the prime minister's assassination saw the government executing more than 200 imprisoned Iron Guard members.

1940–1949

The most important unsuccessful as-sassination in history — the attempt on Adolf Hitler.

1940

March 13. London, England. A Sikh militant named Udham Singh fired five shots at and killed Sir Michael F. O'Dwyer, who had been governor of Punjab in India from 1913 to 1919. O'Dwyer died at a meeting of the East India Association. He had approved the action of Gen. Dyer at the April 1919 Amritsar massacre (above). Udham Singh was tried, convicted, and hanged on July 31, 1940, in London.

Aug. 20. Coyoacán, Mexico. Stalin finally eliminated from the world scene the figure he viewed as his foremost potential rival, the renowned Bolshevik, Leon Trotsky. After exiling him from the Soviet Union in 1929, the Soviet dictator eventually had him assassinated. He lived temporarily in a succession of countries and in 1936 settled near Mexico City in a heavily guarded villa. In 1938, Soviet agents murdered Trotsky's son in Paris. On May 24, 1940, came the first direct attack on Trotsky. The assault, allegedly directed by the famous Mexican painter David Alfaro Sequeiros, resulted in one death (bodyguard Sheldon Harte of New York) and extensive damage to his villa. The principal human target escaped harm, however.

Stalin's secret police earlier introduced an agent, Ramon Mercader, into the scene; he had won Trotsky's trust and now it was his turn. Three months after the failed frontal attack, Mercader lured Trotsky into the latter's study, supposedly to review a draft article. There he struck the exiled leader in the head with an ice ax he had concealed. Trotsky died the following day of the massive wound. Stalin no longer had any reason to fear Trotsky's influence on the world Communist movement. Tried and convicted in a Mexican court, Mercader spent twenty years in prison, gaining his release in 1960. He died in Havana in 1978.

Nov. 29. Bucharest, Romania. Noted historian and former premier Nicolas Iorga, leader of the National Democratic party, was assassinated by terrorists of the Iron Guard.

1941

March 11. Istanbul, Turkey. A bomb planted in the luggage room of the Pera Palace Hotel exploded soon after the arrival of the British embassy delegation recently departed from Bulgaria. Four people died and eleven were wounded, two seriously. Sources indicated that the attack was the work of Bulgarian terrorists and the Nazi Gestapo.

March 23. Lisbon, Portugal. A military court sentenced fourteen alleged terrorists to prison terms up to twenty-eight years.

April 20. Sarajevo, Yugoslavia. The German army upon entering the city took down a memorial table commemorating the assassination in 1914 of Archduke Franz Ferdinand (above) and turned it over to Adolf Hitler, then on the Balkan front. The army announced it would be exhibited as proof of the Serbs' guilt for the onset of World War I.

Aug. 14. Tokyo, Japan. The influential senior political figure Baron Kiichiro Hiranuma was shot and seriously wounded by Nachiko Ishiyama, reportedly a member of the Black Dragon Society. Hiranuma, formerly an ardent nationalist, had taken the position publicly that the nation should adopt a cautious foreign policy. Later in the month, a Tokyo court sentenced nine conspirators to jail terms ranging up to two and one-half years. It was the first assassination attempt on a government figure at that level since the late 1920's.

Aug. 27. Versailles, France. Pierre Laval, Nazi collaborator and former Vichy foreign minister and vice premier, along with a colleague, the editor Marcel Deat, were seriously wounded in an assassination attempt by a Gaullist named Paul Collette. The last-named fired five shots at Laval at a barracks where a French legion was being formed to fight with Germany against Russia. Within three days, the Vichy government had executed eleven persons by firing squad. Laval recovered. He was tried and convicted of treason at war's end; in October 1945 he in turn was executed by firing squad.

1942

Jan. 20. Berlin, Germany. Decisions taken by the Nazi high command made the "Final Solution" with respect to Jews an official German government policy and a major obsession of the Hitler regime.

June 4. Prague, Czechoslovakia. A war-time assassination set off an episode of ferocious state terror — the destruction of the town of Lidice and the murder of all its male inhabitants. Czechoslovaks partisans who had parachuted in from England waylaid the Nazi German "Protector" or governor, Reinhard Heydrich, as he was driven to his office at Prague Castle. He was seriously wounded and died ten days later, setting off fierce reprisals. All of the attacking parachutists died in the endeavor.

Dec. 24. Algiers, Algeria. Adm. Jean-François Darlan, recently designated by American General Dwight Eisenhower as leader of the Free French in North Africa despite his background of collaboration with the German conquerors of France, was shot and killed by a lone gunman, Ferdinand Bonnier de la Chapelle. The fatal shots came as he entered the Free French headquarters building. His anti-Nazi, royalist assassin was trained by British intelligence and had been a member of the French Resistance. No available evidence indicates he acted under the orders of any particular group, but speculation exists that his was a "deniable" action by the British secret service to rid the scene of the controversial admiral.

Gen. Henri Giraud was named to succeed Darlan. The assassin was tried by a military court and summarily executed.

Adm. Darlan, late 1942, flanked by U.S. generals Eisenhower (left) and Mark Clark.

1943

July 11. New York, USA. A radical leftist (but opponent of Stalinism) named Carlo Tresca was murdered in the street, the victim of a never-solved crime. The intellectual and editor had enemies at both ends of the political spectrum.

Aug. 28. Sofia, Bulgaria. King Boris III had survived several attacks and assassination attempts over the years. A reluctant supporter of Germany in World War II, he met his end suddenly after a strained interview with Hitler concerning Bulgaria's further participation in the Axis war effort. The exact cause of his death is not known: possibly a heart attack, possibly assassination.

1944

May 26, Rastenburg, Germany. At his Prussian headquarters, Chancellor Adolf Hitler, addressing the question of the slaughter of Jews, spoke to senior officers of the German army: "By removing the Jew, I abolished in Germany the possibility to build up a revolutionary core or nucleus. One could naturally say to me: Yes, couldn't you have solved this more simply … [or] more humanely? My dear officers, we are engaged in a life or death struggle. If our opponents win in this struggle, then the German people would be extirpated."[1]

July 20. Rastenburg, Germany. Adolf Hitler narrowly escaped death in what has been called "perhaps the most important unsuccessful assassination in history."[2] The episode warrants inclusion here for its potentially crucial bearing on one period of twentieth century history, although not occasioned by terrorists in the usual sense.

Numerous plots throughout Hitler's career aimed at his elimination, but only one happened to come close to success—one calling for a bomb to be set off virtually at Hitler's feet in a staff conference at his headquarters in East Prussia. The ringleader and person who placed a brief case containing the bomb was Lt. Colonel

Klaus Schenk von Stauffenberg, who had long despised Hitler. He and the generals whom he represented clearly had had enough, finally, of the Fuehrer's losing efforts in the war.

Four officers were killed in the explosion and Hitler was injured, but the force of the bomb had been dissipated by its placement. A heavy table leg partially shielded Hitler and he survived. Stauffenberg had set an acid-activated detonator and had left before the explosion. Thinking Hitler was surely dead, he tried to set in train the plot to take over the government from Berlin. Loyal officers and troops backed Hitler once it was known he was alive, however, and the massacre of the conspirators began. This included the renowned Field Marshal Erwin Rommel, who was obliged to take poison, even though only marginally involved in the plot. Stauffenberg was shot by a firing squad. Others died at Hitler's orders in particularly dreadful ways. In the following weeks, some 7,000 arrests were made and as many as 2,000 received death sentences. Germany continued the war ten more months, until May 1945.

1945

Feb. 24. Cairo, Egypt. Premier Ahmed Maher Pasha took the floor of parliament to read a royal declaration of war against Germany and Japan. A young lawyer named Mahmoud Essawy then shot him fatally, evidently because Essawy (among many others) had held that Egypt's best chance for freedom from British rule lay in support for the Axis Powers. A military court found Essawy guilty; he was hanged in September 1945.

Oct. 31. Palestine. With World War II over, a Jewish terrorist offensive against British rule began. Multiple bombings took place on police vehicles, railway sites, and the Haifa oil refinery. One policeman, one soldier, and two civilian railway workers were killed on this date.

Nov. 27. Jerusalem, Palestine. Eight British soldiers died in a bomb attack on a police station. On this occasion, unusually, no civilians were injured. The bombing was blamed on the Jewish terrorist group *Irgun Zvai Leumi*, headed by Menachem Begin (later the prime minister of Israel).

1946

March 11. Tehran, Iran. Historian, prolific author, and reformer Ahmad Kasravi was killed by a fanatical group called the *Feda'iyan-e Eslam*. It was the first of a series of assassinations sanctioned by Iranian religious leaders (see below).

July 22. Jerusalem, Palestine. Shortly after noon, Jewish terrorists, the group Irgun and the Stern Gang, blew up the King David Hotel, in the west wing of which the British had their heavily guarded headquarters. (The Stern Gang was a Zionist terrorist group headed by Itzak Shamir, later prime minister of Israel.) Operatives disguised as waiters that morning had brought seven milk cans packed with TNT through a rear entrance into a civilian restaurant area. Casualties from the tremendous blast, estimated to have the force of a 500-kilogram aerial bomb, totaled ninety-one killed (forty-one Arabs, twenty-eight British, and seventeen Jews) and forty-five injured. The Irgun reportedly telephoned a warning to the hotel fifteen minutes beforehand; according to Begin, his object was to terrorize the British, not to kill indiscriminately. A hotel assistant manager ignored the warning, considering it another false alarm. The British immediately arrested and held for questioning more than 400 Jewish activists and imposed a 6 p.m. to 6 a.m. curfew.

London and much of the rest of the world, including Jewish agencies, reacted with shock and horror, condemning the Irgun. Assessments made later of the attack's effect indicate that the death and destruction at the King David Hotel by no means decided the British to depart Palestine, but it probably advanced the timing.

The bombing of the King David Hotel signaled an intensification of the Zionist push to establish a homeland in Palestine, an effort that was to take the form in-country of an intense terrorist campaign against the British and Palestinian Arab opponents alike. Not for several more years, after the establishment of Israel, were the Palestinians to mount in turn more than a scattering of significant terrorism attacks of their own.

Aug. 5. Beirut, Lebanon. Bombings took place at both the American legation and the British consulate. No casualties resulted. The American diplomatic mission, located in an older building, was virtually destroyed, whereas less damage resulted at the British consulate. Speculation for a motive centered on dissatisfaction with Anglo-American plans for Palestine.

Aug. 9. Beirut, Lebanon. A bomb thrown from a passing automobile exploded on the university campus, but caused no casualties or damage.

Oct. 31. Rome, Italy. The British embassy was damaged by two bombs in suitcases left by Irgun terrorists. There were no casualties.

Oct. 30. Jerusalem, Palestine. Explosives set off at two sites, one on a road north of the city and the other nine hours

later at the railway station, killed two British soldiers and a British police detective. The railway station suffered considerable damage. A police patrol soon arrested three Jews, a woman and two wounded men, near the Jaffa Gate of the Old City.

1947

March 3. Jerusalem, Palestine. Press reports on this date indicate that at least four serious incidents had taken place during the previous twenty-four hours: Near Rishon, a British army truck had been blown up, badly injuring three soldiers; near Ramla a mine was set off under a Royal Air Force truck carrying civilian workers, with four Arabs injured in the attack; and small arms fire at a camp at Hadera wounded two British soldiers. Finally, an explosion was heard outside Haifa, but no details were available. This violence took place despite the martial law imposed by British forces over almost one-third of the Jewish population.

July 19. Rangoon, Burma. Pre-independence leader Prime Minister U Aung San and six leading political colleagues, including his brother, were shot down in the council chamber while the executive council was in session. His principal political rival, the right-wing contender and former premier U Saw hired the gunmen; he and the assassins were executed for the murders on May 8, 1948.

July 31. Nathanya, Palestine. Authorities found the bodies of two British army sergeants, Clifford Martin and Mervyn Paice. After being kidnapped on July 12 and subjected to a "trial," they had been hanged. The Irgun had tried, unsuccessfully, to bargain for the release of three

Irgun members who had been sentenced to death by the British.

Aug. 10. Jerusalem, Palestine. Arab gunmen assaulted a cabaret called the Hawaiian Garden. In the attack and the aftermath of rioting, thirty-one people, Jews and Arabs, died, with a total of eighty-five hurt.

Aug. 23. Jerusalem, Palestine. The British inspector general of police announced that as of July 1, 323 suspected terrorists had been arrested.

Sep. 29. Haifa, Palestine. At 8:00 a.m. on the city's busiest street, two members of Irgun exploded a huge barrel-bomb against the front wall of the district police headquarters. Ten people died and fifty-three were injured, including many civilians.

Sep. 30. Haifa, Palestine. Twenty miles south of Haifa, the main railway to Cairo suffered a bomb blast under the engine of a train. In what was presumed to be the work of the Irgun, the engine, coal car, and two coaches were derailed, but no one was seriously hurt. In Jerusalem, terrorists failed in a bombing effort at a large Arab grocery, possibly in a move by Arabs to impose a boycott on the sale of Zionist-made goods. Further, a Jewish shopkeeper was kidnapped.

Oct. 10. Santiago, Chile. Early in the morning, gunmen in a speeding auto fired several shots at the Soviet embassy. No one was hurt. The attack coincided with a Chilean government crackdown on local communists. Moscow protested formally, calling the incident "shocking."

Oct. 12. Jerusalem, Palestine. Following an attack on the Swedish consulate on Sep. 27, a bomb exploded outside the Polish consulate. No one was injured.

Oct. 13. Jerusalem, Palestine. An attacker threw a bomb over a garden wall onto the doorstep of the U. S. consulate general. The resulting blast wounded two persons and caused extensive damage. Reports indicated that an Arab group had undertaken the bombing because of recently announced U. S. support for the partition of Palestine. The French and the Czechoslovak consular offices reportedly were targeted next.

Dec. 3. Arras, France. An allegedly Communist group derailed the Paris-Lille train, causing sixteen deaths and sixty injuries.

Dec. 12. Ramleh and Haifa, Palestine. Gunmen from Haganah (one of the three best-known Jewish terrorist organizations) attacked Arab quarters, killing twenty-seven — twenty Arabs, two British soldiers, and five Jews.

Dec. 25. Tel Aviv, Palestine. Members of the Stern Gang shot and killed two off-duty British soldiers in a cafe.

Dec. 29. Jerusalem, Palestine. Members of the Irgun group, the third of the most noted Jewish terrorist organizations) threw a bomb from a speeding taxi at the Damascus Gate, killing thirteen people — eleven Arabs and two British police officers — and wounding at least thirty-two Arabs. A similar attack had taken place at the same location sixteen days earlier.

1948

The year during which Great Britain withdrew from Palestine and Israel declared its nationhood, setting up the framework for a partitioned Palestine. Virtual warfare raged, both between the Jews and the Arabs in Palestine and both of those parties separately against what was viewed as foreign interventionists. By this time, violence was rampant. Deadly incidents took place almost daily, each of the two sides furthering the violence. The following accounts set the tone.

Jan. 4. Jaffa, Palestine. The Stern Gang exploded a bomb in a building next to the headquarters of the National Arab Committee. Fourteen persons died and more than 100 were injured.

Jan. 5. Jerusalem, Palestine. Haganah exploded a bomb in the Hotel Sémiramis next to the Arab Quarter. Thirty-six people reportedly were killed. In the nearby town of Safad, Irgun set off a bomb the same day that resulted in fourteen deaths.

Jan. 7. Jerusalem, Palestine. Five Irgun members using a stolen police armored car threw bombs in two attacks near the Jaffa Gate, killing eight Arabs.

Jan. 17. Kfar Etzion, Palestine. Palestinian gunmen opened fire on motorists; thirty-five died.

Jan. 30. New Delhi, India. Mohandas K. "Mahatma" Gandhi, the leading figure in the Indian independence movement and the foremost worldwide advocate of nonviolence, was assassinated by a right-wing Hindu fanatic, Nathuram Vinayak Godse. The assassin was a member of the National Volunteer Force (RSS), the militant wing of *Mahasabha*, a rightist Hindu political party. The group's leaders believed Gandhi's policies leading toward Hindu-Muslim accommodation harmed Hindu interests. Their ultimate aim was to foster civil war, thus opening the way for an assumption of subcontinent-wide Hindu supremacy. He and six RSS colleagues had made an unsuccessful grenade attempt on

Gandhi's life ten days earlier. The bomb went off harmlessly at that time; one of the conspirators, Madanlal Pahwa, was arrested.

On this later date, January 30th, Gandhi insisted on holding a prayer meeting in the Birla House gardens despite police warnings that another attempt would be made on his life. Waiting in the gardens late in the afternoon, Godse, now armed with a pistol, was accompanied by the unarmed Narayan Apte and Vishnu Kakare. He approached the Mahatma, pulled the gun, and fired three shots with a .38 caliber pistol almost point blank. Gandhi died within minutes.

All seven of the conspirators were tried and found guilty of the murder. Godse and Narayan Apte were sentenced to death, the others to life imprisonment. The two died on the gallows on November 15, 1949.

Feb. 22. Jerusalem, Palestine. In retaliation for the Jewish attack in Ramleh on Dec. 22, 1947 (above), Palestinians exploded two truck bombs in Ben Yahuda Street. Heavy damage resulted and fifty-four persons were killed.

Feb. 29. Cairo, Egypt—Haifa, Palestine. The Stern Gang bombed the Cairo-Haifa train. Twenty-eight British soldiers were killed and thirty-five wounded.

March 7. Saigon, Indochina. Two nationalist Vietminh terrorists assassinated an American embassy official. They were tried, condemned to death, and executed on December 14, 1949.

March 11. Jerusalem, Palestine. An Arab group using the official, flag-bearing automobile of the American consul general, exploded a car bomb in the inner courtyard of the heavily guarded Jewish Agency building. Thirteen people died and eight-four were wounded. It was not known for certain whether the usual chauffeur, an Arab Christian, gained entry for the vehicle into the courtyard and then walked away before the explosion or whether the vehicle had been stolen shortly before the attack.

March 31. Haifa, Palestine. The Stern Gang again attacked the Cairo-Haifa train, planting mines on the track and derailing the engine and cars. Forty Arabs reportedly died, with sixty injured.

April 9. Bogotá, Colombia. Leftist Jorge Eliecer Gaitan, presidential candidate and leader of the Liberal Party, was assassinated at a Pan American conference by a man named Juan Roa Sierra. The latter died in the same bomb blast. Savage riots resulted. Down to the twenty-first century, reports surfaced that the U. S. Central Intelligence Agency was somehow involved.

April 9. Deir Yassin, Palestine. In an incident that has come to be notorious worldwide, members of the Irgun and the Stern Gang attacked the Arab village of Deir Yassin near Jerusalem, massacring over 100 civilians. The attack has been roundly condemned over the years; at the time, the Jewish leadership did not deny that there had been a massacre, but that it had been by forces claimed not to be under its control. Jewish political leaders apologized to King Abdullah of Jordan, in whose claimed territory the village fell.

April 9. Bogotá, Colombia. A bomb exploded near the U.S. embassy during an Organization of American States conference.

May 3. Colverhampton, England. Rex Farran was killed by a letter bomb intended for his brother, Roy. The latter had been acquitted in Jerusalem of causing the death of a young Jew. The Stern Gang claimed responsibility and vowed it would in time get the right Farran.

May 14. Tel Aviv, Israel. On the last full day of the British Mandate over Palestine, the Jewish People's Council at 4;00 p.m. issued a proclamation establishing the State of Israel. Five surrounding Arab nations mobilized.

At that point in 1948, Israel entered the ranks of the world's nation states. It remained under attack year after year from Palestinian and other Arab interest groups, which during that time were mostly confined to terrorist tactics. Israel retaliated as a sovereign nation state — if no longer in terrorist kind, with similar tactics.

June 30. Istanbul, Turkey. Retired Bulgarian air force colonel Stahil Mihalakev, with several companions, hijacked to Istanbul an airliner on a domestic flight in Bulgaria. During the incident, one crew member was killed and both pilots wounded. The hijackers requested political asylum in Turkey.

During the period 1945 to 1950, twenty-five air hijackings took place, most of them carried out by refugees from the Iron Curtain countries in Europe.

July 14. Rome, Italy. Palmiro Togliatti, leader of the Italian Communist party, was shot and seriously wounded at the Palazzo di Montecitorio by a Sicilian student, Domenico Antonio Pallante. The latter evidently had only a desire to become famous, but his act had significant political consequences. The communist-dominated Federation of Labor called a general strike in protest of the act. Once the widespread strike — almost a state of civil war — ended, the reaction was swift: The government made 7,000 arrests and during the next two years more than 15,000 Com-

Mohandas K. Gandhi, India, walking with family members, ca. 1947. Library of Congress LC-USZ62-53552.

munists went to prison. The party was effectively stymied for the next fifty years or more.

Pallante was imprisoned but received amnesty and was freed in 1953. Curiously, in November 1955, Togliatti bought (for 600 lire) the pistol that had almost ended his life.

Sep. 17. Jerusalem, Israel. The UN Representative, Count Folke Bernadotte, and an aide died in their car in a hail of bullets fired by members of the Stern Gang. The highly respected Bernadotte

four months earlier had arranged a UN cease fire between the warring Israel and a number of Arab states. One proviso of the truce — that Arab refugees be allowed to return to Israel — led to the assassination; the Israeli assailants feared the UN would seek concessions from Israel that would threaten its existence.

Three days later, the Israeli government outlawed the Stern Gang and Irgun.

Dec. 28. Cairo, Egypt. Premier Mahmoud Fahmy Nokrashy Pasha was a firm opponent of a Jewish state in Israel and of the continued presence of the British in the Sudan. Earlier in the month, however, he had outlawed the Muslim Brotherhood. A Brotherhood member, twenty-one-year-old student Ahmed Hamid Ahmed Hassan, sought out the official in the interior ministry and shot him five times, killing him instantly. The gunman, captured despite his apparent wish to commit suicide, was executed and hundreds of the banned Muslim Brotherhood's members arrested.

1949

Oct. 15 . Budapest, Hungary. In a notorious example of a Stalinist purge — this one indirectly against the separatist tendencies of Yugoslavia's Marshal Tito— Hungarian officials accused Foreign Minister Lázló Rajk of being an American spy and Trotskyite. He confessed under torture and was found guilty in a show trial. He was hanged, along with eighteen others. His wife was imprisoned for five years. Rajk had shown too much of a tendency toward independent thinking.

Jan. 30. Shanghai—Tsingtao, China. During the civil war, six Communists hijacked a Chinese Nationalist airliner to Tsinan, where the aircraft was held.

Feb. 4. Tehran, Iran. Mohammed Reza Shah Pahlavi was attacked at a ceremonial event at the University of Tehran by Fakhr Ara, a member of the Iranian Communist Party, the Tudeh. The assailant stepped out of a row of photographers and fired three shots. The Shah, wounded twice, recovered. His guards killed the would-be assassin on the spot.

Aug. 5. Damascus, Syria. Terrorists threw a bomb into the entrance of a synagogue as preparations were being made for a service. Seven people were killed and twenty-seven injured. The blast caused considerable damage. A possible explanation for the act focused on it being a demonstration against peace negotiations in Palestine conducted by the UN. Officials speculated that it was an effort to embarrass the Syrian government.

Nov. 4. Tehran, Iran. Prime Minister Abdulhussein Hajir died, shot down in a city street by Seyyed Hussein Emami of the ultra-nationalistic Crusaders of Islam (*Fadayan-e Islami*). This was perhaps the first of a succession of assassinations secretly sanctioned by Iranian religious leaders. Enami was hanged five days later, shouting "I pride myself on killing him!"

Dec. 3. Sibu (Cebu), Borneo. The British governor of Sarawak, Duncan George Stewart, was stabbed to death by two Malays after less than a month in office. Authorities arrested the two assassins, plus sixty others charged with conspiracy.

Dec. 9. Belgrade, Yugoslavia. Four hijackers diverted a Soviet-Rumanian DC-3 scheduled to fly to Bucharest. The hijackers killed one security officer aboard the aircraft.

Notes

1. Quoted in Israel Time Line, http://users. iafrica.com/, entry for 1944.

2.Sifakis, *Encyclopedia of Assassinations,* 79.

1950–1959

Control by terror — the Stalin-inspired Soviet government show trials.

1950

Jan. 11. Washington, USA. Oscar Collazo and Griselio Torresola of the Puerto Rican Nationalist Party tried to force their way into Blair House, Pres. Harry S. Truman's temporary quarters across from the White House. Their objective: to bring attention to their cause by killing the American president. Guards fought them off successfully, killing Torresola in the fierce but brief gun battle. One American security officer was killed and two wounded. Pres. Truman suffered no harm.

Collazo was sentenced to death; a week before his scheduled execution in 1952, Truman commuted the sentence to life in prison. President Jimmy Carter commuted his sentence in September 1979, and he was released. Collazo died in Puerto Rico in 1994.

June 5. Saigon, Indochina. The Bao Dai government's education minister, Vong Quang Nhuong, was critically wounded by three gun shots fired by a would-be assassin, who escaped. The minister reportedly had been negotiating secretly to bring nationalist factions over to the French-supported government. Saigon announced the next day a new crackdown on terrorist forces.

Nov. 12. Damascus, Syria. Military authorities of the recently organized (in September) government launched major legal proceedings against twenty-one persons affiliated with the Arab Suicide Redemption Falange. The little-known Falange was a group charged with complicity in a number of assassinations and bombings. Included in the alleged bombings was an attack on the U. S. legation in 1949 in which thirteen people were killed and twenty-one injured, plus an explosive set off at the office of the UN relief agency. Nine of the persons charged faced death penalties.

Nov. 13. Las Mercedes, Venezuela. Col. Carlos Delgado Chalbaud, chairman of the military junta ruling the nation since a 1948 coup, was kidnapped and taken to a house in the suburbs of the capital. There he was shot and killed, almost certainly at the instigation of fellow officers in the upper reaches of government (although reports were circulated that British intelligence had done the deed). Delgado Chalbaud had proven to be too liberal for the Venezuelan military that now headed the nation.

Nov. 16. Rome, Italy. Two bomb blasts wrecked the offices of the Republican and the Socialist Unity parties—the suspected work of a neo-Fascist group called the Italian Social Movement. No one was injured.

Dec. 16. Saigon, Indochina. Communist Vietminh terrorists, some wearing Vietnamese army uniforms, sped through the city's downtown and Chinese areas in the early evening spraying cafés and sidewalks with machine gun fire and tossing grenades. One person was killed and twenty-four wounded in what was called the worst acts of terrorism in months.

Dec. 21. Almendares, Cuba. In this suburb of Havana, a bomb exploded at the home of Interior Minister Lomberto Diaz, wounding his son and damaging the property.

Dec. 27. Belgrade, Yugoslavia. Staff found a crude bomb in the stacks of the U. S. Information Service library. Police disarmed the device, thought to be a fire bomb. There were no clues on who had planted it.

1951

March 7. Tehran, Iran. A twenty-six-year-old member of the militant *Fadayan-e Islami* named Khalil Tahmasebi stepped out of a crowd before the city's principal mosque and shot Premier Ali Razmarra, killing him. Gen. Razmarra had opposed nationalization of the oil industry; with his death, the nationalist Muhammad Mosaddeq soon became prime minister and nationalization proceeded. (The Shah signed a bill in Nov. 1952 freeing Tahmasebi, who had been imprisoned.)

July 16. Amman, Jordan. Riad Bey al-Solh, the prime minister of Lebanon, was assassinated while in Amman for discussions with King Abdullah. Rumors that they were considering a peace treaty with Israel led Arab extremists to slip past his security guards and kill al-Solh.

July 20. East Jerusalem, Jordan. While visiting the al-Aqsa Mosque in Jerusalem for prayers and the funeral of the Lebanese prime minister, King Abdullah was assassinated by an Arab fanatic, Mustapha Shukri Usho, a Jerusalem tailor who feared that the king would make a separate peace with Israel. The gunman fired three fatal bullets into the King's head and chest. Abdullah's teen-aged grandson, Hussein Ibn Talal (king of Jordan from 1953 to 1999) grappled with the assailant. The assassin was shot and killed on the spot.

Thirty Palestinians reportedly soon were executed and hundreds arrested. On August 20, a trial opened in Jordan; Usho evidently had not acted alone. Four conspirators eventually were found guilty and hanged. Indication were that the man behind the assassination was Haj Amin al-Husseini, the former grand mufti of Jerusalem, then living in exile in Egypt.

Oct. 6. Selangore, Malaya. Sir Henry Gurney, the British high commissioner for Malaya, fell victim to the Communist terrorist campaign that had resulted in the party's being banned in 1948. He was ambushed while traveling with his wife in a convoy with armed escort on holiday in the interior. Members of an organization called the Malayan Races' Liberation Army gunned him down when he dashed out of his unarmored Rolls Royce, apparently in order to draw fire away from Lady Gurney.

Oct. 16. Rawalpindi, Pakistan. Prime Minister Liaquat Ali Khan, addressing a large public meeting near the disputed Kashmir frontier, was shot twice in the chest and soon afterward died in a nearby hospital. His assassin, a Muslim fanatic named Syed Azbar Khan, was one of many who objected to the prime minister's friendship with India's Jawaharlal Nehru. The assassin was set upon and killed by the enraged audience.

Nov. 22. Ismailia, Egypt. Reports noted that eight Britons had been killed and at least four wounded during the past week in the Suez Canal zone. Less than two weeks earlier, Egyptian terrorists stabbed three British soldiers in the streets of the town. Pamphlets distributed by the "Defenders of Islam" promised more if the British did not "Pack up and go home."

Dec. 10. Saigon, Indochina. The police warned U. S. Ambassador Donald Heath that Communist forces had marked him for assassination, this being the second warning given to him within the year.

1952

Feb. 15. Tehran, Iran. A second unsuccessful assassination attempt was made on Foreign Minister Hussein Fâtemi, this one by teenager Mohamed Mehdi Abd Koda'i. a member of the *Fadayan-e Islami.* The young Fâtemi was foreign minister during the turbulent era of Premier Mosaddeq. Upon the ouster finally of Mosaddeq, the Shah had Fâtemi tried, convicted, and, on November 10, 1954, executed.

Sep. 6. Nairobi, Kenya. The Legislative council, according to the press, was being summoned to pass emergency laws to strengthen the government's fight against a secret society called "Mau Mau." The society threatened to drive all whites from the colony. Not until the following year, 1950, was Mau Mau mentioned (briefly) in the British government's *African Affairs Department Annual Report.*

The Mau Mau organization arose in 1947 among Kikiyu tribesmen of the north; its first terrorist operations took place in 1949, against Africans who were viewed as collaborators with the British colonists. By 1952, Mau Mau had gained a dreaded reputation and had begun an open uprising against the British.

Oct. 16. London, England. Colonial Secretary Oliver Lyttlelton announced in the House of Commons that forty-three persons had been murdered recently as part of the Mau Mau campaign to drive the white man out of Kenya.

Nov. 27. Prague, Czechoslovakia. "Control by terror," as it was called in the foreign press. The Stalin-inspired show trials of Vladimir Clementis and Rudolf Slansky, former foreign minister and ex-head of the Czech Communist Party, respectively, resulted in their conviction for "Trotskyite-Titoist-Zionist activities in the service of American imperialism" and sentences of death. They and nine other former top officials were hanged in December 1952. Three of those tried received life sentences. The unfortunate fourteen clearly were used as scapegoats for failures in the Czech economy.

Dec. 13. Nairobi, Kenya. British authorities hanged four African Mau Mau murderers. Their victims had been anti-Mau Mau Africans. "Thousands" of Africans were imprisoned for terrorist offenses.

Nine days later, a court sentenced eleven Kikuyus to death for the murder of a British settler, Eric Bowyer, who was hacked to death at his farm in the Kinangop district.

Despite the Mau Mau's reputation for

ruthlessness, by far most of its ferocity was directed against fellow Africans. An official 1954 annual Kenya police report noted that murders of loyal tribesmen took place virtually every day. Throughout the rebellion, 1949 through 1956, by which time the Mau Mau had been greatly diminished in active strength, tens of thousands of Africans were killed — the estimates vary widely; the relatively small total of sixty-three Europeans in all died.

Dec. 30. Quemoy Island, Taiwan. A single hijacker diverted an internal Philippines Airways flight to Quemoy. Two people lost their lives in the incident.

1953

March 25. Naivasha, Kenya. The same night as the Lari Massacre, Mau Mau fighters pulled off a quite different kind of assault. In an operation that went like clockwork, they raided a police station, overwhelmed the garrison, released 150 prisoners, and captured large stores of arms and ammunition.

March 26. Lari, Kenya. Mau Mau partisans, in the single bloodiest incident of the extended struggle, massacred a local chieftain, Chief Luka, his family, and other known loyalists in the village. Ninety-seven people in the village lost their lives, twenty-nine were wounded, and forty-six were reported missing. No reliable information exists on the extent of Mau Mau casualties in these totals, but blame for all fell on them. On the international scene, the attack was viewed as a barbarous Mau Mau atrocity.

1954

March 1. Washington, USA. Four Puerto Rican nationalists smuggled pistols into the gallery of the House of Representatives. Firing twenty to twenty-five rounds down at the floor of the House, they were able to wound five congressmen before running out of ammunition. One of the wounded, Rep. Alvin Bentley (Mich.), was not expected to live but pulled through.

The four assailants — one of whom was a woman named Lolita Lebron — were tried and sentenced to up to seventy-five years in prison each. In 1979, President Jimmy Carter pardoned all four in what was called a "humanitarian gesture."

Oct. 26. Alexandria, Egypt. Many thousands witnessed a Muslim Brotherhood assassination attempt against Col. Gamal Abdel Nasser that failed. Mahmoud Abdel Latif fired eight shots at the premier as he spoke from a third-floor balcony in Republic Square, but missed. Two dignitaries seated nearby were slightly injured by flying glass. Three days later, the government formally dissolved the Brotherhood. On November 13, Nasser ousted the titular head of government, General Mohamed Naguib, who was implicated in the assassination attempt.

In Cairo on December 7, the would-be assassin named Latif, a thirty-year-old tin smith, along with five Muslim Brotherhood leaders, were hanged for their roles in the plot.

1955

Feb. 15. Berne, Switzerland. Six anti-Communist Romanians invaded the Romanian embassy and killed one person, demanding freedom for prisoners held in Romania. They surrendered after several hours of fruitless negotiations. Three of them managed to escape the following day.

March 24. Patish, Israel. Egyptian terrorists threw hand grenades at a marriage ceremony, killing one person and wounding twenty-two.

April 1, Cyprus. A Greek Cypriot EOKA (*Ethnike Organosis Krpriakou Agonos*) terrorist campaign for independence began with a series of bomb explosions around British-controlled Cyprus. Led by Dighenis Grivas, EOKA continued its campaign; Britain granted independence in 1960.

April 11. Off Great Natuna Islands, Indonesia. A time bomb exploded in the wheel well of an Air India Lockheed Constellation, causing the loss of an engine, a fire, and the breakdown of control systems. The airplane, from Hong Kong destined for Djakarta, crashed in the sea, killing sixteen of the nineteen persons aboard. Eight of the passengers were Chinese Communist officials bound for the Bandung Conference. Reportedly Nationalist Chinese agents believed (erroneously) that CPR Premier Zhou En Lai was aboard.

June 11. Casablanca, Morocco. Terrorists from a group called the Red Hand murdered industrialist Jacques Lemaigre-Dubreuil.

Aug. 20. Oued Zem, Morocco. Berber tribesmen killed thirty Europeans in rioting. French Foreign Legionnaires were parachuted in to restore order. On the following day, at the mining town of Khouribga, three Europeans were murdered.

Aug. 20. Philippeville, Algeria. The National Liberation Front (FLN), organized the previous year by exiles in Egypt, to this point in their drive for independence from France had targeted military and government targets. On this date the group began an escalation; the FLN murdered 123 civilians, including women and children. In response, the government under Gov. Jacques Soustelle killed 1,273 terrorists, according to its own reports; the FLN claimed that a massacre of 12,000 Muslims took place.

All-out war had begun, a conflict that was not to cease until Algeria achieved its independence in July 1962.

Aug. 21. Constantine, Algeria. As an adjunct to the uprising noted above, sudden attacks at a dozen locations by insurrectionists resulted in a casualty toll of nearly 400 on both sides. FLN terrorists killed twenty French civilians and wounded thirty.

These figures are not supported by contemporary official data. Incomplete totals issued in Paris indicated that, since the previous November, more than 500 Algerians categorized as "terrorists" had been killed or wounded and 600 captured. Sixty-nine Frenchmen, including civilians, had lost their lives and 158 had been wounded. Whatever the count, the toll was heavy: by the time the war ended, at least 100,000 Muslims and 10,000 French soldiers had been killed.

Oct. 17. Algeria. FLN adherents killed five French soldiers and eight civilians in shooting attacks.

Nov. 16. Tehran, Iran. Members of the nationalist *Fadaiyan-e Eslam* made an unsuccessful effort to kill Prime Minister Hussein Ala as he was about to leave to sign the Baghdad (CENTO) Pact. The perpetrators were arrested; their leaders, after trial in secret military courts, went before firing squads a month later. Minister Ala

"Death on an Algerian Roadway." A French soldier (right) shoots a fleeing nationalist rebel at Ain Abbid, Algeria, August 1955. Photograph by CBS cameraman Jacques Alexander. Library of Congress NYWTS Subj.: Algeria.

served in office until April 1957, one of a succession in the office during the Shah's reign.

1956

March 3. Nicosia, Cyprus. EOKA terrorists bombed and destroyed a British Hermes aircraft at the airport. On April 27, the terrorists repeated the feat, destroying a Dakota transport aircraft.

Sep. 21. Managua, Nicaragua. In an historically unusual father-and-son episode, dictator (since 1937) Anastasio Somoza Garcia fell to an assassin, and his second son, Anastasio Somoza Debayle, exiled in Paraguay, suffered the same fate twenty-four years later. The senior Somoza, who indicated his intention to stay in office indefinitely, was shot four times while attending a social function and died a week later. The assailant, a poet, was killed on the spot; his body was mutilated and eventually it disappeared.

The younger Somoza assumed power in 1976, only to be ousted in 1979. He and two aides were killed in Asuncion, Paraguay, by a rocket fired at his chauffeured Mercedes.

1957

July 26. Guatemala City, Guatemala. In reaction to increasing Communist influence in the government, a group sponsored by the United States' CIA and led by Col. Carlos Castillo Armas invaded from Honduras in 1956 and ousted Col. Jacobo Arbenz. The right-wing Castillo Armas became president, but he was assassinated the following year in the Presidential House by military rivals.

Sep. 27. Santa Cruz, Bolivia. Prisoners being flown from the eastern lowland to La Paz in the Alto Plano took charge of the aircraft, forcing the pilots to fly to Argentina. There the prisoners were granted political asylum.

Oct. 10. Kuwait City, Kuwait. About twenty Palestinians met to form al-Fatah. The name is the reverse of an acronym standing for *Harakat Al-Tahrir Al-Watani Al-Filastini* — the Movement for the National Liberation of Palestine. (In Arabic, HTF means death; when reversed to FTH, it means victory.) Yasser Arafat, then an engineer in Kuwait, soon emerged as the leader. In 1967-68, Fatah joined the PLO and won the leadership role in 1969.

Oct. 29. Jerusalem, Israel. A hand grenade exploded in the Knesset, wounding Prime Minister David Ben Gurion and several others. No clear motive was established for the would-be assassin.

1958

Feb. 24. Havana, Cuba. Two armed men from Fidel Castro's Twenty Sixth of July movement kidnapped Argentine motor racing champion Juan Manuel Fangio from a hotel lobby. The object was to stop him from taking part in a Grand Prix race and thus to embarrass the Cuban government of Fulgencio Batista. Legend has it that the group planned to kidnap the equally famed driver Stirling Moss as well,

but Fangio told them that Moss was on his honeymoon. The terrorists forbore to interrupt the honeymoon. Fangio was released when the race had been run.

May 10. Beirut, Lebanon. The U. S. Information Service library was set ablaze by fire bombs thrown by unknown persons.

July 14. Baghdad, Iraq. In a sudden predawn coup, the military under Brigadier Abdul-Karim Qassim and Colonel Abdul Salam Arif, inspired by the example of Egypt's Nasser, overthrew the monarchy. Their troops killed King Faisal II and Prince Abdul Ilah (who had served as regent from 1939 until 1953). Many members of the royal family were assassinated, as well. The bodies of the king and Abdul Illah, along with those of the royals, were hanged upside down outside the palace in a public display.

Two days later, the revolutionaries foiled Prime Minister Nuri al Said in his attempt to escape, murdered him, and had his corpse dragged through the streets behind a motor vehicle until virtually nothing was left.

Sep. 15. Paris, France. Three Algerian nationalists ambushed French Information Minister Jacques Soustelle's automobile on a busy street near the Arc de Triomphe. The minister escaped unhurt from the shoot-out, but one bystander was killed and three wounded. Police captured two assailants on the spot and the third the following month.

Two months previously, Soustelle had announced plans for the integration of Algeria and the French Sahara into a "Union for French Renewal" under the aegis of Gen. Charles De Gaulle. At the time, the latter was viewed by the French right as committed to keeping Algeria French.

Sep. 25. Colombo, Ceylon. A Buddhist monk shot Prime Minister Solomon W. R. D. Bandaranaike three times with a .45 caliber pistol. Bandaranaike died the next day. The attack at the prime minister's private bungalow came just before he was to depart for New York to address the UN General Assembly. Speculation on the motives of the assassin centered on the assassin's view of the value conflict between Eastern and the Western medical systems.

Oct. 3. Famagusta, Cyprus. In probably the most notorious of attacks during Cypriot efforts to oust the British, gunmen attacked three women, two British and one German, in a crowded street. They shot and killed one, Catherine Mary Cutliffe, and gravely wounding another. EOKA denied responsibility, a denial not widely believed. At least 2,000 Cypriots were already under detention and many more were subjected to total house curfew.

Nov. 1. Miami, USA. A Cubana Airlines Viscount bound for Havana was hijacked en route by five members of Fidel Castro's Twenty Sixth of July Movement and forced to attempt a night landing in a remote Cuban airfield. The aircraft crashed, killing seventeen of the twenty people on board. (Note: Two months later, Castro came to power.)

Nov. 17. Mt. of the Beatitudes, Israel. Terrorists thought to be from Syria killed the wife of the British air attaché in Israel. She was staying at the guest house of the Italian Convent on the Mount.

1959

April 18. Algiers, Algeria. A bomb exploded in a fashionable European shopping street, the rue Michelet, killing one person and injuring six. Timed to take place on the eve of French-sponsored municipal elections, it was the first sizable bombing attack in over a year. Six people were wounded when a grenade exploded in front of a Muslim quarter café.

The following day, April 19, when polling began under the aegis of the French army, Algerian nationalist insurgents outside the capital city caused the deaths of at least eight persons, injured about eighty people, and kidnapped more than twenty. Virtually all of the victims were Muslims. The terrorists sought to make the army's inability to protect civilians the most important issue in the election.

July 8. Bienhoa, Vietnam. Still early in the American involvement in Vietnam, members of the U. S. Military Assistance Advisory Group came under submachine gun fire late at night while watching a movie in the officers' mess in their compound. Two Americans were killed: Maj. Dale R. Buis and Master Sgt. Chester M. Ovnand. Two Vietnamese guards and a child also were killed. Capt. Howard B. Boston was wounded. Nearly all of the five or more Vietminh attackers escaped; one was killed when a homemade bomb exploded by accident.

This was believed to be the first time the Communists had carried out a successful mission of this kind against Americans. During this period the Vietminh assassinated an estimated total of twenty to thirty lower ranking South Vietnamese officials per month, however.

Sep. 25. Algiers, Algeria. Rebel terrorists killed nine French civilians and wounded at least twelve in a twenty-four-hour period. A time bomb exploded just outside the city's largest department store, killing five people, including three members of a police bomb disposal squad. A hand grenade attack at a café resulted in one death. On September 24, at the village of Baraki, terrorists murdered four people.

Investigators were faced with the possibility that European counter-terrorists might have instigated the violence, but soon announced that possibility had been eliminated.

Oct. 16. Paris, France. A reported assassination attempt (his political enemies disputed the facts) on leftist former minister Jacques Soustelle supported warnings that extremists were preparing a wave of violence to block a liberal settlement in France's disputed province of Algeria. Soustelle escaped harm by abandoning his automobile near the Luxembourg Gardens when, after midnight, he noticed a car following; he jumped a low fence and fled, avoided the hail of bullets.

Gaullist political figure Lucien Neuwirth — no friend of Soustelle's — warned that only unity behind De Gaulle would stay the potentially dangerous rise of far-Right extremists bent upon retaining Algeria at all costs.

1960–1969

In 1968 alone, eighty to ninety terrorist incidents reportedly took place worldwide.

1960

March 4. Havana, Cuba. The French freighter SS *La Coubre* loaded with arms and ammunition from Belgium, blew up during its unloading. As many as 100 dock workers were killed and more than 300 injured; six crewmen died and four were wounded, including the captain. Reports had it that the explosive device had been installed in the Belgian port. The newly installed Castro government was quick to call the act sabotage by "enemies of the Cuban revolution." The United States quickly and categorically denied any involvement in the matter.

March 21. Sharpeville, South Africa. Police shot and killed sixty-nine people (of some 300) demonstrating at a rally in the township of Sharpeville in the Transvaal against the government's apartheid pass laws. As many as 180 more were injured.

June 24. Caracas, Venezuela. President Rómulo Betancourt survived an assassination attempt with minor wounds, but two people were killed and several other injured. A car bomb placed along the route of a parade in which the president participated exploded in flames. After a roundup of more than 100 people, police focused on three suspects in particular: Manuel Vicente Yanes Bustamante, Luis Cabrera, and Lorenzo Mercade, all Venezuelans, as well as a disaffected Venezuelan naval officer, Capt. Eduado Morales Luengo.

Venezuela accused the Dominican Republic under dictator Gen. Rafael L. Trujillo Molina of organizing the plot and Capt. Morales later admitted that the bomb was prepared in the Dominican Republic. The attempt on the president's life was made presumably as an act of retaliation against Venezuela for having petitioned the OAS four months earlier to censure Trujillo for "flagrant violations of human rights."

Aug. 29. Amman, Jordan. Pro-Western Prime Minister Hazza al Majali and eleven others were killed by the explosion of a time bomb concealed in his desk. King Hussein appointed a new conservative prime minister. The plot was traced to Syria and/or Egypt. Four suspects were caught, convicted, and hanged.

Oct. 12. Tokyo, Japan. Socialist Party Chairman Inejiro Asanuma, stabbed twice with a sword on live television while making a speech, died within a few hours. Police immediately arrested his assassin, teenager Otoya Yamaguchi, a right-wing extremist. He committed suicide in his jail cell. Reports had it that more people attended his funeral than Asanuma's.

1961

Jan. 22. Caribbean, off Curacão, Venezuela. A group of twenty-nine Portuguese and Spanish exiles led by former navy captain Henrique Malta Galvão, took control of the Portuguese cruise ship *Santa Maria* on its way to Port Everglades, Florida. The ship carried 607 passengers and 360 crew members. One ship's officer was killed and two crewmen wounded in the takeover. Galvão was acting on the orders of a loser in the 1958 Portuguese presidential elections, Lt. Gen. Humberto Delgado, exiled in Brazil. The object possibly was to raise the flag of revolt in Portugal and Angola to the long-standing Salazar regime. In this they failed; despite disturbances, no effective opposition developed.

After negotiations at sea between Galvão and U. S. and British warships, he decided to take the *Santa Maria* to Recife, Brazil. There after eleven days, he turned over the ship, passengers, and crew. The newly elected Brazilian president, Jânio Quadros, had offered asylum. Morocco later expelled Galvão for revolutionary activities and in November 1961 he and his followers accepted safe haven in Brazil.

May 1. Miami, USA. An airliner en route from Miami to Key West, Fla., was forced by Puerto Rican named Abntulio Ramirez Ortiz to detour to Cuba, the first of a spate of such hijackings. By the end of the year, four airplanes had been diverted to Cuba. (Ramirez Ortiz was jailed for twenty years upon his return to the United States in 1975.)

Airline service between the United States and Cuba was suspended indefinitely in 1961.

Sep. 8. Pont-sur-Seine, France. The far-right *Organization Armeé Sècrete* (OAS), protesting moves toward Algerian independence, was unsuccessful in bombing the car of President Charles De Gaulle. en route between Paris and his home at Colombey des Eglises. A device on the side of the road threw up a wall of fire, but his driver sped through to safety. It was one of the approximately thirty attempts on his life that he survived during a long public career.

Oct. 17. Paris, France. Police reportedly killed or injured dozens of Algerian demonstrators. At least thirty bodies were thrown into the River Seine and later recovered, but the authorities claimed they had died in fighting between rival Algerian nationalist groups.

Dec. 16. South Africa. The African National Congress launched a bombing campaign against government buildings throughout the country. Some 200 attacks took place over the next eighteen months.

1962

Jan. 22. Paris, France. One woman was killed and thirteen people wounded in an OAS bomb attack on the French Foreign Ministry building on the Quai d'Orsay.

April 8. Persian Gulf. The British liner SS *Dara* exploded and sank as it steamed on the return segment of a round-trip voyage Bombay-Basra-Bombay. Two hundred and thirty-six people died, mostly Indians, Pakistanis, and Arabs; 584

persons were saved. The UK Ministry of Transport ascribed the explosion to a time bomb, with "little doubt" that Omani rebels were responsible.

Aug. 22. Petit-Clamart, France. Another of the attempts by the OAS on President De Gaulle's life, all unsuccessful, took place. On his way home in the evening, De Gaulle in his chauffeured vehicle with motorcycle escorts was raked with machine gun fire by OAS attackers. More than a hundred shots were fired, but he and his wife managed to emerge unhurt when his chauffeur engaged in defensive driving tactics. De Gaulle had proclaimed Algeria's independence the previous month.

Fifteen suspects, all former French soldiers, subsequently were tried in a military court. With two exceptions, all were convicted and ended up with prison sentences; one was found innocent and one, Lt. Col. Jean-Marie Bastien-Thiry, sentenced to death. He was executed before a firing squad in March 1963.

1963

Feb. 12. Caribbean, off Venezuela. Nine far-left gunmen, including Second Mate Wismar Medina Rojas, hijacked the Venezuelan freighter SS *Anzoategui* and took its thirty-six-man crew hostage. The incident began seventy miles off the coast. The Caracas government asked for international aid in tracking down and rescuing the vessel. Authorities noted insurgents had been pressing a terrorist campaign in the capital for the past week, including running gun battles, fire bombings, and a holdup and murder of bank messengers. The principal aim of the hijackers was to force a cancellation of President Betancourt's visit to Washington, but Medina Rojas' brother had been jailed for

participation in an uprising the previous year and his release also was at question.

Six days later, the *Anzoategui* reached Belem, Brazil. The hijackers left the ship and were taken into custody. There had been no casualties. In June, five of the terrorists, including their leader, were allowed to fly to Castro's Cuba; the four remaining had asked for asylum in Brazil, much like the circumstances of the hijacking of the cruise ship *Santa Maria* two years earlier (above).

July 30. Madrid, Spain. A bomb explosion at the crowded passport office located in the central police station wounded thirty-seven people. Another at the national unions headquarters caused damage, with no one hurt. Barely two weeks later, two men, Francisco Granados Gata and Joaquin Delgado Martinez, were sentenced by a military court to death for the crime of "terrorism with violence."

Sep. 24. Bogotá, Colombia. Nineteen small bombs went off in the capital, along with others in Cali, Manizales, and Ibague. No one was hurt, but Colombians were nervous about the rise in urban violence. A newspaper columnist wrote that these particular terrorists were not trying to kill anyone, but to frighten a few bourgeois, embarrass the authorities, and force them into some angry error.

Oct. 17. Madrid, Spain. A military court sentenced three young Frenchmen, described as Anarchists or Socialists, to prison terms for bombings to sabotage tourism carried out or planned. Guy Bataux, twenty-three years old, received fifteen years; Alain Pecunia, eighteen, got two twelve-year sentences, and Bernard Ferry, twenty, was sentenced to thirty years.

Nov. 22, Dallas, USA. U. S. President John F. Kennedy died, the victim of a gunshot wound inflicted by a sniper named Lee Harvey Oswald, himself a murder victim two days later. While a tragic event, one that has given rise to various conspiracy theories, the assassination has never been shown to have had a political motivation.

Vice President Lyndon B. Johnson assumed office the day Kennedy died.

Nov. 28. Ciudad Bolivar, Venezuela. The hijacking of airliners fell off in the early '60s. The year 1963 saw only one incident, compared with as many as ten two years previously. Six gunmen diverted an Avensa Convair flight bound for Caracas to Trinidad. No one was injured and the aircraft was allowed to continue its flight within one day.

1964

April 5. Phuntsholing, Bhutan. Having antagonized military and clerical leaders with his proposed reforms, Prime Minister Jigme Palden Dorji met death at the hands of an assassin. An army corporal shot and killed him. Army officers made up most of those arrested; the chief of staff, Namgyal Bahadur, was executed for his part in the plot.

June 2. Jerusalem, Palestine. The First Palestinian Conference established the Palestine Liberation Organization (PLO), which was to provide an umbrella infrastructure for various activist groups in years to follow.

Sep. 9. Montevideo, Uruguay. The leftist, peasant-oriented Tupamaros exploded a bomb outside the First National City Bank and the U. S. embassy. There were no casualties. Uruguay had just broken relations with Cuba. The following

day, the Tupamaros exploded a bomb in the garden of the Brazilian embassy.

Oct. 3. Caracas, Venezuela. The extreme leftist Armed Forces of National Liberation (FALN) kidnapped the American embassy military attaché, Lt. Col. Michael Smolen. He was released ten days later.

Nov. 3. Venezuela. The FALN exploded seven bombs at American oil installations.

Dec. 12. New York, USA. Anti-Castro Cubans fired a bazooka at the UN building as a means to protest a speech given to the General Assembly that day by the Cuban minister of industry, Ernesto (Che) Guevarra. The police arrested three Cubans ten days later.

1965

Jan. 8. El-Beitout, Israel. Fatah/PLO terrorists dynamited a dam at Lake Tiberias. The attack was considered the first made by this combination of groups; Yasser Arafat was said to have participated.

Jan. 15. Bujumbura, Burundi. Premier Pierre Ngendandumwe was shot in the back and killed as he left a hospital after visiting his wife and newborn baby. Regarded as a political moderate, he represented a likely reduction in Chinese Communist influence in the former Belgian colony. Within a week, a Watusi tribe clerk at the U. S. embassy confessed to the assassination, throwing doubt on whether a political aim was involved.

Jan. 21. Tehran, Iran. A radical cleric with ties to Ayatolla Khomeini "authorized" the assassination of Prime Minister Hassan-Ali Mansour, which was duly carried out by a twenty-year-old student, Mohamed Boukharai. Mansour died in hospital from two gunshot wounds on January 26. Boukharai and two accomplices, Saffar Harandi and Morteza Niknejar, were soon arrested. A military tribunal sentenced a total of six people charged with the crime to death and others implicated to long prison terms.

Feb. 9. Guatemala City, Guatemala. Terrorists of the Revolutionary Movement of November 13 (MR-13) tried unsuccessfully to assassinate Col. Harold Hauser, chief of the U. S. military mission at the American embassy.

April 10. Tehran, Iran. A soldier named Sham-Abadi fired at Shah Mohamed Reza Pahlavi while the latter was working in his office. Two guards were killed and a gardener wounded, but the Shah escaped harm. Reportedly the attack was organized by a group of students who were graduates of British universities. A tribunal sentenced the assailant to ten years in prison.

May 6. Montevideo, Uruguay. The extremist National Liberation Movement Tupamaros set off a bomb at the offices of All American Cable and at Western Telegraph. There were no casualties.

May 18. Rio de Janeiro, Brazil. Police disarmed a bomb placed at the American embassy.

May 25. Ramat Hakovash, Israel. Al Fatah attacked a Jewish settlement, killing three civilians.

June 7. Córdoba, Argentina. American Consul Allison Temple Wanamaker was wounded when shot by an unknown assailant. He was on his way home driving his own auto when another car overtook him and shots were fired. Wanamaker was hit in the cheekbone and hand, but managed to keep his car under control and get away. The attackers fled.

July 10. Montevideo, Uruguay. The Tupamaros set off a bomb at the Brazilian embassy. No casualties resulted.

Sep. 1. Aden, Federation of South Arabia. Arab nationalists opposed to federation moves then underway in the British protectorate killed a ranking British official as he drove to a tennis club. A month earlier an assassination attempt was made against a British police superintendent. Two weeks later, seven British children were injured in a grenade attack at the Aden airport.

Oct. 31. Guatemala City, Guatemala. Expected presidential candidate Mario Méndez Montenegro, an anti-Communist reformer, was found shot to death in his home at the start of the election campaign. His younger brother, Julio César Méndez Montenegro, took his place and won the presidency in a three-man race. (The winning candidate finished his term and lived on in Guatemala until April 1996, when he died of a heart attack.)

1966

March 27. Havana, Cuba. A hijacker named Angel María Betancourt Cueto tried to divert an internal flight from Santiago de Cuba to the United States. The pilot, Fernando Álvarez Pérez, instead landed in Havana. The hijacker thereupon shot and killed Álvarez and a security officer and seriously wounded the copilot. The Castro government later executed the hijacker, whose motives were not publicized.

Aug. 4. Bogotá, Colombia. Left-wing rebels set off a bomb in the Colombian-American Cultural Center. The blast killed one American, English-language instructor Robert Smeteck, and at least three Colombians. Fifteen persons were hurt, six seriously.

Sep. 25. Buenos Aires, Argentina. Nineteen Argentine nationalists, protesting British rule over the Falkland Islands, hijacked an Areolineas Argentinas DC-4 from its run to Rio Gallegos and diverted it to the Falklands. The incident lasted only one day before the hostages were released. British authorities returned the hijackers to Argentina.

Nov. 22. Aden, Federation of South Arabia. A Yemen Airways DC-3 airliner exploded and crashed twenty minutes out of Meifah, bound for Aden, killing all thirty people aboard. A bomb had been placed aboard.

1967

Oct. 9. Vallegrande, Bolivia. For almost a year, Ernesto "Che" Guevarra, the famed Argentine-born Cuban revolutionary, led a small guerrilla movement in Bolivia against that country's military regime. Tracked down with C. I. A. assistance, wounded, and captured by the Bolivian army, he was killed on this date, one day later.

Oct. 12. Athens, Greece. A British European Airways Comet, bound for Nicosia, had a bomb explode in the tourist cabin. The aircraft broke up and crashed into the sea, killing all sixty-six persons aboard.

Dec. 11. West Bank, Palestine. The Popular Front for the Liberation of Palestine (PFLP) was founded, headed by George Habash. A left-wing nationalist Palestinian organization, it was organized after the Six-Day War and Israel's occupation of the West Bank.

1968

Jan. 16. Guatemala City, Guatemala. A spate of leftist- and rightist-generated terrorism climaxed with the shooting deaths of U. S. Army Col. John D. Webber, Jr., and U. S. Navy Lt. Cdr. Ernest A. Munro, both attached to the U. S. Military Assistance Group. Two senior American non-commissioned officers were wounded in the attack, which took place at mid-day a short distance from the airport. A car pulled alongside and gunmen sprayed the Americans' car with machine-gun fire. A communist group claimed responsibility.

Five days earlier, rightists killed Miss Guatemala of 1950, Regelia Cruz Martinez, apparently for her leftist sympathies, and on the 16th machine-gunned a leftist lawyer, Alejandro Silva Falla, and his bodyguard, killing both. That same day, the right-wing former labor minister, Carlos Castillo Armas, narrowly escaped the fate of Col. Webber, having his car subjected to machine-gun fire. And the following day, a left-wing group machine-gunned and killed a leading conservative businessman, Alfonso Alejos. The Guatemalan government declared a "state of alarm."

Feb. 21. Havana, Cuba. In the first hijacking of a U.S. airliner in seven years, a Delta airliner bound from Tampa to West Palm Beach, Florida, was diverted to Havana and spent one day there. No one was injured. The hijacker received asylum in Cuba.

[Note During the rest of the year, the spate of diversions to Cuba continued (see

below). Eighteen more flights were hijacked, with up to three hijackers aboard. No one was injured on these flights. Each of the incidents lasted only a day before the aircraft and passengers were released.]

March 12. Tampa, Fla., USA. A National Airlines Tampa to Miami flight was diverted to Cuba by three hijackers.

March 18. The Negev, Israel. A school bus ran over a land mine in the desert. Two adults died and twenty-eight children were hurt. Israel attributed the action to Al Fatah.

March 21. Caracas, Venezuela. An Avensa flight to Maracaibo was diverted to Cuba by three hijackers.

April 2. Frankfurt, West Germany. Radicals who are later to form the Red Army Faction set fires in two department stores in protest of America's involvement in Vietnam.

June 5. Los Angeles, USA. Sirhan Sirhan shot and mortally wounded presidential candidate Senator Robert F. Kennedy (brother of the late president) in the Ambassador Hotel in Los Angeles as the candidate was leaving a campaign rally. He died the next day. Sirhan, an Arab who had emigrated to the United States in the 1950s, reportedly was disturbed by Kennedy's pro-Israel positions. After a 1969 trial, Sirhan was convicted and sentenced to death, a sentence that was later commuted to life in prison.

June 19. Santo Domingo, Dominican Republic. A solitary hijacker diverted to Cuba a VIASA flight scheduled for Curaçao.

July 23. Algiers, Algeria. Three armed members of the PFLP took over an Israeli El Al airline bound for Tel Aviv from Rome. They diverted the airplane with its eleven crew members and twenty-one passengers to Algiers. Remaining there for five weeks, the hijackers obtained the release of sixteen Arab prisoners in Israel. Those abducted were then released and Algerian authorities set the hijackers free.

June 29. Miami, USA. A solitary hijacker diverted a Southeast Airlines flight bound for Key West to Cuba.

July 1. Chicago, USA. A hijacker diverted a Northwest flight to Cuba from its scheduled destination of Miami.

July 17. Los Angeles, USA. A National Airways flight bound for Miami was diverted to Cuba by a single hijacker.

July 23. Rome, Italy. Three members of the PFLP hijacked an El Al flight en route to Tel Aviv and forced it to land in Algiers, the first aircraft hijacking by a Palestinian group. The hijackers, a Syrian and two Palestinians, reportedly thought Israeli General Ariel Sharon was on the flight (he was not). The passengers and crew were held in Algeria for six weeks. Algerian authorities arrested the hijackers when the incident had ended, but soon released them.

Aug. 28. Guatemala City, Guatemala. U. S. Ambassador John Gordon Mein was murdered in the streets of the capital as a rebel faction stopped his official sedan on the way to the embassy after lunch at his residence. At gunpoint, the career diplomat was forced to exit the car. Rather than submit to a kidnapping, however, Mein abruptly tried to escape on foot, but was shot and killed.

He was the first of five American ambassadors to be killed by terrorists in the next twenty years. Others were Cleo Noel in Sudan (1973), Rodger Davies in Cyprus (1974), Francis Meloy in Lebanon (1976), and Adolph Dubs in Afghanistan (1979). See below. In addition, Ambassador Arnold Raphel in Pakistan died in 1988 in an attack on President Zia's airplane.

Sep. 4. Tel Aviv, Israel. Three bombs exploded in the center of the city, killing one and wounding seventy-one civilians.

Sep. 20. San Juan, Puerto Rico. A hijacker diverted an Eastern Airlines flight bound for Miami to Cuba.

Sep. 22. Barranquila, Colombia. One hijacker took an Avianca flight scheduled for Santa Maria, Colombia, to Cuba instead.

Oct. 6. Cozumel, Mexico. Three hijackers diverted to Cuba an Aeromaya flight bound for Merida.

Nov. 4. New Orleans, La., USA. A National flight to Miami was hijacked to Cuba by one person.

Nov. 8. Merida, Mexico. Two hijackers diverted to Cuba a Mexicana flight bound for Mexico City.

Nov. 22. Jerusalem, Israel. Al Fatah Palestinian terrorists set off a bomb in the Mahaneh Yehuda market that killed twelve civilians and injured fifty-two.

Nov. 23. Chicago, USA. Nine hijackers took an Eastern Airlines flight due for Miami on to Cuba.

Nov. 24. New York, USA. Three hijackers diverted a PanAm flight from its intended destination, San Juan, Puerto Rico, to Cuba.

Nov. 30. Miami, USA. An Eastern flight to Dallas was hijacked to Cuba by one person.

Dec. 3. Tampa, Fla., USA. One hijacker diverted a National flight bound for Miami to Cuba.

Dec. 11. Nashville, USA. A TWA flight to Miami was taken to Cuba by two hijackers.

Dec. 19. Philadelphia, USA. An Eastern flight to Miami was diverted to Cuba by two hijackers.

Dec. 26. Athens, Greece. PFLP terrorists machine-gunned an Israeli airliner at the Athens airport. One passenger was killed and a flight attendant wounded. Two days later, Israeli commandos raided Beirut airport, destroying thirteen parked airliners valued at $43 million. Two Palestinians received long prison sentences for the Athens attack, but were freed in 1970.

1969

Jan. Cuba. During the month, a dozen airliners were hijacked to Cuba. Nine of the flights originated in the United States.

Feb. Cuba. Five hijacked U. S. flights ended up in Cuba.

Adding the 1969 total to that of 1968, the number of flights hijacked to Cuba in those two years comes to more than sixty. A rapid decline in numbers took place after Castro's Cuba began to crack down on hijackers and a 1973 U. S.-Cuban accord undertaking to punish hijackers. In 1969, two of the hijackings were by Black Panther members: When William Brent diverted a plane to Cuba, the Cuban government put him in jail for two years; when Anthony Garnet Bryant forced a flight from New York due to land in Miami to Havana instead, he was jailed for a year and a half. Both were Black Panther members.

Feb. 18. Zurich, Switzerland. An El Al passenger jet preparing to take off for Tel Aviv was machine gunned on the runway by five assailants. Two people were killed, including the pilot and one terrorist, and five were wounded. Of the surviving Palestinian attackers, one (a woman) was soon released; the other three were imprisoned, but released sixteen months later as a result of a hijacking of a Swissair airliner.

Feb. 21. Jerusalem. Israel. A bomb set off in a busy market killed two people and injured twenty.

March 11. Cartagena, Colombia. An SAM Colombian airliner from Medillin was taken over by a single hijacker. He, however, was foiled in his intent to fly to Cuba by the passengers. One person died.

Four other flights of U. S. origin ended up in Cuba during the month.

In March in Sao Paulo, Brazil, small leftist terrorist groups began a campaign of kidnapping and ransoming diplomatic figures to embarrass the military government of Brazil. The People's Revolutionary Vanguard (VPR) kidnapped the Japanese consul and traded him for five political prisoners. After his release, the consul stayed on at his post. In April, the VPR wounded the American consul in an unsuccessful kidnapping.

April–May. Havana, Cuba. During this two-month period, six scheduled airliners from the United States ended up in Cuba.

May 22. Copenhagen, Denmark. Police forestalled a possible assassination attempt on the visiting former Israeli premier, David Ben Gurion, Danish authorities arrested a Jordanian woman, an Iraqi, and a Swede with a firearm and a grenade in their possession; they were released after three weeks.

June. Havana, Cuba. Hijackers succeeded in taking five airliners from the United States to Cuba during the month.

July 10. Barranquilla and Bogotá, Colombia. In two separate incidents, hijackers failed in their attempts to take over an airliner; passengers and crew overcame them, preventing a diversion to Cuba.

During the month three other airlines—Mexicana, Continental, and TWA—were taken to Cuba, each by a sole hijacker.

July 18. London, England. The Marks and Spencer department store on Oxford Street in central London was firebombed, reportedly by Arab terrorists. PFLP leader Habash threatened the firebombing of Jewish-owned stores worldwide.

July 31. Tokyo, Japan. A young man attacked U. S. Ambassador Armin H. Meyer with a knife at the international airport. Amb. Meyer was knocked to the floor in the attack, but guards subdued the assailant before he could injure the envoy, who was seeing off U. S. Secretary of State William P. Rogers.

Aug. 11. Khartoum, Sudan. A group of seven hijackers diverted an Ethiopian Airlines flight from its intended destination of Addis Abbaba. No one was injured.

Aug. 16. Valona, Albania. Four hijackers diverted an Olympic airlines flight from its destination, Athens. The hijackers surrendered in Albania.

Aug. 18. Cairo, Egypt. Six hijackers caused a Misrair flight from Cairo to Luxor to land in the desert at El Wagah.

Aug. 23. Izmir, Turkey. Two Jordanian students attempted a bomb attack on an Israeli commercial fair. One of them was killed in the blast and the other injured.

Aug. 29. Damascus, Syria. Two Palestinians — one of them Leila Khalid, the first woman to be involved in such an operation — hijacked a TWA flight from Rome to Tel Aviv (originating in Los Angeles, Cal.) and diverted it to Damascus. There all passengers except six Israelis were freed; the latter were exchanged for the release of two Syrian pilots held in Israel and freed in December 1969. Khalid had escaped by quietly boarding the bus with the freed hostages.

From August to the end of 1969, only ten aircraft ended up in Cuba rather than at their scheduled destinations.

Sep. 4. Rio de Janeiro, Brazil. A group called the MR-8 (Revolutionary Movement of October 8)and the ALN kidnapped the U. S. ambassador to Brazil, C. Burke Elbrick, in broad daylight on his way from his residence to the embassy. This was construed as an act of protest against the Brazilian military regime. Three days later, Elbrick was traded for fifteen prisoners. After his kidnapping, the Brazilian government restored the death penalty for terrorism-related crimes. By that time arbitrary arrests were common and the media were kept under strict control.

Amb. Elbrick suffered thereafter from the effects of a pistol whipping he had undergone while a prisoner.

Sep. 8. Brussels, Belgium. Al Fatah mounted a hand grenade attack on El Al offices carried out by two teenagers. They took refuge in the Iraqi embassy.

Sep. 13. Addis Ababba, Ethiopia. An Ethiopian airlines flight bound for Djibouti was diverted to Aden by three hijackers. One person died.

Oct. 19. Warsaw, Poland. Two hijackers took over a LOT aircraft schedule to land in East Berlin and directed it instead to West Berlin.

Oct. 22. Haifa, Israel. Bombs exploding at two apartment buildings killed four Israeli civilians.

Nov. 27. Athens, Greece. A grenade attack at the El Al office resulted in one child killed and thirteen persons wounded. Two Jordanians arrested and sentenced to eight and eleven years imprisonment, respectively, were released in 1970 after an Olympic Airways hijacking.

Dec. 12. Milan and Rome, Italy. A satchel bomb exploded in the crowded lobby of a bank in Milan's Piazza della Scala; seventeen people died and seventy were injured. That same day, in Rome, three bombs exploded, one at a bank and two others in the city's center, injuring fourteen persons.

1969 from April onward saw an upsurge of violence in Italy, beginning in April when an explosion at the International Milan Trade Fair injured twenty persons. Eleven people were hurt when bombs exploded on seven trains. Police blamed "extremists of all directions," both left and right. By year's end, more than 100 terrorists had been jailed.

Dec. 12. West Berlin, Germany. The German terrorist group called the Baader Meinhof gang exploded a bomb in a U. S. officers' club.

Dec. 5 and 17. London, England. Authorities forestalled two planned attacks on airliners. They arrested a total of six would-be terrorists.

Dec. 12. Milan, Italy. A bomb blast at the Banca Nazionale dell'Agricultura killed sixteen people and injured eighty-four. It was one of Italy's worst-ever terrorist attacks. Shortly thereafter, police arrested an Anarchist, Giuseppe Pinelli, who subsequently fell to his death from a police station window. The incident became the basis for Nobel Prize winner Dario Fo's play, "Accidental Death of an Anarchist."

Thirty-one years later, trials for those implicated in the bank attack began in Milan which resulted, in June 2001, in three right-wing defendants receiving life sentences and one, a three-year term, with another getting off as state's witness. Earlier trials of both Anarchists and right wingers had resulted in no convictions.

Dec. 21. Athens, Greece. An attempt to hijack an airliner bound for Paris failed. The three Lebanese arrested in the incident were released after an Olympic Airways hijacking the following year.

1970–1974

During a span of only eleven days in 1970, airline hijackings resulted in 400 hostages being held for up to a week and four jet aircraft being destroyed.

1970

Feb. 21. Zurich, Switzerland. Authorities suspected Palestinian PFLP members were of putting a bomb on a Swissair flight from Zurich to Tel Aviv. The explosion caused a crash that killed all forty-seven persons aboard the aircraft.

Feb. 27. Guatemala City, Guatemala. A radical leftist group called the Rebel Armed Forces took prisoner the foreign minister of Guatemala, Alberto Fuentes Mohr, as he left in his car a meeting with Organization of American States officials. The abductors issued a demand for the release of a twenty-two-year-old student named José Vicente Girón Calvillo. The demand was met the following day, with Girón obtaining asylum at the Mexican embassy and the foreign minister gaining his freedom. Two days before the kidnapping, three persons were shot to death as they put up political posters in the city.

March 6. Guatemala City, Guatemala. The Rebel Armed Forces abducted the U. S. embassy second secretary, Sean Holly, as he drove in the city streets. The terrorists demanded — and obtained — asylum in the Costa Rican embassy for student José Manuel Aguirre Monzón and his nineteen-year-old girlfriend, Vitalina Monzón. Holly, like Foreign Minister Fuentes (above), was released unharmed.

March 11. São Paulo, Brazil. Terrorists abducted the Japanese consul general, Nobuo Okuchi, demanding the freedom of five prisoners. He was released after four days upon the prisoners in question obtaining permission to take up exile in Mexico. Okuchi stayed on as consul in São Paulo.

March 24. Santo Domingo, Dominican Republic. Leftist kidnappers took Lt. Col. Donald J. Crowley, an Air Force attaché at the U. S. embassy. He was freed two days later upon the Dominican government releasing into Mexican exile, as demanded, twenty prisoners.

March 31. Guatemala City, Guatemala. Terrorists seized the West German ambassador, Count Karl von Spreti in the embassy Mercedes Benz near his residence. The kidnappers demanded $700,000 in ransom money and the release of twenty-two prisoners. Although the West German government later announced that it would be willing to pay the ransom money, Guatemalan officials took a position ignoring the demands.

Following up on a telephoned tip, police found Von Spreti's body in the village of San Raimundo six days later. He had been shot.

April 4. Porto Alegre, Brazil. American Consul Curtis C. Cutter narrowly escaped kidnapping or worse by several men armed with submachine guns riding in a car that tried to force his vehicle off the road. Cutter drove defensively, knocking down and running over one assailant, and escaped in a hail of bullets with a bullet wound in his shoulder. His two passengers, his wife and a friend, were unharmed.

April 12. Frankfurt, West Germany. The Red Army Faction (RAF), formed in 1968 and also known as the Baader-Meinhof Gang, set fire to a department store to protest materialism in society. In the following two years, the group robbed banks to fund their operations.

May 4. Asuncion, Paraguay. Two Palestinian gunmen broke into the Israeli consulate. They killed an Israeli clerk, Edna Pe'er, and wounded a local employee. Sentenced to three years in prison, the terrorists served their terms and were released.

May 17. Istanbul, Turkey. Four members of the Turkish People's Liberation Army, said to have ties with Palestinian militants, kidnapped Israeli Consul General Efraim Elrom, subduing him after he put up a fight as he returned to his apartment from lunch. The abductors demanded the released of "all revolutionaries" in Turkey. Mrs. Elrom issued two appeals that he be released, while the government refused to bargain. Six days later, after a massive search by police, his body was found in a small Istanbul apartment; he had been shot in the head with his hands tied behind his back.

May 29. Buenos Aires, Argentina. Two men disguised as army officers abducted at gunpoint former provisional president Pedro Eugenio Aramburú, a leader in the military's move to oust Juan Perón as president fifteen years earlier. Confusion reigned for days over who had kidnapped the former general and what that was expected to accomplish. The political situation became even more unstable. Speculation on who had kidnapped Aramburo included the current president, Juan Carlos Ongania. Communiqués received from a Peronista organization, the Juan José Command, convincingly indicated Aramburú was being held, to be tried for his part in the execution of twenty-seven Perónist leaders in a failed 1956 coup. He was shot to death on June 1 and two weeks later his body was found near Timote, 300 miles west of Buenos Aires.

Police later charged three men in the assassination, all Perón sympathizers: Carolos Maguid, Ignacio Velez, and Fr. Alberto Carbone. Tried and convicted, Maguid was sentenced to eighteen years imprisonment, Velez to thirty-two months; the priest, Fr. Carbone, got a suspended sentence.

Many terrorist attacks from both the right and left took place in Argentina during the period 1970-74: An Organization of American States report[1] lists fifteen names, with dates, of prominent Argentineans who were assassinated, leaving aside military and police officers.

June 11. Rio de Janeiro, Brazil. Two leftist terrorist groups combined to snatch West German Ambassador Ehrenfried von Holleben from his official car. One Brazilian guard was killed and two wounded. The abductors demanded the release of forty prisoners and the publication of their manifestos in the Brazilian media. Unlike the Guatemalan government two and a half months earlier (above), Brazilian authorities agreed, and von Holleben was released on the 15th.

July 22. Beirut, Lebanon. Six members of the Palestine Popular Struggle Front hijacked an Olympic flight bound for Athens and diverted it to Cairo. There they demanded and obtained freedom for six members of their group in Greek jails. No one was injured in the encounter.

July 31. Montevideo, Uruguay. The Tupamaros kidnapped USAID police advisor Dan Mitrione. They demanded the release of some 150 prisoners. With the backing of Washington, the Uruguayan government refused. Mitrione's body was found in a stolen car on August 10. In 1970, the person charged with his murder, Antonio Mas Mas, was sentence to thirty years in prison.

Aug. 2. New York, USA. On a PanAm flight bound for San Juan, Puerto Rico, a man named Rudolfo Rivera Rios, hoping to publicize the cause of Puerto Rican independence, diverted the aircraft to Havana by showing a pistol and claiming to have a bottle of nitroglycerine. He surrendered to Cuban police and was jailed for seven years. None of the 377 passengers was harmed.

Upon release and return to the United States, the luckless hijacker was sentenced in December 1978 to life in prison, with a possibility of parole after ten years.

Sep. 6. Zurich, Switzerland. Two PFLP hijackers took control of a Swissair flight bound for New York. The airplane, with 155 passengers aboard, was directed to Dawson Field (Zerqa), a military airfield twenty miles north of Amman, Jordan. After seven days, the hijackers released their hostages and blew up the plane. This exploit led directly to the expulsion of the Palestinian Fatah organization from Jordan.

Sep. 6. London, England. A pair of terrorists tried to hijack an El Al airliner out of London, but failed due to the presence of armed marshals on board. One member, the famous (or notorious) Leila Khalid, was captured; her partner in the hijacking was killed. The aircraft landed at Heathrow Airport. After a month, the German, Swiss, and British governments acceded to PFLP demands for the release of prisoners, including Khalid. (She was to have a total of six cosmetic operations on her notably pretty face in order to continue her hijacking career.)

Sep. 6. Amsterdam, the Netherlands. Two Palestinian terrorists took control of a Pan Am flight scheduled for New York with 170 passengers and redirected it to Beirut. There, seven more gunmen came aboard and the flight continued to Cairo. Everyone left the plane and it was immediately blown up. No one was hurt.

In this month during a span of eleven days, airline hijackings resulted in 400 hostages being held for up to a week; four jet aircraft were destroyed on the ground.

Oct. 5. Quebec, Canada. This date marked the beginning of the "October Crisis." Two armed men kidnapped British Trade Commissioner James Cross. A note identified those responsible as being members of the Front de Libération du Québec (FLQ). Their demands included the release of twenty-three "political prisoners," payment of $500,000 in gold, publicity for the FLQ manifesto, and an aircraft to take the kidnappers to Cuba or Algeria. Authorities immediately began rounding up suspects and enacting emergency measures.

On October 10, two masked gunmen kidnapped provincial minister of labor Pierre Laporte at his home in Quebec. The two also were FLQ members, but evidently from a more radical wing of the organization. Negotiations continued on the release of the two officials, and the national authorities invoked the War Measures Act; more than 250 people were arrested.

The FLQ murdered Laporte. His body was found in Montreal on October 18. The police rescued Cross, however, retrieving him on December 3 from captivity near Montreal, unharmed but twenty-two pounds lighter.

Some of the perpetrators escaped to Cuba and eventually Paris, only later to return and stand trial. Those connected with the Cross kidnapping received relatively light sentences. Francis Simard and Paul Rose, however, were convicted and sentenced to life in prison for their roles in the Laport murder, and Jacques Rose got eight years as an accessory. Bernard Lortie received a twenty-year sentence for kidnapping. (Jacques Rose was released in July 1978 and Paul Rose paroled in December 1982.)

Nov. 26. Manila, the Philippines. A knife-wielding Bolivian artist attempted to stab Pope Paul VI during the latter's pilgrimage to West Asia, Oceania, and Australia. The Pope narrowly escaped and continued the trip, but reportedly may have received a minor wound. It was the last such trip he made during the following eight years of his life.

Dec. 7. Rio de Janeiro, Brazil. The VPR kidnapped the Swiss ambassador, Giovanni Enrico Bucher. His Brazilian police escort died in the ambush. Bucher was the fifteenth political kidnapping victim in the Western Hemisphere in fifteen months.

The Brazilian government, after protracted negotiations, ransomed the ambassador for seventy prisoners who were flown to asylum in Chile. On January 16, He was released on a deserted street near the center of Rio. This proved to be the final such major urban terrorist operation

in Brazil, but it marked a total of 130 terrorist or terrorist-suspect prisoners the Brazilian authorities had released and sent abroad because of diplomatic kidnappings.

During 1969-70, the activities of the far-left U. S. terrorist organization called the Weathermen reached a peak. Violent, small, and ineffectual, the group set off more than 4,000 bombs in that two-year period, amazingly not causing any deaths except among Weathermen themselves. The last such attack took place in 1975.[2]

1971

Jan. 8. Montevideo, Uruguay. Tupamaro terrorists kidnapped the British ambassador, Sir Geoffrey M. Jackson and held him for eight months. Their demand: the release of political prisoners. On September 8, the Tupamaros released him following a jail break that freed 106 members of that organization.

Jan. 30. Lahore, Pakistan. Hashim and Asharaf Quereshi, brothers, of the Jammu and Kashmir Liberation Front hijacked an Indian Airline flight from Srinagar scheduled for Jammu. Armed with a pistol and a hand grenade, they forced the pilot to land instead at Lahore. There Pakistani Foreign Minister Zulfiquar Ali Bhutto met with the two, furthered their effort at publicity, and persuaded them to release the crew and passengers. On February 1, these latter proceeded to Amritsar by road. No one was hurt.

March 1. Washington, USA. The Weather Underground claimed responsibility for a bomb blast in a U.S. Capitol building lavatory. The explosion caused damage, but no casualties.

April 15. Stockholm, Sweden. Yugoslav Ambassador Vladimir Rolovic died in the Karolinski Hospital after being grievously wounded the previous week when three gunmen burst into the Yugoslav embassy and shot the diplomat three times. The Croatian Ustasha claimed responsibility. Police arrested two men, Andejelko Barajkowic and Miro Baresic, and temporarily detained three others. Sweden found Baresic, an almost legendary figure in Ustasha circles, guilty of murder and sentenced him to eighteen years in prison. (After he had served half of that term, the authorities released him in December 1987, but promptly deported him to Paraguay, where he had previously resided.)

May 8. Tel Aviv, Israel. Four members of Black September, two men and two women, took over an airliner from Brussels, Belgium, and demanded the released of certain prisoners. The demand was refused. Israeli commandos stormed the plane and killed the two male terrorists. The two women were later sentenced to life terms in prison.

Skyjacking peaked in the period 1968-72, with more than 300 attempts around the world in 1972. In the following ten years, numbers dropped to an average of about nine attempts per year in the United States. The dramatic drop may be attributed to the implementation of deterrent and prevention measures and international agreements.

Nov. 28. Cairo, Egypt. In their first significant terrorist act, Black September operatives assassinated Jordanian Prime Minister Wasfi al-Tal at the Sheraton Hotel. Police captured the assassins, but heavy outside pressure, especially from Libya, brought the Egyptian government to free them. The following year Black September mounted its attack at the Olympic Games.

Dec. 4. Belfast, Northern Ireland. Fifteen civilians died in a bombing by Loyalist paramilitaries at McGurk's Bar in the northern part of the city. The bomb apparently had been planted by the Protestant Ulster Volunteer Force (UVF).

Dec. 15. London, England. A Palestinian hit squad wounded Jordanian Ambassador Zaid al-Rifai in a failed kidnapping attempt.

1972

In 1972, a chronicle of twentieth century events in the United States year-by-year began classifying certain events as relating to "terrorism."[3]

Jan. 30. Londonderry, Northern Ireland. "Bloody Sunday." British paratroopers shot and killed thirteen civilian demonstrators during a protest march. Another man died later of his wounds, and thirteen additional people were injured. Tempers ran so high that the British embassy on Merrion Square in Dublin was burned by an irate crowd.

March 4. Belfast, Northern Ireland. Protestant terrorists bombed the Abercorn Restaurant, killing two people and injuring 131.

April 10. Buenos Aires, Argentina. The general manager of the Fiat company, Dr. Oberdan Sallustro, was assassinated by terrorists of the Peoples' Revolutionary Army (ERP).

May 8. Tel Aviv, Israel. Four Palestinian Black September gunmen commandeered a Belgian airline at Ben Gurion Airport. Israeli commandos stormed the plane and killed all of the terrorists, freeing the hostages. One passenger and five Israeli soldiers died.

May 11. Heidelberg, West Germany. A time bomb explosion at the American headquarters resulted in the deaths of four U. S. servicemen. The Red Army Faction (RAF) claimed responsibility. The RAF set off other explosions during the month, the most destructive at U. S. Army offices in Frankfurt, where there were one death and thirteen injuries; a publishing office in Berlin and a police building in Augsburg also were hit.

May 30. Lod, Israel. Three members of the Japanese Red Army (JRA) dressed in business suits and carrying violin cases arrived at Lod Airport near Tel Aviv on an Air France flight. They suddenly opened fire with automatic weapons in the airport terminal, killing twenty-six civilians and wounding seventy-eight. One gunman ran out of ammunition and was killed by his companions; another committed suicide with a hand grenade. Police captured the third, Kozo Okamoto, one of the top leaders of JRA. He was jailed in Israel until May 1985, when Israel and the PFLP agreed to exchange captives. (The Lod Airport massacre was organized by the PFLP.)

Okamoto, along with four Japanese colleagues involved peripherally in the Lod attack, dropped out of sight in Beirut; in 1997 they were jailed there for three years for using forged passports. In March 2000, Lebanon granted asylum to Okamoto, but expelled the other four, who were arrested upon return to Japan.

July 2. Saigon, South Vietnam. A solitary hijacker armed with a knife tried to take over a PanAm jetliner with 151 aboard at Tonsonnhut Airport. He sought to redirect the aircraft to Hanoi, but was shot dead by an American reserve policeman aboard the flight, which had arrived from Hawaii. An unusual aspect of the incident was that the police reservist was specifically ordered by the American pilot, as he grappled with the student, to shoot the would-be hijacker — and he did. Later investigations cleared both the pilot and the police reservist of any wrongdoing.

July 8. Beirut, Lebanon. Popular Front for the Liberation of Palestine spokesman, editor, and novelist Ghassan Kanafani died, along with his niece, in a bomb explosion set off in his car. The PFLP charged that he had been assassinated by Israel's Mossad.

July 21. Belfast, Northern Ireland. "Bloody Friday." The IRA Provisionals set off twenty-six bombs, including two powerful car bombs. In a little more than an hour's time, eleven people died and about 130 more were injured, nearly all civilians. Ten days later, three IRA car bomb attacks in the village of Claudy left six dead.

July 31. Miami, USA. Five Black Panther Party members hijacked a Delta Airlines jet aircraft and forced it to fly to Algeria after releasing the passengers in Miami. They received a $1 million ransom. Most of the hijackers were arrested and tried in France four years later.

Sep. 5. Munich, West Germany. In a setting of unexpectedly (and unfortunately) relaxed security arrangements for the Olympic Games, Palestinian Black September terrorists, organized by Abu Daoud, had little difficulty in taking control of the delegation of Israeli athletes. Before dawn that morning, the attack group of eight Palestinians forced their way into the ground-floor quarters of the athletes and coaches. They soon shot dead two of the Israelis who tried to resist and captured the other nine (at least one athlete had escaped through a window just as the kidnapping started).

Shortly after 5:00 a.m., the terrorists made known their demands: the release of 234 prisoners held in Israeli jails, plus the notorious German terrorists Baader and Meinhoff in German prisons. They announced they would kill one hostage for each hour of noncompliance after 8:00 a.m. At 8:15 a.m., the next scheduled Olympic event, an equestrian trial, started on time.

During the day, Black September (a name chosen by this particular group of militants from a heavy military defeat Palestinians suffered in Jordan two years earlier) pushed back the deadline, contented, as they saw it, to make world headlines for the Palestinian cause. Late in the afternoon of the 5th, the terrorists made a new demand: an airplane to fly them and their hostages to Cairo. The authorities appeared to agree, meanwhile stationing police around the area of the military airport near Furstenfeldbruck where the hostages and their captors would be helicoptered. In a failed rescue mission, however, all seven Israelis surviving to that point and all eight Palestinians, plus a German police officer, died. It was a complete fiasco of poor planning. Nevertheless, the Games continued the next day, the 6th.

In September 2002, the families of the slain Israeli Olympic team members accepted $3 million in compensation that the German government had offered the previous year. In the years after the massacre, Israel's secret service, the Mossad, tracked down and killed all the Palestinians who had participated in the mounting of the mission, including Abu Daoud.

Dec. 28. Bangkok, Thailand. Four Black September gunmen took six hostages after seizing the Israeli embassy. After nineteen hours, the hostages were released in exchange for safe conduct. They were unable to effect the release of thirty-six terrorists in Israeli jails.

1973

In 1973 alone, by one count 221 significant terrorist incidents occurred worldwide.[2]

Jan. 27. Santa Barbara, Cal., USA. The Turkish consul general, Mehmet Baydar, and Consul Bahadir Demir were assassinated at a private luncheon held by Gurgen Yanakian, an elderly U. S. citizen of Armenian extraction. He was tried, convicted, and sentenced to life in prison. Yanikian was paroled at the end of 1984 and died soon thereafter.

In 1975, two bombs planted in Beirut, Lebanon, were associated with demands for the release of Yanakian. The Armenian Secret Army for the Liberation of Armenia (ASALA) claimed responsibility.

March 1. Khartoum, Sudan. Seven members of the Palestinian Black September faction of the PLO, led by a Sudanese, Rizik Kass, seized the Saudi Arabian embassy. Armed with pistols and submachine guns, about 7:00 p.m. they burst and took more than a half dozen hostages at the reception. Several senior diplomats escaped in the initial confusion, but before it was over they had assassinated U.S. Ambassador Cleo A. Noel, Jr., George C. Moore, the outgoing American chargé d'affaires, and Belgian diplomat Guy Eid. The assailants demanded the release of Sirhan Sirhan, convicted assassin of U. S. presidential candidate Robert Kennedy, all prisoners held in Israel, some sixty-seven imprisoned in Jordan, and two in Germany.

With none of their demands being met, the terrorists scaled back their demands, and with no avenue of escape with their hostages apparently available to them, the terrorists told their three chosen victims to write their wills and farewell messages. On March 2 they fired some forty bullets into the three diplomat victims. The following day, the terrorists dropped all their demands, seeking only to escape alive. Ordered by PLO leadership to surrender after the murders had been committed, they did so early in the morning of March 4. Sudanese authorities released two immediately due to what was called lack of evidence. The other six were tried and convicted of murder, but later were released into PLO custody and flown out of the country.

May 4. Guadalajara, Mexico. Four members of the People's Revolutionary Armed Forces kidnapped American Consul General Terrence Leonhardy, taking him prisoner at gunpoint in the evening as he drove home from a police exhibit. The kidnappers demanded the release of thirty prisoners in seven jails that they termed "political," even though they included kidnappers and bank robbers. The Mexican government acceded to the demand. On May 6, the prisoners—twenty-six men and four women—were flown to asylum in Cuba in a Mexican Air Force plane. Consul General Leonhardy was freed.

July 1. Washington, DC, USA. Yosef (Joe) Allon, air force attaché at the Israeli Embassy, was shot to death outside his home.

Aug. 4. Between Bologna and Florence, Italy. The Black Order bombed the Rome-to-Munich express packed with holiday travelers. The blast and train wreck killed twelve people and injured forty-eight. The group asserted the act was in protest of an Italian government political ban on fascist groups.

Six years later, in August 1980, a judge in Bologna indicted eight rightist-wing activists for the crime, and shortly thereafter another deadly bomb blast took place (below).

Aug. 5. Athens, Greece. A Black September suicide squad attacked the airport passenger terminals and killed three civilians, injuring fifty-five.

Sep. 5. Paris, France. For the first time, Palestinians carried out an act of terrorism in the country that had generally favored Arab causes. Five armed men occupied the Saudi Arabian embassy near the Bois de Boulogne for twenty-eight hours (the Saudi ambassador was not present), holding thirteen hostages. They demanded that Jordan free from prison Mohammed Daoud Odeh, a leader of Al Fatah. Evidently they hoped by the invasion of the Saudi embassy to bring pressure on that government to support their demand. After throwing one hostage from a second story window, negotiating with French authorities, setting and then changing ultimatums, accepting Iraqi envoy Naama al-Naama as a voluntary hostage, releasing a slightly wounded hostage, and apologizing to France for their actions—after all this, the gunmen arranged an exit. They quit the embassy and left with five trussed-up Saudi hostages from Le Bourget Airport on a Syrian airliner.

The group flew to Cairo, then to Kuwait. There they obtained a Kuwait Airways airplane to fly over Riyadh, Saudi Arabia, threatening to throw out their hostages if their demand for the release of Odeh were not met. They were unsuccessful. On September 8, the terrorists surrendered in Kuwait. They were not arrested, however, and possibly were simply delivered to the Iraqi border.

Dec. 17. Rome, Italy. Five Palestinian terrorists suddenly began shooting up a terminal lounge at Fiumicino airport, killing two people. At that point, they threw an incendiary bomb aboard a Pan American aircraft loading for departure; the bomb destroyed the plane and killed all twenty-nine people aboard. Next the terrorists captured five Italian hostages, herded them aboard a Lufthansa flight ready to depart. The gunmen killed another person as he tried to flee. They took more hostages and hijacked an aircraft to Athens, where the Palestinians' demand for the release of two prisoners in a Greek jail was not met, before flying to Damascus. Next the aircraft proceeded to Kuwait. (One of the hostages had been killed.) At Kuwait the terrorists released their remaining hostages in return for safe conduct for themselves to an unknown country.

Dec. 20. Madrid, Spain. Members of the Basque separatist organization called "Basque Homeland and Liberation" (in the unique Basque language), or ETA, assassinated Prime Minister Luis Carrero Blanco, dictator Francisco Franco's number-two man and presumed successor. Through months of preparation that involved thirty-foot tunneling under a street where Carrero Blanco's car passed after he attended mass each morning, and the gradual introduction of 175 pounds of explosives into the site, the plotters prepared a huge and deadly bomb. When it exploded, set off by remote control, the blast killed Admiral Carrero Blanco and two people with him, blew a twenty-five-foot hole in the street, and tossed his car over a five-story church. Authorities did not think to look for what was left of the automobile, on the other side of the Church of San Francisco de Borja, for several hours.

Fourteen ETA members were arrested and tried, five of whom were executed. The remaining eleven were imprisoned, but amnestied in 1978, after the death of General Franco.

Dec. 27. Managua, Nicaragua. At a birthday dinner for U. S. Ambassador Turner B. Shelton held at the home of a former agriculture minister, José María Castillo, nine members of the Sandinista Liberation Front, including three women, took hostage some of the most important figures on the national scene. (Amb. Shelton, having left earlier, just avoided being captured.) After killing Castillo and three guards, they settled in for sixty-one hours of negotiations. Their demands included money — initially $5 million — but centered on the release of fourteen political prisoners of the Anastasio Somoza regime.

With agreement reached, most of the hostages were freed. The terrorists, the released prisoners, and four volunteer hostages flew to Havana, arriving December 30.

1974

Feb. 4. Berkeley, USA. Members of the domestic terrorist group the Symbionese Liberation Army (SLA) kidnapped heiress Patricia C. Hearst. The Hearst publishing family agreed to the initial demands, which included the distribution of millions of dollars worth of food, but negotiations reached a stalemate. Later, on April 15, apparently brain washed, the nineteen-year-old Hearst joined the group, participating as an armed robber in a raid on the Hibernia Bank in San Francisco, Cal. An assault on the group by police later that year left most SLA members dead, but Hearst escaped. Arrested in 1975, she was convicted of bank robbery and sent to jail; in 1979 her sentence was commuted.

May 15. Maalot, Israel. Three gunmen from a far-left offshoot of the PDFLP, disguised as Israeli soldiers, infiltrated

Galilee from Lebanon. They took over a school at Maalot in northern Israel after killing at least one adult, a guard. Eleventh-grade students on a field trip were spending the night there. Some few students escaped by jumping out second story windows, but the terrorists held the bulk of the students and teachers hostage. The next day they demanded that Israel release three jailed Palestinian terrorists and threatened to begin executing hostages at 6:00 p.m.

Prime Minister Golda Meir ruled out any negotiations; she ordered the army to take the school. At 5:45 that afternoon, Israeli troops attacked. In the ensuing brief but violent clash, Israeli soldiers killed the three terrorists, but concurrent losses among children and teachers were high: As many as twenty-three children and five Israeli adults died. Of these, some likely were killed by Israeli bullets in what has been termed a bungled rescue operation.

May 17. Dublin and Monaghan, Ireland. A series of explosions set off by Loyalists killed thirty-three civilians. Three car bombs exploded in rush-hour traffic almost simultaneously in Dublin's Parnell, Talbot, and South Leinster streets, causing most of the casualties. Another car bomb went off a few hours later at Monaghan, near the boundary with Northern Ireland.

The death toll of thirty-three was the highest during any single day of the conflict.

May 28. Brescia, Italy. A high-explosive time bomb went off at a rally of some 3,000 workers and students—the worst terrorist attack Italy had seen since the December 1969 bombing of a Milan bank. Eight people were killed—at least four of them women—and ninety-four injured. The blast coincided with a police inquiry into the Black Order, a right-wing extremist organization.

Aug. 19. Nicosia, Cyprus. U.S. Ambassador Rodger P. Davies was killed in the embassy by a burst of machine gun fire from a nearby building during an anti-American protest by Greek Cypriots. The bullets sent through his office window proved fatal for the career diplomat, recently arrived, even though at the time he was standing with other employees in a nearby central hallway. An embassy clerk, Antoinette Varnavas, also died. Three days previously, a cease-fire had been proclaimed in the strife-ridden island.

Three men who fired the shots, two or more of which proved fatal, were identified through film taken by a local news crew. After trial, two of the gunmen were convicted to long prison sentences.

Sep. 15. Phan Rang, South Vietnam. A solitary hijacker armed with two hand grenades took over an Air Vietnam jetliner en route from Da Nang to Saigon with sixty-two passengers. He demanded to be flown to Hanoi. The pilot, however, decided to land at Phan Rang, north-east of Saigon in South Vietnamese territory. He overshot the runway, tried to come around again, but the plane stalled out and crashed. Everyone aboard was killed.

Oct. 5. Guildford, England. An exploding IRA bomb in the Horse and Groom pub killed four British soldiers and a civilian. Forty-four people, mostly civilians, were injured. Four suspects—one Englishwoman and three Irishmen—were tried, convicted, and imprisoned for the crime. The "Guildford Four," however, eventually were found to have been wrongly convicted. They were released in 1989. In June 2000, all four received apologies from Prime Minister Tony Blair. No one else was ever charged.

Nov. 10. Berlin, West Germany. The RAF attempted to kidnap the president of the West German Superior Court of Justice, Gunter von Drenkmann, from the doorstep of his home. Von Drenkmann and his family were celebrating his sixty-fourth birthday and he opened the door to what appeared to be a delivery man. In a struggle, RAF members shot him three times. He died soon thereafter in hospital.

Nov. 21. Birmingham, England. Twenty-one people were killed and nearly 200 injured by the explosion of bombs planted in two pubs, the Mulberry Bush and the Tavern in the Town. Although the IRA denied responsibility the following day, that organization was widely held to be the instigators. Public outrage at the carnage brought the British government under pressure to act more forcefully against the threat of further bombs. Eight days later the House of Commons passed the Prevention of Terrorism Act.

Within months six Irishmen were arrested and convicted of the crime. They served sixteen years in prison before being freed on appeal on March 14, 1991.

Nov. 23. Dubai, United Arab Emirates. Four Palestinian Rejectionist Front terrorists hijacked a British Airways VC-10 airliner scheduled to fly to Calcutta. Demanding the release of prisoners, they forced the pilot to fly to Tripoli, Libya, and then to Tunis. Notwithstanding the acceptance of their demands, the terrorists killed one German passenger at Tunis before surrendering.

Notes

1. www.cidh.oas/org/countryrep/argentina
2. Laqueur, A History of Terrorism, p. 85.
3. Gordon and Gordon, American Chronicle.

1975–1979

During the '70s, armed men on both sides of the dispute over Ireland engaged in at least fifty incidents involving in each case a loss of life of five or more civilians.

1975

Jan. 2. Samastipur, India. In the most significant political assassination (a fairly rare occurrence in India) since the shooting of Gandhi in 1948, Railway Minister Lalit Narayan Mishra was fatally injured by a bomb thrown at him at a public rally in his home state. He died the next day; two other people were killed. His brother, a state minister, was wounded. The police promptly arrested seven persons, reportedly Anang Marg terrorists. It was not clear, however, who was responsible for the killing of the controversial Mishra, who had become something of an embarrassment for the Congress Party due to financial irregularities.

Jan. 19. Paris, France. At Orly Airport, Arab gunmen tried a grenade attack on an El Al jumbo jet. Twenty people were injured in a gun battle that broke out. They seized ten hostages and held them in a terminal bathroom. Eventually the French government provided the terrorists with a plane that flew them to safety in Baghdad, Iraq. The hostages meanwhile were released.

Jan. 24, New York, USA. A bomb set off during lunch at the historic Fraunces Tavern in lower Manhattan killed four and injured sixty-three people. The Puerto Rican nationalist group FALN claimed responsibility. New York police tied thirteen other bombings to the group. No one was ever charged with this particular blast.

A 1983 FBI report lists dozens of FALN bombings in New York, starting with an explosive device that maimed a policeman, Angel Poggi, on December 11, 1974, and continuing through a fatal 1977 blast at the Mobil Oil headquarters (below).

Jan. 29. Washington, USA. The Weather Underground domestic terrorist group claimed responsibility for an explosion in a bathroom at the U.S. Department of State. No one was hurt.

Feb. 19. Córdoba, Argentina. American Consul John Patrick Egan, kidnapped earlier and held by Montoneros terrorists, was executed by firing squad.

Feb. 27. West Berlin, Germany. The extremist Second of June Movement kidnapped the head of the Christian Democrat Union, Peter Lorenz. They demanded the release of six prisoners, a demand that was met. On March 3, Berlin Vicar Heinrich Albertz flew with the freed prisoners to South Yemen; the following day, Lorenz was released.

March 5. Tel Aviv, Israel. Eight PLO gunmen, who had arrived undetected by sea, entered the Savoy Hotel and took dozens of hostages. The terrorists barricaded themselves in the top floor of the hotel and demanded the release of their followers from Israeli jails. Israeli troops mounted a rescue mission that afternoon in the course of which three soldiers were killed and eight hostages wounded. The terrorists retreated to a room and blew themselves up when the commandos broke in. Seven terrorists were killed and only one captured. In all, eight hostages died and eleven were wounded. The surviving PLO assailant said they made the attack to sabotage forthcoming talks between Israel and Egypt.

April 4. New York, USA. The Jewish Defense League set off a bomb at the Iraqi mission to the UN. No casualties resulted.

April 5. Belfast, Northern Ireland. Republican loyalists set a bomb in the Mountainview Tavern. Its explosion killed five civilians.

April 24. Stockholm, Sweden. Six Red Army Faction terrorists seized the West German embassy and took twelve hostages. One hostage and one terrorist died when a bomb exploded prematurely. Their demands for the release of twenty-six terrorists in prison, including Baader Meinhof members, and an escape airplane were not met. The terrorists murdered two embassy staff members, but an accidental explosion provided the police an opportunity to storm the embassy. They captured or killed the assailants and freed the remaining hostages; extradited to West Germany, they were all imprisoned. In 1979, another RAF member involved in the planning for the raid received a West German prison term of fourteen years.

This episode led to the development of the famous "Stockholm syndrome," which posits that hostages in time often come to sympathize and identify with their captors.

July 31. Belfast, Northern Ireland. In what was called the "Miami Showband Massacre," the loyalist United Volunteer Force (UVF) staged an official roadblock and stopped the bus of a professional musical group. A bomb the terrorists loaded on the bus, apparently intended to throw suspicion on the band, the Miami Showband, exploded prematurely, killing two UVF men. The others in that group thereupon shot dead three band members.

In retaliation, two weeks later, on August 13, the IRA shot up the Bayardo Bar in Belfast, killing several civilians.

Aug. 4. Kuala Lumpur, Malaysia. Members of the Japanese JRA took fifty-two hostages at the U. S. and Swedish embassies. After their demand for the release of five JRA prisoners in Japan was met, the hostages were freed. Further negotiations resulted in the JRA terrorists being flown to Libya.

Oct. 22. Vienna, Austria. Three ASALA gunmen killed Turkish ambassador Danis Tunalz'gil in his study at home.

Two days later, in Paris, the Turkish ambassador to France, Ismail Erez, and his driver, Talip Yener, were shot and killed. The ASALA and the Justice Commandos for the Armenian Genocide (JCAG) disputed responsibility.

Nov. 27. London, England. British publisher Ross McWhirter offered a large monetary reward for information leading to the arrest of terrorist bombers. Gunmen showed up at his home and shot him dead. Two years later, four IRA members were sentenced to life in prison for that and other murders.

Dec. 2. Beilen, the Netherlands. Six young South Moluccan terrorists, protesting their homeland being integrated into Indonesia, hijacked a train and held it and twenty-three of its passengers for twelve days. Three of the hijackers were killed before the surviving terrorists surrendered on December 14. After serving fourteen-year prison sentences, by the beginning of the 1990s they had been set free.

Dec. 4. Amsterdam, the Netherlands. Another group of seven Moluccan terrorists seized the Indonesian embassy and held thirty-six people hostage (one of the hostages died in a leap from an upper story window). Two weeks after it began, the siege ended. As many as twenty South Moluccans were imprisoned for these acts.

Dec. 21. Vienna, Austria. In an internationally publicized incident, the notorious terrorist-for-hire "Carlos the Jackal" (Venezuelan-born Ilich Ramírez Sánchez) led a group of six PFLP terrorists in the take-over of OPEC's Vienna headquarters. They stormed in, killing three people, wounding seven (in addition, one terrorist was shot), and taking at least seventy hostage, including eleven OPEC nation oil ministers gathered for a conference. The terrorists demanded $5 million in ransom — and may have ended up receiving even more. They also voiced vague demands about the need for relief to Palestinians. The terrorists soon released forty-one Austrian OPEC staff hostages, but the rest were flown to Algeria. Some of the ministerial-level hostages were released there. Others were released after an onward flight to Tripoli, Libya. There the group of six, including a German woman, ran out of options and had to return to Algiers. There the remaining hostages were released, all unharmed.

The kidnappers' relations with Algerian officials were cordial to a fault: no armed guards or troops were at the airport. Although Austria demanded their extradition, Algeria appeared ready to grant them political asylum. The terrorists disappeared. In following years "Carlos" dropped from sight on the world terrorist scene.

The PFLP likely had inside help in planning the operation from Libya or Iraq, strong supporters of higher oil prices. The terrorists planned to ransom the ministers for needed cash, but the expectation was they would then murder the ministers representing Saudi Arabia and Iran for those countries' lack of dedication to the twin causes of Palestine and higher oil prices. The last of the hostages were released in Algiers after a ransom was paid, estimated at between $20 and $50 million (probably a high estimate). None was murdered, to the outrage of PFLP Palestinian leadership.

In August 1994, Sudanese officials turned "Carlos" over to French agents, who took him to Paris in chains. He was tried for killing two (unarmed) French intelligence officers and a Lebanese PFLP figure in 1979. Found guilty, in December 1997 he was sentenced to life in prison (below). German terrorist Hans Joachim Klein had been his deputy at Vienna and had been wounded in the stomach in that attack; he was captured in France in 2000 and deported to Germany. There a repentant Klein was sentenced to nine years in prison for his part in the attack on OPEC headquarters.

Dec. 23. Athens, Greece. A masked gunman, using an automatic pistol, shot to death U.S. embassy official Richard Welch, the CIA station chief, outside his home in an Athens suburb. The Greek organization November 17 subsequently took responsibility for his assassination.

1976

In Argentina under military rule from 1976 to 1983, the government arrested thousands of people, most of them dissidents and civilians unconnected with terrorism, who then vanished without a trace.

Jan. 1. Dubai, United Arab Emirates. A bomb destroyed an MEA airliner bound from Beirut to Muscat, Oman, killing eighty-two persons. The explosion took place while the jetliner was in the Dubai airport. Sabotage was suspected.

Jan. 5. County Armagh, Northern Ireland. A faction of the IRA termed the Republican Action Force stopped a minibus in a fake security check. They then shot to death ten civilian workmen.

Feb. 16. Beirut, Lebanon. Oktar Cirit, Turkish embassy first secretary, was shot to death in a restaurant by ASALA operatives.

May 11. Paris, France. Gunmen from a previously unknown group that called itself the "Brigade Internationale Che Guevara" assassinated the Bolivian ambassador, Joaquin Zenteno Anaya. The ambassador was hit by three pistol shots. He was one of the senior commanders of the troops that captured Ernesto (Che) Guevara in 1967, and it was he who gave the order to execute the fabled Argentinean terrorist.

May 27. Beirut, Lebanon. Armed men broke into the apartment of Linda Joumblatt, Druze political leader Kamal Joumblatt's sister, and opened fire on her. She was killed and her two daughters were wounded.

May 28. Zurich, Switzerland. A bomb explosion at the office of the Turk-

ish labor attaché resulted in extensive damage. Another explosive device planted at the Turkish Tourism Bureau was defused. The JCAG claimed responsibility.

June 5. Belfast, Northern Ireland. Loyalist Ulster Volunteer Force (UVF) gunmen killed at least five civilians in a bar on Gresham Street. Less than a month later, the UVF killed a similar number of civilians in an attack on an inn near Antrim, Northern Ireland.

June 16. Beirut, Lebanon. PLO terrorists abducted U. S. Ambassador to Lebanon Francis E. Meloy, Economic Officer Robert O. Waring, and the driver of the embassy car, Mohammed Moghrabi, en route to an informal meeting with new President Elias Sarkis. (Meloy, newly arrived at the post, had not yet formally presented his credentials.) Shortly after passing through a militia checkpoint between East and West Beirut, the car disappeared. The bullet-riddled bodies of all three men soon were soon found in the mainly Muslim section of the city. Rumors circulated later that the son of the embassy driver had set the party up for the hit, thereby deliberately sacrificing his father's life.

In 1996, an appeals court freed two former Muslim terrorists convicted in 1976 of the kidnappings (but not the murders). The ruling held that a 1990 amnesty on the commission of political crimes during Lebanon's civil war applied to Bassem Farkh and Namek Kamal.

June 16. Soweto, South Africa. Police put down forcefully a demonstration of thousands of black students gathered near Johannesburg, fatally shooting several. The students were protesting a requirement that they be taught in Afrikaans. The incident, which became a *cause célèbre* around the world, touched off nationwide riots and boycotts that lasted more than a year and claimed during that time the lives of at least 575 people.

June 27. Athens, Greece. The German RAF and the Palestinian PFLP cooperated in hijacking an Air France flight bound for Paris from Tel Aviv with fifty-three persons aboard. A young woman traveling with a Ecuadorian passport in the name of Ortega, a young blond man with a Peruvian passport in the name of A. Garcia, and two dark-complected young men, one with Bahraini and the other with Kuwaiti travel documents, took over the Airbus. They diverted it first to Benghazi, Libya, for fuel and then to Entebbe, Uganda, arriving the next day. (One woman managed to talk her way off the aircraft at Benghazi.) Terrorist colleagues awaited the hijacked airplane at Entebbe, as did supporting Ugandan soldiers and dictator Idi Amin. The passengers and crew were off loaded into what was called the airport's Old Terminal.

The terrorists' demanded the release of RAF and Palestinian prisoners in Israel, France, Germany, Switzerland, and Kenya. They set a deadline for compliance of July 1; if not met, the plane with its passengers, they said, would be blown up. Israeli officials decided to extricate the hostages and mounted a lightning raid on the Entebbe airport.

On July 3, four Israeli transports made their way in utmost secrecy to Entebbe loaded with paratroopers and armored vehicles. When the first aircraft landed, the lead contingent in just three minutes took over the terminal. The other three combat teams secured the airport. The shocked and traumatized hostages were quickly loaded and the four planes departed just before and just after midnight for Nairobi on the way back to Israel. The Israeli force lost only one man: Lt. Col. Yoni Netanyahu, the commander. Six terrorists were killed, including a

woman and a German called Wilfried Boese, plus an undetermined number of Ugandan soldiers. Three hostages perished, one in Nairobi after leaving. The daring rescue mission had very largely succeeded, to much world acclaim for the Israeli Defense Forces.

July 2. Buenos Aires, Argentina. The Montoneros set off a bomb in the dining room of the federal police building. The explosion killed eighteen and wounded sixty-six, most of them civilians. Soon thereafter, the right-wing Argentine Anti-Communist Alliance murdered eight foreign-born priests, nuns, and seminarians as revenge.

March 21. Dublin, Ireland. An IRA land mine blew up the car of and killed newly appointed British Ambassador Christopher Ewart Biggs, along with an assistant, Judith Cook. Two people were seriously injured. Ewart-Biggs had been in Dublin only twelve days.

Sep. 10. New York, USA. Six terrorists from the Croatian National Liberation Forces, one of several splinter separatist groups, hijacked a TWA flight to Paris. There they surrendered to authorities, were returned by France to the United States, and ended up serving long prison sentences.

Sep. 21. Washington, USA. A car bomb killed leftist Chilean political figure Orlando Letelier, an exiled former foreign minister, along with an aide, Ronni Moffit, as they drove down Massachusetts Avenue less than a mile from the White House. Moffit's husband was injured in the blast. Before the 1973 coup that brought Gen. Augusto Pinochet to power, Letelier had also filled the posts of Chilean ambassador to the United States and defense minister.

Although the affair was (and remains)

shrouded in mystery, there was no doubt that the secret police of the Pinochet government arranged the assassination, carried out by anti-Castro Cuban exiles. As late as 1990, a third man was arrested in Florida: José Dionosio Suarez y Esquivel was tried and convicted for complicity in the assassination plot; he served seven years of an eight-year sentence and was released in 1997. Two other conspirators, Virgilio Paz and Jose Dionisio Suarez, had already served prison time. In 1995, under pressure from Washington, Chile tried the then-chief of Chilean secret police, Col. Manuel Contreras; he was convicted and sentenced to seven years imprisonment.

Sep. 26. Damascus, Syria. Abu Nidal's Palestinian terrorists seized the Semiramis Hotel, taking ninety hostages. When Syrian troops moved against them, four hostages and all of the terrorists were killed by gunfire. Thirty-four hostages were injured.

Oct. 6. Bridgetown, Barbados. A Cubana Airlines aircraft with seventy-three people on board blew up in mid-flight shortly after leaving the airport and crashed in the Caribbean. Fifty-seven passengers were Cuban, including the twenty-four members of the junior fencing team that had just won gold medals in a Central American championship. Eleven passengers were young people from Guyana, six of whom had been chosen to study medicine in Cuba. Five passengers were North Koreans. No one survived.

Cuba immediately alleged sabotage, and the crash raised embarrassing questions for Venezuelan and American intelligence authorities. Police in Trinidad and Venezuela arrested sixteen Cuban exiles, one of whom confessed to placing a bomb on the airplane before he deplaned at the Barbados airport. The group's leader reportedly was Orlando Bosch, who had

been arrested for terrorist activities in Miami in 1968 and linked with the assassination of Chilean Orlando Letelier earlier in 1976 (above).

Oct. 17. Buenos Aires, Argentina. A Montoneros group headed by Numa Laplane, the son of a former army commander, placed a bomb at the cinema of the Army Club at a function attended by civilians and the families of officers.

More than fifty people were wounded.

Nov. 18. Amman, Jordan. Four Palestinians, members of a group opposed to Syrian intervention in Lebanon, tried to make a statement by seizing the Inter-Continental Hotel. They were overpowered by Jordanian soldiers; three of the terrorists were killed, along with four Jordanians, and one wounded.

Dec. 4. Beirut, Lebanon. During the civil war, a violent explosion next to the home of Druze leader Kamal Jumblatt in the Mousseytbeh district killed four people and injured twenty others. He was unhurt, but was to be assassinated by Syrian agents the following year (below).

1977

March 9. Washington, USA. Seven heavily armed Hanafi Muslims led by Hamaas Abdul Khaalis seized the headquarters of the Jewish charitable organization B'nai Brith and took more than 100 hostages. Later that day, two other small groups of the same Muslim body took over the mosque on Embassy Row and part of the District Building, holding as many as forty-nine additional hostages. One of these, radio newsman Maurice Williams, was shot and killed. The main reason for the takeovers was to stop the showing of

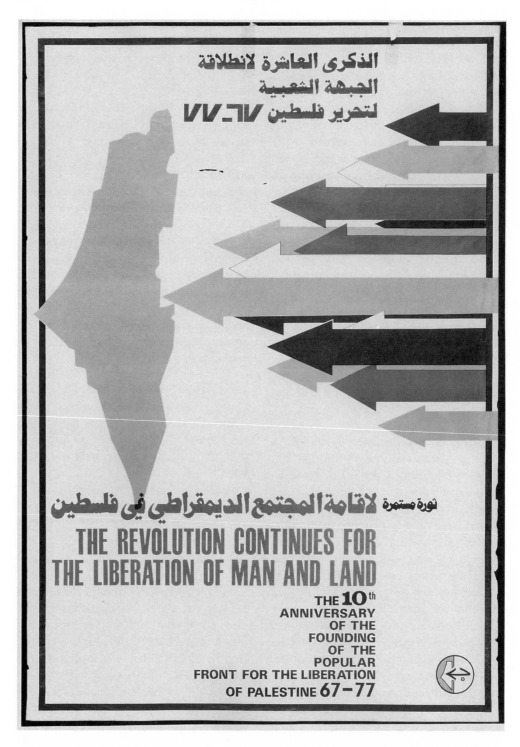

Poster marking the tenth anniversary of the founding of the Popular Front for the Liberation of Palestine, 1977. Library of Congress POS 6, Palestine, no. 50.

the film "Mohammad, Messenger of God," but also Khaalis wanted handed over to him for punishment five Black Muslims convicted of killing members of his family in 1973.

Three ambassadors from Muslim countries acted as intermediaries and talked the twelve terrorists into surrendering early on March 11. All were tried for at least conspiracy to commit armed kidnapping. In July, all were convicted, with Khaalis and two followers found guilty of murder.

March 16. Beirut, Lebanon. Kamal Jumblatt, leftist political leader and critic of Syria's role in Lebanon, was assassinated by a car bomb set off at the College Haiyazian in West Beirut. Syrian agents were blamed.

April 7. Karlsruhe, West Germany. The chief federal prosecutor, Siegfried Bubock, was killed by a machine-gunner riding post on a motorcycle. As Bubock's Mercedes stopped for a traffic light, the two motorcyclists drew alongside; a fusilade of bullets killed all three occupants of the car. (One of them, the bodyguard, died after five days.) The chief prosecutor had been successful in bringing to trial a number of terrorist leaders, including the notorious Andreas Baader. The long-running trial, continued after Bubock's death, culminated in life terms handed out to the three principals accused.

A suspect, Gunther Sonnenberg, sought for the murder of the prosecutor, was wounded by police near the Swiss border.

May 23. Bovensmilde, Groningen, the Netherlands. Gunmen pressing the case for improved conditions for South Moluccan in Holland, if not their independence from Indonesia, took hostage more than 100 children and six teachers at a primary school. Other demands were thought to be freedom for twenty South Moluccan terrorists imprisoned for the hijacking of a train in 1975 (above).

In a reprise of that attack, seven other South Moluccans seized a train at the same time with about fifty passengers on board in open countryside near the city of Groningen. A South Moluccan girl brought the express to an abrupt halt by pulling the emergency cord. Five armed men boarded the train from surrounding fields. They promptly released children and the elderly.

On May 27, an outbreak of influenza brought the release of the primary school children. Four teachers remained. Twenty days after the beginning of the crisis began, Dutch marines successfully stormed both the school and the train. Two hostages died in the clashes, along with six terrorists.

June 9. Rome, Italy. Justice Commandos of the Armenian Genocide (JCAG) gunmen assassinated the Turkish ambassador to the Vatican, Taha Carz'm.

July 30. Oberursel, West Germany. Three RAF members—two of them females—attempt to kidnap Jürgen Ponto, head of the Dresdner Bank. Ponto died defending himself.

Aug. 3. New York, USA. An FALN Puerto Rican nationalist named Marie Haydee Torres placed an umbrella stuffed with explosives in a coat rack at the Mobil Oil building on East 42nd Street. When set off, the blast killed one company executive and injured several other persons. After a trial, she was convicted to life in prison.

Sep. 5. Cologne, West Germany. The RAF kidnapped and eventually, more than a month later, murdered the German employers' federation director, Hans-Martin Schleyer, in an unsuccessful attempt to free three of their leaders from prison. His driver and three body guards were killed during the kidnapping. With this failure, after protracted negotiations, Andreas Baader, Ensslin, and Raspe committed suicide in prison. Further, a major Lufthansa hijacking effort failed (below). His captors thereupon murdered Schleyer.

Almost exactly a year later, in Dusseldorf, German police shot and killed Willy Peter Stoll, believed to have organized Schleyer's kidnapping.

Oct. 4. Los Angeles, USA. The "Armenian Group of 28" claims responsibility for a bombing attack on the home of Prof. Stanford Shaw, a specialist in Ottoman history at the Univ. of California at Los Angeles.

Oct. 13. Palma de Mallorca, Spain. The PFLP, cooperating with the RAF, mounted a four-person hijacking of a Lufthansa jet bound for Frankfurt loaded with German tourists and six beauty queens. They took it to Rome, Cyprus, Bahrain, Dubai, Aden (where the pilot was killed), and finally Mogadishu, Somalia. Their demand: release of RAF terrorists in prison in West Germany, as well as two Palestinians held in Turkey. At Mogadishu, twenty-eight West German special counter-terrorist commandos, accompanied by a small contingent of British Special Air Services troops, stormed the plane. Using stun grenades, they freed the hostages unharmed, killed three of the hijackers, and seriously wounded the fourth. It was hailed as a classic rescue operation.

Partly because the West Germany government refused the terrorists' demands in this incident, the kidnappers of the West German industrialist Hans-Martin Schleyer murdered their victim (above).

In late 1979, Armenian terrorist groups exploded a series of bombs in Milan, Rome, *Paris, Madrid, Amsterdam, and London. More than twenty people were injured and property damage in some instances was heavy.*

1978

Jan. 4. London, England. In one of the periodic flare-ups of internal rivalries, a group called the "Voice of the Palestinian Revolution" claimed it had assassinated Said Hammami, PLO representative in London. The PLO nonetheless held the United States indirectly responsible.

Jan. 17. County Down, Northern Ireland. The IRA carried out an incendiary bomb attack at a restaurant that resulted in the deaths of twelve civilians.

March 11. Tel Aviv. Israel. Eleven Fatah adherents landed by rubber dinghy at the beach of Kibbutz Ma'agan Michael, killed two people, and hijacked a passing bus. Its passengers, including children, were on a day-trip to the north. The hijackers forced the driver to return to Tel Aviv. A shootout took place when the bus reached a police blockade outside the city. The terrorists left the bus and fired missiles that set it on fire; most of the passengers died. The deadly raid left thirty-five civilians dead in all and 100 injured. Nine of the terrorists were killed and two captured.

March 13. Assen, the Netherlands. Three South Moluccan terrorists took over a government building, holding hostage seventy-one government workers. Their demand: the release of colleagues in Dutch jails. When negotiations failed, Dutch marines took the building and freed the hostages, with several casualties, and captured the terrorists.

March 16. Rome, Italy. The Italian Red Brigades kidnapped Christian Democratic leader and former premier Aldo Moro, killing all five of his bodyguards. Held hostage to try to influence the Communist Party into more radical policies, a goal that was not achieved, the terrorists murdered Moro on May 9. The brutality of their action turned much of Italian public opinion decisively against the radical leftist group.

June 2. Madrid, Spain. In a machine gun attack on the automobile of the Turkish ambassador, assassins killed the ambassador's wife, Necla Kuneralp, retired Ambassador Besir Balcz'oglu, and the chauffeur, Antonio Torres. The ASALA and JCAG both claimed responsibility.

July 28. London, England. Two terrorists threw a hand grenade under the auto of the Iraqi ambassador, but he escaped injury. (Iraq and the PLO were at odds at the time, with the Iraqi position on Israel more adamantly hard line.) Authorities arrested Khoujoud Mograbi, a teenager from Algeria, and Lebanese national Abou-Namma Mahmoud for the crime.

June 29. Jerusalem, Israel. A bomb blast at the Mahane Yehuda market killed two people and wounded at least thirty-five. Reports from Beirut indicated that a Palestinian group named after a leader, Ali Yasin, killed two weeks earlier in Kuwait as a result of factional strife, had taken responsibility.

July 31. Paris, France. An al-Fatah gunman named Hammami took control of the Iraqi embassy located in the Sixteenth Arrondisement and held a number of hostages for most of the day. Initially he demanded an airplane to fly to London to rescue the female terrorist Mahmoud involved in the attempt the previous week

on the life of the Iraqi ambassador (above). As he finally gave up to police, Iraqi security guards opened fire. A French police inspector was killed and the terrorist wounded. French security forces returned fire, resulting in the death of one Iraqi. An Arab League official who had offered his services as a mediator also was wounded. The assailant, Hammami, told police that his brother had been assassinated in London the previous January (above). On August 2, the French government expelled three Iraqi officials with diplomatic immunity involved in the shooting.

On August 3, two gunmen firing submachine guns killed two senior PLO officials in their office. Promptly apprehended, the two assassins, Hatem Abdul Kadir and Kayed Hassad, both in their twenties and both of Palestinian origin, said they had taken their orders from Abu Nidal. The pair faced the death penalty.

Aug. 3. Karachi, Pakistan. Shooting broke out in front of the Iraqi consulate general. One attacker, described as an Arab, and one Pakistani guard were killed; one Iraqi diplomat was wounded.

Aug. 5. Islamabad, Pakistan. Four terrorists burst into the PLO office and killed four persons, including two students. The terrorists escaped. The PLO representative, Yousef Abu Hantash, who was away from the building, ascribed the violence to the "Iraqi regime."

Aug. 12. Zamboanga City, the Philippines. The Moro Islamic Liberation Front (MILF) led off an insurrection that was to last for years by hijacking a ferry off Olutanga Island. Five people were killed and eight wounded.

Aug. 20. London, England. The Palestinian PFLP attacked with submachine guns and grenades an El Al airline coach parked outside the Europa Hotel in Mayfair. A flight attendant was killed and six fellow crew members injured; one of the terrorists was killed.

Aug. 20. Nicosia, Cyprus. Two Abu Nidal Organization gunmen shot and killed the editor of the Cairo newspaper *Al Ahram*, Yusuf al-Sibai, who was also the leader of the Committee for Afro-Asian Solidarity and an old friend of Egyptian President Anwar Sadat. Al-Sibai was in Nicosia to attend a conference.

Aug. 22. Managua, Nicaragua. A large contingent of armed men from the Sandinista National Liberation Front seized the national palace and managed to hold more than 1,500 people hostage. Headed by Eden Pastora, the FSLN demanded publicity and amnesty for all political prisoners, plus a ransom. After the government met the demands, the terrorists departed on safe passage to Mexico and Cuba, a mission successfully accomplished.

Dec. 18. London, England. After a lull of two years, a wave of violence believed to be IRA-instigated erupted in England and Northern Ireland (below). Three car bombings occurred in the capital, along with seven in five other cities the previous day. Eleven people were injured. The object was to bring attention to the future of Northern Ireland in forthcoming general elections.

Dec. 20. Northern Ireland. The IRA was held responsible for a series of hotel bombings. Four hotels in four different towns were damaged and two others required the services of army bomb squads to defuse explosive devices. Nine people suffered injuries.

Dec. 30. New York, USA. Two bombs exploded for which Omega Seven, an anti-Castro group, later claimed responsibility. One was at the Lincoln Center, where two of a Cuban orchestra's performances of the evening had to be canceled, and the other at the Cuban mission to the UN on East 67th Street. There was property damage, but no injuries. The same group acknowledged responsibility for a similar bombing at the Cuban mission the previous September.

1979

Jan. 22. Beirut, Lebanon. A Palestinian involved in the planning for the Munich Olympic Games terrorist attack in 1972 (above) died in a car bomb explosion, along with nine other people. Ali Hassan Salameh evidently was targeted by an Israeli Mossad hit team.

Feb. 14. Kabul, Afghanistan. In the early morning, U. S. Ambassador Adolph Dubs, on his way to the embassy in a bullet-proof sedan, was stopped by men dressed as Afghan police. They persuaded the driver to open his window, thus being enabled to kidnap the ambassador. Men later described as Muslim extremists took him to a top floor of the Kabul Hotel in the city's center. As the standoff continued and negotiations got underway for the release of jailed prisoners, a shot rang out. Afghan police thereupon opened up a fusilade of shots into the room where Dubs was held. Later, he was found dead, his body riddled with bullets.

Although it was known that the Soviet KGB was deeply involved in Afghanistan even before Moscow decided to invade that year, and although three of the kidnappers were taken alive, no definite information was developed on the degree of KGB involvement in the abduction.

Feb. 14. Tehran, Iran. Islamic extremists, in a what might be called a dress rehearsal for their later takeover of the U. S. embassy, occupied the mission for one day. On orders from the Ayatollah Khomeini, they withdrew.

March 22. The Hague, the Netherlands. British Ambassador Sir Richard Adam Sykes and a servant were shot and killed by two gunmen outside the official residence as Sykes entered his chauffeured auto. Officials were baffled as to motive and the terrorist group involved, but noted the ambassador was responsible for a report on Irish security questions following the 1976 killing of the British envoy in Dublin (above).

March 30. London, England. An IRA car bomb killed the prominent politician Airey Neave, MP, the shadow Northern Ireland secretary and a friend of Tory leader Margaret Thatcher. The explosion took place in the House of Commons car park.

Aug. 22. Geneva, Switzerland. Terrorists threw two grenades at the automobile of the Turkish consul general, Nyazi Adalz'. Two bystanders were wounded, but he escaped injury.

Aug. 27. Donegal Bay, Ireland. The explosion of a fifty-pound bomb planted by the IRA on Lord Louis Mountbatten's sport fishing boat *Shadow V* killed Mountbatten, the cousin of Queen Elizabeth II, and three others. Included were his fourteen-year-old grandson Nicholas, the boy's grandmother, Lady Barbourne, and a teenaged boat hand, Paul Maxwell. The bomb injured Mountbatten's daughter and another grandson — Nicholas' twin, Timothy — and their father, Lord Brabourne. The IRA immediately announced it had detonated the bomb by remote control from the coast. It also took responsibility for the same-day bombing attack against British troops in County Down, Ireland, that claimed eighteen lives.

The assassination of war-hero and elder statesman Mountbatten was the first blow struck by the terrorists directly at the royal family. It did much to toughen attitudes in Britain and strengthened the government's decision to take a hard-line against the IRA.

An IRA member with considerable notoriety, Thomas McMahon, was later arrested and convicted for his role in the bombing. Authorities believed the Mountbatten assassination was the work of many, but McMahon was the only individual convicted. Sentenced to life in prison, in 1998 he was released under a provision of Northern Ireland's peace arrangement.

Oct. 12. The Hague, Netherlands. Ahmet Benler, son of the Turkish ambassador, Ozdemir Benler, was shot to death by assassins, who escaped. Both the JCAG and the ASALA claimed responsibility.

Nov. 4. Tehran, Iran. Following the decision of U.S. President Jimmy Carter to admit the exiled shah of Iran to the United States for medical treatment, hundreds if not thousands of militants, prominently including students, overran the U.S. Embassy in Tehran and captured sixty-six American staff members (some few managed to avoid capture, not being in the building at the time). Thirteen hostages were released, but the remaining fifty-three were held. It was a climactic point in the deteriorating relations between the United States and the new rulers of that nation. The head of state, the Ayatollah Khomeini, praised the mob's action. The captors of the embassy demanded that the shah (who had fled) be turned over to them, along with his wealth, and that the United States apologize for crimes against

Iran. It was the beginning of a 444-day siege.

In April 1980, a U. S. military mission sent to rescue the hostages failed, never reaching Tehran. Finally, on January 20, 1981, immediately after the inauguration of President Ronald Reagan, the hostages were released.

Nov. 13. Buenos Aires, Argentina. At a time when terrorist movements were considered to be on the wane, gunmen were able nonetheless to murder businessman Francisco Soldati and his chauffeur, Ricardo Durán, in the center of the city.

Nov. 13. Lisbon, Portugal. An attempt was made on the life of Israeli Ambassador Ephraim Eldar, who was wounded. A guard at the embassy was killed, and the embassy chauffeur and a local policeman were injured.

Nov. 20. Mecca, Saudi Arabia. Two hundred and fifty-nine Sunni Muslim extremists seized the Grand Mosque, taking hundreds of pilgrims hostage. They denounced the legitimacy of the Saudi government, claiming that it was not Islamic enough. Saudi security forces retook the shrine after a battle in which some 250 people died and 600 were wounded. Control was reestablished only after ten days. The group's leader, Juhayman al-'Utaybi, and most of his followers were executed. However, the government in effect began to adopt some of the very ideological measures the insurgents had demanded.

Nov. 22. Islamabad, Pakistan. Islamic militants attacked the U. S. embassy following rumors that the United States was involved in the violent takeover of the Grand Mosque in Mecca, Saudi Arabia (above). The government's delayed response enabled the attackers to burn the embassy. Four people were killed. The American cultural center in Lahore also was destroyed by fire.

Dec. 22. Paris, France. While strolling on the Champs Elysées, Turkish embassy attaché Yilmaz Çolpan was assassinated by machine gun- wielding terrorists. Several Armenian groups claimed responsibility.

Dec. 24. Rome, Italy. The Armenian ASALA set off three bombs, two in front of Air France and TWA airline offices and the third in the stairwell of a small hotel, claiming by telephone it was in protest of France's repressive measures against resident Armenians. No one was injured.

1980–1984

By 1980 approximately one-third of all terrorist attacks were targeted directly at U.S. personnel or installations.[1]

1980

Jan. 25. Silverton, South Africa. Three African National Congress members took over the Volkskas Bank in a Pretoria suburb, along with twenty-five hostages. According to a later ANC statement, they explained the organization's policies to those being held and pledged not to hurt them, but demanded Nelson Mandela's release. When the police stormed the building, all three of the intruders were killed. Two hostages lost their lives; more than twenty others were wounded. South African authorities then arrested nine ANC members for their involvement in the incident, and all received long prison terms.

March 17. Bogotá, Colombia. Two dozen armed guerrillas of the M-19 extreme-left movement, led by Rosemberg Pabón Pabón and including four women, stormed Dominican Republic Ambassador Diógenes Mayol's residence at noontime during that nation's independence day reception. Charging in with weapons concealed in gym bags, they bagged more than a dozen members of the senior diplomatic corps. An initial exchange of gunfire with Colombia police resulted in a reported one dead and four wounded.

In a siege that was to last sixty-one days, Ambassador Fernando Gómez Fyns of Uruguay leapt to his freedom from a second story window, but the rest, including American Ambassador Diego C. Ascencio, had to settle in for the long haul of protracted negotiations and uncertainty. The terrorists initially demanded the release of more than 300 leftists facing charges and a ransom of $5 million; eventually they settled for the release of eight suspects held in Colombian jails, a commitment by the Colombian government to have the Organization of American States monitor jail conditions, and an undetermined amount of money furnished through privates sources.

On April 27, the M-19 group, still with the last twelve of its senior hostages, left by air for Cuba and the asylum offered by Castro, if desired. In Havana the hostages were released. When he reached Florida from Havana, Ambassador Ascencio was bearded and twenty pounds lighter than when the ordeal began.

March 24. San Salvador, El Salvador. Archbishop Oscar Arnulfo Romero y Galdamez was killed by a single rifle shot as he celebrated mass in a small hospital chapel. A 1991 UN report found the far-right Major Roberto D'Aubuisson responsible for ordering the execution.

On March 30, at the archbishop's funeral attended by 30,000 people, explosions and gunfire lasting nearly a hour set off a mass reaction that resulted in twenty-six deaths and at least 200 injuries. The ruling junta blamed left-wing terrorists.

April 17. Rome, Italy. Armenian gunmen staged a shooting attack on the Turkish ambassador to the Holy See, Vecdi Turel, and his chauffeur. Turel was seriously wounded and driver Tahsin Guvenç slightly hurt.

April 30. London, England. Five Iranian Arabs seized the Iranian embassy in Prince's Gate, facing Hyde Park, taking twenty-one people hostage. The terrorists represented a group they called the "Arab Popular Movement in Arabistan," the place name they used for the Iranian province of Khuzistan. They demanded the release of ninety-one prisoners being held in Iran and safe passage for themselves. British SAS special forces, along with local authorities, stood by during the negotiations that followed. On May 5, minutes after the terrorists murdered two hostages, the SAS troops stormed the building, killed three of the gunmen, and rescued the remaining nineteen hostages.

July 17. Paris, France. Two people died, a neighbor and a policeman, in a failed attempt by Iranian followers of the Ayatollah Khomeini to assassinate the Shah's last prime minister, Shahpour Bakhtiar. Another policeman was seriously injured. The police killed two of the terrorists and captured five.

In 1991, retired in Paris, Dr. Bakhtiar was murdered by unknown assailants.

Aug. 2. Bologna, Italy. In the worst terrorist incident in Italian history, neo-Fascists bombed the railway station on a busy weekend of holiday travel, killing seventy-six persons and hospitalizing at least 160. On August 6, French police in Nice arrested four suspects in connection with the attack.

Aug. 10. Miami, USA. A single hijacker diverted an Air Florida jet servicing Key West to Havana. None of the thirty-five people aboard was injured. The hijacker surrendered to police upon arrival.

Three days later the same scenario was played out on the same airline, with the only difference being that seven hijackers and seventy-four passengers were involved.

Aug. 14. Miami, USA. On a National Airlines flight scheduled for San Juan, Puerto Rico, two hijackers diverted the airplane and its 224 passengers to Havana. No one was hurt.

Aug. 16. Miami, USA. Hijackers, like others before them evidently Cubans disenchanted with life in the United States, hijacked three airliners in a single day, forcing all to proceed to José Marti Airport in Havana rather than their scheduled destinations in Florida. All three soon returned to Miami and the hijackers were apprehended in Cuba. This brought to six the number of airplanes diverted to Cuba in a week and eleven the number hijacked in a little over a month. U. S. authorities said new security measures were being installed at airports, including the limited use of behavioral profiles.

Sep. 17. Asuncion, Paraguay. Gunmen from the Argentinean Revolutionary Workers' party (ERP) shot and killed former Nicaraguan dictator Anastasio Somoza Debayle, who had fled his country in the wake of a mass uprising. Some reports indicated Paraguayan officials may have been complicit in the assassination, given that Somoza was an embarrassment to the government.

Oct. 3. Paris, France. Four worshipers were killed and twelve injured by a bomb placed by Palestinians that exploded outside a synagogue in rue Copernic.

Oct. 5. Madrid, Spain. The Armenian ASALA bombed the Alitalia airline offices, injuring twelve people.

Oct. 13. Dyarbakir, Turkey. Four Iranian hijackers diverted a flight scheduled from Istanbul to Ankara to a landing in eastern Turkey. Security forces thereupon stormed the aircraft. One of the one hundred and fifty five hostages was killed by the terrorists.

The above was one of thirty-nine aircraft hijackings in 1980, fifteen of which involved flights to or from Cuba.

Oct. 26. Munich, West Germany. A member of the neo-Nazi terrorist Hoffman Military-Sports Group set off a bomb at the famous Oktoberfest, killing himself and thirteen others. As many as 215 reportedly were wounded.

Dec. 2. El Salvador, San Salvador. A right-wing death squad abducted and killed four American church workers: nuns Ita Ford, Maura Clarke, and Dorothy Kazel, plus lay worker Jean Donovan. Their bodies were unearthed two days later. Five national guardsmen eventually were convicted of the murders.

Dec. 17. Sydney, Australia. Two Armenian gunmen of the JCAG murdered the Turkish consul general, Sarz'k Arz'yak, and his driver, Engin Sever.

Dec. 31. Nairobi, Kenya. PLO terrorists bombed the prestigious Jewish-owned Norfolk Hotel. Eighteen people died.

1981

March 2. Karachi, Pakistan. On a PIA flight scheduled to fly to Peshawar, three Pakistani activists of the Al-Zulfikar organization, opposed to Pakistan's ex-military ruler Zia-ul-Haq, hijacked the plane with its 111 passengers and forced it to land at Kabul, Afghanistan. Later they took the aircraft to Damascus, Syria. Their demand: the release of prisoners in Pakistani custody. One hostage was killed. On March 14, after Islamabad agreed to free fifty-four supporters of former premier Zulfikar Ali Bhutto's Pakistan People's Party, the hijackers released the remaining hostages and surrendered. This fourteen-day episode was the longest aviation hijacking to that time.

March 28. Bangkok, Thailand. Five Muslim members of a group called Jihad Commandos hijacked an Indonesian airliner flying on an internal route bound for Medan on the island of Sumatra. The terrorists diverted the flight to Penang, Malaysia, where the they made known their demands for the release of members of their group held in Indonesian prisons and a payment of $1.5 million. The Indonesian government secretly sent thirty-five specially trained troops to Medan; in the early hours of March 31 they mounted an attack on the aircraft. All five hijackers died in the shootout, as did the pilot and one soldier. All passengers escaped unharmed.

May 13. Rome, Italy. Riding in an open automobile in St. Peter's Square, a would-be assassin shot and seriously wounded Pope John Paul II, who survived. Police captured his assailant, Mehmet Ali Agca, reportedly a member of a Turkish rightist terrorist group called the Grey

Wolves; speedily tried and convicted to life in prison, the would-be assassin at the behest of the Pope was pardoned in 2000 and extradited to Turkey. There he was imprisoned for a 1979 killing.

Rumors abounded that the Soviet and Bulgarian secret police were involved; Agca's unclear motivation, expressed at the time of his arrest, was a protest against the imperialism of both the United States and the Soviet Union

May 17. New York, USA. A previously unknown group called the Puerto Rican Resistance Army planted a bomb in a washroom at the Pan Am terminal of John F. Kennedy Airport. The resultant explosion killed one person, twenty-year-old airport worker Alex McMillan. Two other explosive devices discovered in the same terminal brought evacuation of the facility; both bombs were disarmed. The Puerto Rican group's telephoned claim at the same time that it had placed a bomb on a specific airplane scheduled for departure caused several flights to be delayed or diverted.

New York City police revealed shortly afterward that they had received more than 170 bomb threats or reports on May 19, the majority coming in Manhattan. Seven separate bomb threats were made against the World Trade Center. Police noted that such reports always increased after an explosion such as that at the airport.

June 6. Bangkok, Thailand. Three bombs exploded almost simultaneously in a crowded shopping center, injuring more than fifty people. Police had no immediate information on who was responsible.

The use of suicidal fighters in unconventional warfare has long been known in history. It was about this time, 1981, however, that the term "suicide bomber" in the terrorist context came into widespread use.

June 9. Geneva, Switzerland. An ASALA terrorist murdered Turkish consulate official Mehmet Savas Yergus. The prompt arrest of the assailant, Mardiros Jamgotchian, occasioned the formation of an ASALA splinter group, the Ninth of June Organization.

Aug. 10. Vienna, Austria; Athens, Greece. In two separate incidents, bombs exploded at Israeli embassies, the first in the early morning hours in Vienna. One woman was injured. Later that day, two bombs went off outside the diplomatic mission in Athens. Only slight damaged was caused in the latter incident.

Aug. 29. Vienna, Austria. Two Abu Nidal terrorists armed with automatic pistols and hand grenades attacked the Synagogue Seitenstettengasse, killing two worshipers and wounding twenty.

Sep. 4. Beirut, Lebanon. Near the place where U. S. Ambassador Meloy was assassinated in 1979, four men gunned down and killed the ambassador of France, Louis Delamare. Speculation about the killers focused on Palestinians opposed to PLO Chairman Arafat, who had met recently with the French foreign minister. A spokesman for the French embassy, however, was quoted as saying, "Here everyone kills everyone else and it would be difficult to determine who your enemies are."

At the end of the year, a bomb exploded close to the residence of Delamare's replacement, Ambassador Paul March-Henry, the fourth bomb blast in Beirut in two days. Two people were killed and six injured in that attack.

Sep. 28. Beirut, Lebanon. An explosives-packed Mercedes-Benz blew up outside a crowded restaurant adjacent to a Palestinian guerrilla checkpoint yesterday, killing at least fifteen persons. The driver had immediately beforehand departed the automobile and walked through the restaurant. Militia officials said forty persons, women and children among them, were wounded in the blast. Some sources blamed the Israelis; others, the Abu Nidal Group.

Oct. 6. Cairo, Egypt. Thousands witnessed a fatal attack on President Anwar Sadat at a military review marking the 1973 October War against Israel. Rushed to the military hospital at Maadi, after being gunned down, he was pronounced dead on arrival. In the midst of tight security measures, the five assassins, an officer named Khaled el Islambouly and four soldiers, all members of a Islamic fundamentalist sect, had jumped from a truck in the parade, firing automatic weapons and tossing two hand grenades as they ran toward the stands just as a flight of jets passed noisily low overhead. Those attending the event were thunderstruck. Eleven dignitaries in the stands including Sadat died and more than thirty others were wounded.

Evidently Sadat was not murdered for his famed peace overture to Israel four years previously, a move that led to the Camp David agreement providing for a peace settlement between Egypt and Israel. Rather, it was as the key element in an attempt by extremist Muslim forces to install a religious government in Egypt, as in Iran. It did not come to pass, however. More than 800 suspects were rounded up, two dozen indicted for murder and conspiracy, and all but two convicted. The courts sentenced five to death and the rest to prison for terms up to life at hard labor. The actual conspirators were tried and convicted; in April 1982, two were shot and three, hanged. A leader among those who called for the president's assassination, Karam Zohdy, received a life sentence in prison, but was released twenty-two years later, in September 2003.

Sadat's vice president, Hosni Mubarak, was elected his successor.

Oct. 10, London, England. An IRA remote-controlled bomb in a parked van, when detonated in a deafening explosion as a British army bus passed, killed two civilians and wounded forty other persons, about half of them civilians, including two children, near the Chelsea Army Barracks. There was speculation that the IRA missed their real target; if the bombers had triggered the device a few minutes later, they would almost certainly have caught two bus-loads of Irish Guards. A further stroke of luck in a sense was that a group of about thirty boy cadets missed the blast because they approached the Barracks at that time from a different direction.

Nov. 21. Beverly Hills, USA. A bomb exploded during the night at the Turkish consulate. No one was hurt. A group called Armenian Genocide claimed responsibility.

Dec. 4. San Salvador, El Salvador. Three American nuns and one lay missionary were found murdered outside the city, believed to be the victims of a right-wing death squad.

Dec. 17. Verona, Italy. Four members of the Red Brigades led by Antonio Savasta kidnapped from his home Brig. Gen. James L. Dozier, a U. S. Army officer assigned to a NATO staff position. Two men initially entered the general's apartment passing as plumbers; the group tied up his wife and carried him away to six weeks of captivity. Police rounded up over 800 suspects and launched an intensive search for Dozier. It is not clear what the Red Brigades' objective was, but he was interrogated, subjected to a "proletarian trial," and denounced for America's role in Vietnam.

An elite anti-terrorist commando

squad rescued Dozier in Padua on January 28, 1982. Seven of nine suspects in custody soon thereafter confessed, including Savasta. Eight other suspects were still at large.

1982

Jan. 28. Los Angeles, USA. The Turkish consul general was assassinated by members of a group calling itself the "Justice Commandos for the Armenian Genocide."

During the early 1980's U. S. authorities linked the political advocacy group ANCA (Armenian National Committee of America) with four terrorist incidents: on October 12, 1980, at the UN Plaza in New York; June 3, 1981, at a Los Angeles, California, convention center; November 22, 1981, at the Turkish consulate in Beverly Hills, California; and the October 22, 1982, attempted assassination of the Turkish consul at Philadelphia, Pennsylvania.

April 3. Paris, France. A young woman shot and killed Ya'acov Bar-Simantov, Israeli Embassy attaché, outside his home. The Revolutionary Armed Factions of Lebanon claimed responsibility. The assailant escaped. In February 1986, however, a French court convicted a Lebanese, Georges Ibrahim Abdallah, a principal figure in the Lebanese Armed Revolutionary Faction, for involvement in the killing.

June 3. London, England. Israeli Ambassador Shlomo Argov was critically wounded as he left a dinner at the Dorchester Hotel on Park Lane. Police captured his assailant and later arrested two Jordanians and an Iraqi in connection with the assassination attempt. Shot in the head, the ambassador survived but was permanently incapacitated. The three terrorists were tried and sentenced to thirty to thirty-five years imprisonment.

Two other similar incidents had taken place in Europe in recent weeks: On March 31 in Paris, attackers shot up the Israeli military attaché's office; additionally, Israeli officials in Vienna had been attacked.

June 17. Rome, Italy. A car-bomb explosion killed the deputy director of the Rome PLO office, Kamal Hussein; a bystander was wounded. The previous night, gunmen in a passing car shot and killed Nazeh Matar, a Palestinian student and part-time journalist. An organization called "The Jewish Armed Resistance" claimed responsibility for both attacks.

July 19. Beirut, Lebanon. David Dodge, acting president of the American University in Beirut, was abducted and transported first to Damascus and then, via Iran Air, to Tehran. He was held in the Iranian capital for six months before being released.

July 23. London, England. The IRA touched off two large nail bombs in Hyde and Regent's parks, killing eleven soldiers of the Household Cavalry and Royal Green Jackets (and seven horses). Fifty people were injured, many of them civilians in attendance at the Regent's Park band stand.

Aug. 7. Ankara, Turkey. Nine people were killed and more than eighty-two were wounded in an attack at Ankara's Esenboga Airport by the "Armenian Secret Army for the Liberation of Armenia." Two gunmen opened fire in a crowded passenger waiting room. Police killed one of the terrorists and captured the other, Levon Ekmekchian. He was tried, convicted, and in January 1983, executed.

Aug. 11. Honolulu, Hawaii, USA. A bomb planted on a PanAm flight exploded as the aircraft was about to land. One person was killed and several other injured. Almost ten years later, in January 1992, a Greek court convicted Mohammad Rashid of murder in the case. He had been arrested in May 1988.

Aug. 22. Paris, France. As many as six *Action Directe* terrorists threw a grenade and then machine gunned fleeing lunchtime diners at the kosher Goldenberg Restaurant not far from Notre Dame. Six people died. The Paris representative of the PLO condemned the attack.

Sep. 14. Beirut, Lebanon. President Bashir Gemayel, elected only a month earlier, was killed by the explosion of a powerful car bomb outside his party's headquarters placed by pro-Syrian Lebanese. Scores of people were injured.

Two days later, in retribution Lebanese Christian militia occupied Palestinian refugee camps called Sabra/Shatilla; a massacre began and before it was over, approximately 460 civilians had been murdered. The Israeli government received widespread condemnation for it's failure to intervene.

Oct. 9. Rome, Italy. Gunmen fired and threw grenades at worshipers leaving Rome's imposing synagogue on the banks of the Tiber. A child was killed and thirty-four people wounded. Ten hours later, a bomb exploded outside the Syrian embassy and shortly afterward, another bomb went off outside the Islamic Center in the northern part of the city. In neither of the latter cases were there casualties.

Dec. 6. Ballykelly, Northern Ireland. An IRA bomb blast at a bar killed seventeen people and injured sixty.

Dec. 12. Paramaribo, Surinam. The military-backed government executed without trial fifteen political opponents, including journalists, lawyers, and a trade union leader. The Netherlands and the United States suspended their assistance programs.

1983

March 9. Belgrade, Serbia-Montenegro. Armenian gunmen attacked the Turkish ambassador, wounding him and his driver and killing a Yugoslav student.

April 18. Beirut, Lebanon. Islamic Jihad claimed responsibility for a suicide truck bomb attack on the U. S. embassy. The detonation of the 400-pound device, driven virtually into the embassy lobby in a stolen pickup truck, killed sixty-three people, of whom eighteen were Americans and the rest, Lebanese; those injured totaled 120.

May 20. Pretoria, South Africa. The African National Congress (ANC) exploded a car bomb outside an office building killing nineteen people. Two terrorists also died (the bomb went off prematurely).

May 25. San Salvador, El Salvador. The Farabundo Marti National Liberation Front assassinated Cmdr. Albert A. Schaufelberger, deputy chief of the U.S. military advisory group. In civilian clothes, the officer had driven to the University of Central America, where a car pulled alongside and gunmen fired four shots, killing him instantly.

July 23. Paris, France. Eight people were killed and sixty-three injured when a suitcase bomb exploded at Orly Airport. Known Armenian terrorists were later arrested by French security forces.

July 27. Lisbon, Portugal. Five gunmen belonging to the Armenian Revolutionary Army tried to seize the Turkish embassy but managed only to take hostage Counselor of Embassy Yurtsev M'hç'oglu and his family. With the police about to storm the site, a terrorist bomb exploded prematurely, killing the diplomat's wife, Cahide, and four terrorists, and wounding the diplomat and his son. The remaining terrorist and one policeman were killed and one policeman wounded in the subsequent assault.

In the aftermath, the ARA threatened the life of the prime minister.

Aug. 21. Manila, the Philippines. Benigno Aquino, political opposition leader, was shot dead as he was escorted by airport security off an airliner upon his return from three years of virtual exile in the United States. President Ferdinand Marcos was widely believed to have arranged the assassination despite the government's claim that a solitary communist gunman, Rolando Galman, committed the act. (Galman was killed on the spot by security forces.) After months of political turmoil, including a disputed national election, in February 1984 Marcos fled the country and Corazon Aquino, Benigno Aquino's widow, took office as president.

In September 1990, a Philippine court sentenced sixteen military officers, including a general named Luther Custodio, to life in prison for the murder of Aquino.

Oct. 9. Rangoon, Burma. Three North Korean commandos detonated a bomb in Rangoon during a state visit by senior Republic of Korea officials. Twenty-one Burmese and Koreans were killed and forty-eight injured. Two of the terrorists were captured, confessed to acting on orders from Pyongyang, and were executed.

Oct. 23. Beirut, Lebanon. In what might best be termed a paramilitary action rather than terrorism in the strictest sense, a suicide bomber drove a Mercedes truck loaded with 2,600 pounds of TNT into U. S. Marine headquarters at the international airport, a building that also served as a barracks. At 6:20 a.m., the explosives-laden vehicle crashed through a wrought-iron plate, hitting the sand-bagged guard post, smashing through another barrier, and ramming over a wall of sandbags into the lobby, exploding with terrific force. The death toll from the explosion eventually came to 241 marines.

Less than two minutes after the initial attack, another suicide truck bomber with 600 pounds of TNT plowed into a French paratrooper barracks two miles north and collapsed the building with its blast. Fifty-eight French soldiers died. (France and the United States composed part of the four-nation international force acting as peace keepers.) A group that called itself the Free Islamic Revolution claimed responsibility for both attacks. A Shi'ite organization owing allegiance to Iran's Ayatollah Khomenie called Islamic Amal, suspected of the deed, denied accountability; its leader, Hussein Husavi, nonetheless called the attack "this good deed."

In February of the following year, the United States withdrew its Marine presence from the country, as did Great Britain. This move was seen by many Islamic militants as proof that the use of terror would succeed.

Nov. 7. Washington, USA. A bomb exploded in the Capitol building on the Senate side after 11:00 p.m. No one was hurt. A group calling itself the Armed Resistance Movement claimed it had set off the device to protest the American invasion of Grenada and the presence of U. S. marines in Lebanon.

Nov. 15. Athens, Greece. One of two men on a motor scooter shot and killed U.S. Navy Captain George Tsantes while on his way to the embassy, where he was assigned. His chauffeur also died in the attack. The "November 17" organization took credit for the killings.

Dec. 12. Kuwait City, Kuwait. The American and French embassies were bombed. Similar attacks took place at an American housing compound, a Kuwaiti oil facility, an airline terminal, and a Kuwaiti government office. Islamic Jihad claimed responsibility. Six people in all died and more than eighty were injured. Seventeen pro-Iranian terrorists eventually were convicted of the crime.

Dec. 17. London, England. At the famed Harrod's Department Store, a Provisional IRA bombing during the Christmas shopping season resulted in six people killed, including three policemen, and ninety injured. Reportedly an IRA attempt to send a warning failed to get through. The IRA later issued a statement claiming that the attack had not been authorized and that it regretted the deaths.

1984

Various sources indicate that in 1984, approximately 600 international terrorist incidents occurred, resulting in more than 300 dead and approximately 1,000 wounded.

Jan. 17. Beirut, Lebanon. Terrorists kidnapped Saudi Arabian consul Hussein Farrash, an action ascribed to Muslim fundamentalists. Over a year later, on May 20, 1985, he was released.

Jan. 18. Beirut, Lebanon. Two gunmen killed Malcolm H. Kerr, Lebanese-born American president of the American University of Beirut, outside his office. The assassination reportedly was part of the Hizballah's plan to drive all Americans from Lebanon. Two years previously (see above), the university's acting president had been kidnapped by pro-Iranian terrorists and held for six months.

Feb. 15. Rome, Italy. The Red Brigades assassinated Leamon R. Hunt, the American director general of the Sinai multinational peace-keeping force.

March 16. Beirut, Lebanon. Three members of the Islamic Jihad kidnapped at gunpoint U. S. embassy political officer (and C.I.A. station chief) William Buckley as he left his apartment. They held him for eighteen months, subjected him to extended, extreme torture for information. Buckley also contracted pneumonia. American efforts to locate him, including a request to Israel's Mossad for assistance, were unavailing. Buckley died in captivity, reportedly in October 1985, either because of physical injuries and illness, or in a ritual murder by his abductors. His body was not found until December 27, 1991, in southern Beirut, nearly eight years after his abduction.

Analyzing kidnapping in Lebanon, one scholar of terrorism noted that diplomacy is the "most dangerous profession of all."[1]

April 12. Torrejon, Spain. Eighteen off-duty American servicemen were killed and eighty-three people injured in a bomb attack on a restaurant near a U.S. air base. Hezbollah claimed responsibility, although the Basque separatist ETA (*Euskadi Ta Askatasuna*) would appear to be a more logical suspect.

The ETA was being phased out, however. Four years previously, in 1980, in its bloodiest year of insurrection ever, ETA terrorists caused the deaths of more than 100 people in numerous incidents.

June 3. Amritsar, India. On Prime Minister Indira Gandhi's orders, army units and paramilitary forces surrounded the holy seventeenth-century Golden Temple not far from the site of a massacre in 1919. Sikh extremists had occupied the complex, converting it into a haven for terrorists. One of the leaders of this revivalistic and nationalistic movement was Jamal Singh Bhindranwale, a politically ambitious itinerant Sikh preacher. After demands that they surrender were ignored, army tanks and heavy artillery were used to suppress the insurgents' antitank and machine-gun fire. After a twenty-four-hour fire fight, the army was successful. Indian government sources put the casualties at eighty-three army personnel killed and 249 wounded; extremist Sikh casualties were 493 killed and eighty-six injured. Bhindranwale's body was found riddled by more than a dozen bullets.

Significant segments of the Sikh community around the world swore vengeance. Two months later, on August 9, Sikh terrorists assassinated the commander of the force attacking the Temple. Just over four months later, Gandhi herself was assassinated by her trusted Sikh bodyguards (below). The following year, Canadian Sikhs planted a bomb that caused an Air India flight to blow up en route from Canada to London (below).

Sep. 20. Aukar, Lebanon. A suicide truck bomb explosion at a U. S. embassy annex near Beirut killed sixteen people and injured Chargé Reginald Bartholomew and visiting British ambassador David Miers. As many as seventy people were hurt. The Islamic Jihad claimed responsibility. The attack came in response to the

U.S. veto September 6 of a U. N. Security Council resolution.

Oct. 11. Los Angeles, USA. Members of the Jewish Defense League (JDL) bombed an office of the Arab-American Anti-Discrimination Committee. Its director, Alex Odeh, died from the explosion of a pipe bomb when he opened the door to his office. Three suspects identified by the FBI fled to Israel, where they remained. One of these, however, later was extradited to the United States to serve a life sentence for an another, unrelated crime.

Oct. 12. Brighton, England. The IRA placed a bomb on the fifth floor of the Grand Hotel in Brighton during a Conservative Party conference. The aim was to kill Prime Minister Margaret Thatcher, and perhaps indeed the entire cabinet, the first time the IRA had made an attempt on the lives of political figures at that level. By chance the prime minister escaped unharmed, but five others died in the explosion and three dozen were injured. Heretofore Thatcher had been accompanied for protection by a single police constable. The shock of this attack caused security to be considerably increased.

The IRA released a statement to the effect that, as a result of the bombing, the prime minister would now realize that Britain could not occupy Ireland and abuse its people and hope to get away with it. "Give Ireland peace and there will be no war."

Oct. 31. New Delhi, India. Prime Minister Indira Gandhi was shot to death as she walked in the morning in the Birla Gardens. The assassins were two of her trusted Sikh bodyguards, driven by resentment over the government's invasion of the Golden Temple in Amritsar in June (above). She had refused to heed warnings that Sikh members of her guard detail

Amritsar Sikh shrine, India, site of mid–1984 clashes between Indian troops and Sikh militants.

should be replaced. The prime minister, the daughter of the former prime minister, Jawaharlal Nehru, was riddled with sixteen bullets fired at close range and died instantly. One of the assassins was shot dead by other guards and the other one wounded.

Gandhi's son, Rajiv, was sworn in as her replacement twelve hours after his mother's death. Widespread anti-Sikh rioting following the assassination resulted in thousands of deaths throughout India. The new prime minister appealed for calm.

In January 1986, the surviving assassin, Satwant Singh, and two other men were sentenced to death for the murder.

Nov. 25. Lisbon, Portugal. The Popular Forces of 25 April fired four sixty-millimeter mortar rounds at the U. S. embassy.

Nov. 27. Bombay, India. Gunmen thought to be from an Abu Nidal Palestinian faction murdered Sir Percy Norris, Britain's deputy high commissioner. Press reports linked the killing with the attack on the Israeli ambassador in London, Schlomo Argov, in 1982 (above). Three terrorists who took part in that assault were serving long prison sentences in Britain and the Norris assassination was seen as a move to force London to release them. Associated with the campaign was the March murder in Greece of Deputy Director Kenneth Whitty of the British Council.

Dec. 4. Tehran, Iran. Four Islamic Jihad terrorists hijacked a Kuwaiti Airbus with 161 aboard bound for Karachi from Kuwait via Dubai and ordered it flown to Tehran. Two American aid officials were killed during the hijacking. The terrorists tortured two other Americans, an aid official and a businessman, during the ordeal. There demand was for the release of prisoners. After four days, Iranian troops stormed the aircraft, retaking it from the hijackers and freeing the hostages.

Notes

1. Kenneth A. Duncan, "Terrorism," in Jentleson and Paterson, sr. eds. *Encyclopedia of U. S. Foreign Relations*, vol. 4, p. 189.
2. Taheri, *Holy Terror*, p. 148.

1985–1989

Acts of terror by movements struggling for national independence comprised the single most important category of terrorism in the 1980s.[1]

1985

Jan. 15. Paris, France. Action Directe (AD)— Red Army Faction (RAF) gunmen shot and killed the head of French international arms sales, Gen. René Audan, at his home. Two weeks later in Munich, Germany, four RAF terrorists murdered an industrialist, Ernst Zimmerman, and his wife in their home.

Feb. 2. Glyfada, Greece. An organization called the National Front set off a bomb at a night club frequented by Americans; sixty-nine people were wounded.

Feb. 21. Athens, Greece. A car with two men intercepted the chauffeured Mercedes of conservative publisher Nikos Momferato in the center of the city. Two automatic pistol-wielding assassins killed him and seriously wounded his driver before making their escape. Responsibility was assigned to the 17 November group.

March 8. Beirut, Lebanon. A suburban car bomb explosion killed more than eighty people, injuring scores. It went off outside a block of flats and close to a mosque as worshipers were gathering for Friday night prayers in a densely populated suburb. A leading fundamentalist Shia Muslim cleric, Sheikh Muhammad Husain Fadlallah, may have been the target, but he was not hurt. Reports indicated that Lebanese government agents trained by the CIA carried out the attack in an instance of the use of state terror.

March 12. Ottawa, Canada. Three gunmen stormed the Turkish embassy, killing a Canadian security guard. Ambassador Coskun Kz'rca escaped but was injured. His wife and daughter were taken as hostages and held for a period of time; eventually they were released and the terrorists surrendered.

March 16. Beirut, Lebanon. Islamic extremists kidnapped Terry Anderson, Associated Press bureau chief, and held him as a negotiating card for more than six years, until December 4, 1991, when he was released. Two other high-profile captives were held nearly as long: Thomas Sutherland, dean at the American University, and Terry Waite, an Anglican Church negotiator from England. (See below.)

April 12. Madrid, Spain. A bomb blast at the El Descanso Restaurant near a U. S. air base killed eighteen Spanish civilians and wounded eighty-two people.

May 25. Kuwait City, Kuwait. The emir of Kuwait, Sheikh Jaber al-Ahmed al-Sabah, escaped death at the hands of a suicide car bomber. The bomber drove a car loaded with explosives into the emir's motorcade in the streets of the city. The explosion killed, aside from the suicide bomber, two bodyguards and a bystander, but not the sheikh. A caller later claimed responsibility for the Islamic Jihad.

May 28. Beirut, Lebanon. David P. Jacobsen, director of the American University hospital, was seized at gunpoint and held captive for almost eighteen months by the group Islamic Jihad. He was released in November 1985, at which time Islamic Jihad was still holding three Frenchmen, Jean-Paul Kauffmann, a journalist, and Marcel Carton and Marcel Fontaine, both diplomats.

June 10. Beirut, Lebanon. A Jordanian airliner schedule to fly to Amman, Jordan, was seized by six gunmen and flown first to Larnaca, followed by Palermo, and then back to Beirut. They released the hostages and blew up the aircraft.

June 14. Athens, Greece. A TWA flight was hijacked en route from Athens to Rome by two Lebanese Hezbollah terrorists and forced to fly to Beirut. The eight crew members and 145 passengers were held for seventeen days, during which one American hostage, U.S navy diver Robert D. Stethem, was murdered and his body thrown out on the tarmac. After being flown twice to Algiers, the aircraft was returned to Beirut following Israel's release of 435 Lebanese and Palestinian prisoners. The remaining hostages were released in stages, the last being freed on June 30th.

Four Hezbollah agents later were indicted, including the senior officer believed to be involved, Imad Mughniyah. In January 1987, Mohammad Ali Hamadei was arrested at the Frankfurt, Germany, airport. Tried and convicted of the kidnapping and the murder of Stethem, he received a life sentence in prison.

June 19, San Salvador, El Salvador. Thirteen people were killed in a machine gun attack at an outdoor café, including four off-duty U. S. embassy marine guards.

June 23. Montreal, Canada. An Air India flight bound ultimately for New Delhi via London exploded over the Irish Sea 110 miles west of Cork, Ireland, and crashed in the Atlantic. All 329 persons aboard were killed. Included was U. S. Congressman Lawrence P. McDonald (D-GA) . According to evidence cited in the accident report, Sikh separatists planted a bomb in luggage on the airplane. It was believed to be in retribution for the Indian government's attack on the Sikh holy place, the Golden Temple, the previous year (above).

The tragedy set off Canada's longest ever criminal investigation. In February 2003, one of three suspects charged was Inderjit Singh Reyat, who had already served ten years in a British prison for his role in a blast that killed two baggage handlers at Tokyo's Narita Airport an hour before the Air India Flight went down. He received a five-year sentence for conspiracy. Two Canadian Sikhs from British Columbia, Ripudaman Singh Malik and Ajaib Singh Bagri, held since October 2000, were scheduled to be tried on first degree murder and conspiracy charges.

This act of sabotage resulted in the highest death toll in the history of aviation, other than the 9/11 attack on New York's Twin Towers.

July 22. Stockholm, Sweden. Bomb explosions at a synagogue and at a Northwest Orient Airlines office injured twenty-seven people. A caller attributed the attacks to the Islamic Jihad in retribution for Israeli raids in southern Lebanon.

Aug. 8. Frankfurt, Germany. A large car bomb explosion near an American air base killed two people; twenty were injured.

Aug. 17. Beirut, Lebanon. A car bomb exploded outside a crowded supermarket in an eastern Christian area of the city. At least fifty people died and 100 were wounded.

Aug. 20. Cairo, Egypt. A group called Egypt's Revolution claimed credit for killing an Israeli diplomat and wounding two embassy employees. The terrorists sprayed an Israeli embassy car with machine gun fire. The motive given was to drive Israel "colonists" from the country.

Aug. 20. Tripoli, Lebanon. A car bomb exploded in this northern Lebanon city, killing forty-four people and wounding ninety. Speculation on who did it centered on the possibility that it was a Syrian government move to crush the PLO in Tripoli.

Sep. 30. Beirut, Lebanon. Terrorists kidnapped three Soviet diplomats and the Soviet embassy doctor from their official cars. The next day a group not previously heard of, the Islamic Liberation Organization, delivered to the press photographs of the four — Dr. Nicolai Virsky, Arkady Katakov, Valery Mirkov, and Oleg Spirin — with guns held to their heads. The name suggests the abductors were Sunni Muslims. Their demand: that leftist forces backed by Syria withdraw from Tripoli in northern Lebanon. Moscow denounced the kidnapping as a heinous crime carried out by bandits. One of the Soviets was killed and three later were released.

Oct. 7. Off Port Said, Egypt. Four heavily armed Palestinian Liberation Front

(a faction of the PLO) gunmen hijacked the Italian cruise ship *Achille Lauro* in the eastern Mediterranean, taking more than 700 hostages. Near the Syrian port of Tartus, the terrorists summarily shot and killed an elderly disabled American, Leon Klinghoffer, and pushed his body and wheelchair overboard. After some confusion as to their purpose, the hijackers demanded that Israel free fifty Palestinian prisoners. The Egyptian government offered the terrorists safe haven in return for the release of the hostages.

After two days of drama and with nowhere else to go, the terrorists surrendered to Egyptian authorities in return for safe passage out of the country. After their release, U.S. fighter planes intercepted an Egyptian jet carrying the hijackers to Tunisia and forced it down at a base in Sicily where they were arrested. Tried and convicted to thirty years in prison, in 1996 Klinghoffer's killer, Youssef Magied al-Molqi, disappeared temporarily on a twelve-day "furlough" from a high-security prison in Rome, but was caught and returned. The other three members of the party received lighter sentences. The terrorist group's organizer (although not a member of the kidnapping party), Abu (Muhammad) Abbas, was allowed to depart Sicily, reportedly because he carried an Iraqi diplomatic passport. Later an Italian court sentenced him in absentia to a life term. In 1996, Abbas apologized publicly for the hijacking and the murder. The United States formally rejected the apology.

In 1994, the ill-fated *Achille Lauro* caught fire in the Indian Ocean off Somalia and sank. At the end of the war in Iraq in 2003, American troops captured Abu Abbas in Baghdad; a contest immediately began on who would have legal jurisdiction over him.

Nov. 6. Bogotá, Colombia. Thirty-five leftist M-19 terrorists seized the

Palace of Justice and took 100 people hostage, including a number of judges. When Colombian army troops stormed the building, all of the terrorists and ninety-seven of the hostages, including eleven supreme court justices, died in the shooting and ensuing fire. The M-19 group's purpose was to force President Belisario Betancur's government to release investigation reports said to show the movement had been victimized by the Colombian armed forces during a cease-fire period.

Nov. 23. Luqa Airport, Malta. Three Palestinians hijacked to Malta an Egyptian jetliner flying from Athens bound for Cairo. The hijackers killed two hostages, but the worst came when Egyptian security forces stormed the plane: fifty-eight more of the total ninety-eight aboard died before the hijackers were subdued. Abu Nidal's Arab Revolutionary Command took responsibility for the action.

In 1986, the sole surviving hijacker, Mohammed Ali Rezaq, was captured in Nigeria, tried and convicted in the United States for the murder of U. S. citizens, and sentenced to life in prison.

Dec. 7. Paris, France. The Armenian ASALA took responsibility for bombs that exploded at two leading department stores, Galeries Lafayette and Printemps. At least thirty-five Christmas shoppers were injured. The ASALA may not have been the perpetrators, however; police found indications that both bombs may have been have been of Middle Eastern, specifically Kuwaiti, origin.

Dec. 23. Durgan, South Africa. The African National Congress (ANC) set off a bomb in a shopping area that killed five people and injured an additional forty-eight.

Dec. 27. Rome, Italy, and Vienna, Austria. In virtually simultaneous attacks, PLO terrorists of the Abu Nidal Organization attacked two major airport terminals with grenades and automatic weapons, killing sixteen people and wounding more than 100. At Vienna, three gunmen concentrated on the El Al ticket counter area, while at the Leonardo da Vinci airport in Rome, four screaming terrorists sprayed with gunfire and bombed two adjacent U. S. airline counters. The three terrorists at Vienna tried to escape by car; one was killed and the other two arrested. Of the four at Rome, three died and one was wounded and arrested.

1986

From 1973 to 1986, Armenian terrorist organizations claimed responsibility for 200 attacks on Turkish diplomatic and other institutions. They murdered fifty-five Turkish and sixteen non-Turkish people, wounding hundreds of others.[2]

Feb. 5. Paris, France. A bomb went off for the third time in three successive days, this one in an underground shopping complex near the Centre Georges Pompidou; nine people were injured. The two previous blasts took place in a shopping area on the Champs Elysées and at a book store on the Left Bank; eleven injuries resulted. Additionally, a bomb at the Eiffel Tower was found and disarmed by police. A previously unknown group called the Committee of Solidarity with Arab and Middle Eastern Political Prisoners claimed responsibility and demanded the release of three prisoners serving time in French jails for terrorist acts.

Feb. 18. Lisbon, Portugal. The Popular Forces of 25 April (FP-25) exploded a car bomb at the American embassy. No one was injured.

March 30. Athens, Greece. An Iraqi-backed group called the May 15 Organization set off a bomb as a TWA flight from Rome approached the Athens Airport. Four people were killed although the airplane managed to land. The splinter group was headed by Mohammed Rashid, a Palestinian.

March 31. West Berlin, Germany. The German-Arab Friendship Association site was bombed, injuring seven people, in an attack allegedly organized by Syrian agents.

April 2. Athens, Greece. A bomb exploded in the cabin area of a TWA airliner flying from Rome, blowing a hole in the fuselage. Four passengers, including an infant, were sucked out of the aircraft by the change in pressure and killed. The aircraft landed safely at Athens. the bombing was attributed to the Fatah Special Operations Group headed by Abdullah Abd al-Hamid Labib.

April 5. West Berlin, Germany. The La Belle Discotheque in Berlin was bombed, killing two off-duty American soldiers and a Turkish woman. An additional 229 people suffered injuries. Communication intercepts by American, British, and German intelligence groups confirmed Libyan sponsorship of the bombings. Eventually two Palestinians and two Germans were tried in German courts.

In reprisal, U.S. President Ronald Reagan ordered an Air Force bombing attack on Tripoli and Benghazi, Libya. The raid, launched from England, took place April 14 and resulted in thirty-nine people being killed, including an infant daughter of Libya's ruler, Col. Mu'amar Qadhafi.

May 3. Cuzco, Peru. Members of the far-left Sendero Luminoso set off a bomb on a train with tourists bound for the historic Inca site Machu Picchu in the Andes. Seven people were killed and numerous others injured. Afterward, the trains were heavily guarded.

July 18. Madrid, Spain. The Basque separatist group ETA carried out a car bomb attack on a bus carrying Civil Guards. Twelve were killed and twenty were wounded.

Sep. 5. Karachi, Pakistan. Four members of the Palestinian Fatah Revolutionary Council of Abu Nidal hijacked a Pan Am aircraft at the airport with 389 on board after it landed from Bombay, destined for Frankfurt and then New York. Disguised as security guards, they drove what appeared to be a security van directly to the aircraft steps. Firing shots as they ran up the stairs, the four took control of the plane. For the next sixteen hours the hijackers held the passengers at gunpoint. Their demand for the release of prisoners was not satisfied; police stormed the airplane and freed the hostages, but not before twenty-two people died and more than 120 were injured. All four of the terrorists were captured and jailed for long prison terms.

In October 2001, Pakistani authorities released one of the hijackers, Zayd Abdel Latif Safarini, a Jordanian, to U. S. custody after he had served fifteen years in prison. He was transported to Alaska and indicted there on two federal murder charges related to the execution-style killings of American citizens Rajesh Kumar and Surendra Patel during the hijacking.

Sep. 9. Beirut, Lebanon. Hezbollah kidnapped Frank Reed, director of the American University in Beirut, accusing him of being a CIA agent. Three days later, the same group kidnapped Joseph Cicippio, the university comptroller. His captors released Reed forty-four months later; Cicippio was not freed until December 2, 1991, after Israel had released twenty-five prisoners from a prison in southern Lebanon.

Sep. 14. Seoul, South Korea. North Korean agents detonated a bomb at Kimpo Airport, killing five persons and injuring twenty-nine others.

Nov. 17. Paris, France. Two female members of the left-wing *Action Direct* (AD) terrorist group murdered George Besse, president of the state-owned Renault car company. Riding a motorcycle, they gunned him down as he arrived at his home. Four months later, Nathalie Menigon and Joelle Aubron were arrested for the crime at an isolated farmhouse in northern France; in January 1989, the two, along with two others convicted as accomplices, were sentenced to life in prison.

1987

Jan. 10. Beirut, Lebanon. Islamic Jihad terrorists abducted Terry Waite, a British representative of the Archbishop of Canterbury on a mission to secure the release of other western hostages held in the city by Iranian-backed groups. He was concerned in particular with journalist Terry Anderson, kidnapped March 16, 1985, for publicity purposes (above). Eventually, on November 18, 1991, Waite was released; Anderson gained his liberty shortly thereafter, following nearly seven years as a prisoner of the Iran-backed terrorists.

By 1987, hostage-taking has become commonplace in Lebanon. The International

Committee of The Red Cross estimated that 6,000 Lebanese had been kidnapped and or had disappeared since 1975.

Jan. 30. Zaragoza, Spain. The Basque separatist organization ETA exploded a car bomb, killing an army officer and a bus driver and wounding thirteen civilian passersby, plus twenty-eight military personnel. Two days later, 35,000 people staged a silent march of protest in the city against violence and terrorism.

April 21. Colombo, Sri Lanka. Tamil Tiger terrorists exploded a car bomb at the main bus terminal during the peak of rush hour, killing as many as 150 people (later reports set the figure at 105). Some 200 people were injured; scores of the victims were trapped inside buses and either burned to death or suffocated.

The government launched military attacks on Tamil areas of the country and announced that the next elections. scheduled for 1989, might be canceled if the problem of terrorist violence could not be resolved.

June 9. Rome, Italy. The Japan-based Red Army terrorists launched a rocket attack, coupled with a car bombing, against the U. S. and British embassies. No one was hurt and only minor damage resulted.

June 19. Barcelona, Spain. In the Basque ETA's bloodiest attack, fifteen people — seven men, five women, and three children — died immediately in a car bomb attack in a supermarket's parking garage. At least twenty-nine were injured, five critically. The eventual death toll went as high as twenty-four people. A ceiling collapsed in a shopping area, setting off a large fire. The incident caused Prime Minister Felipe González to cut short a visit to Brazil and return to Spain. Sympathy among Basques for the extremists, already limited, diminished further following the deadly attack.

Up to this time, ETA had taken responsibility for killing 600 people in Spain since 1968, most of them military and police officials. The campaign over two decades involved seven major attacks in Barcelona. ETA later was to apologize for the June 19 car bombing, calling it a mistake.

Aug. 18. Colombo, Sri Lanka. President Jayewardene survived a grenade attack in the parliament building, but one legislator was killed. Tamil Tiger terrorists were believed to be responsible.

Nov. 8. Enniskillen, Northern Ireland. The IRA Provisionals killed thirteen people with a bomb detonated during the town's Sunday observance of Remembrance Day.

Nov. 29. Andaman Sea, near Burma. Two North Korean agents who deplaned at Abu Dhabi left a radio and a liquor bottle containing explosives aboard a Korean Airlines flight bound for Bangkok. The time bomb blast in the passenger cabin caused the aircraft to crash into the sea, killing all 115 persons aboard.

Dec. 26. Barcelona, Spain. Catalan separatists bombed a bar frequented by U.S. servicemen, resulting in one person killed.

1988

Feb. 17. Lebanon. U. S. marine Lt. Col. William R. Higgins, while serving as an observer with the UN Truce Supervisory Organization, was kidnapped and eventually murdered by an Iranian-backed Hezbollah group. Its leader, Sheikh Abbas Musawi, claimed responsibility. The same group kidnapped an Englishman, Alec Collett, and an Italian, Alberto Molinari; two years later both were believed dead. On July 31, 1989, a pro-Iranian group released a videotape showing the body of Higgins dangling from a rope. Although the exact date of his death is uncertain, he was officially declared dead on July 6, 1990.

In October 1997, the U.S. Navy christened the Guided Missile Destroyer *Higgins* (DDG 76) at the Bath Iron Works in Bath, Maine, USA.

March 1. Athens, Greece. A gunman firing a .45 caliber automatic from the back of a motor scooter killed business leader Nokos Momferato when the latter stopped for a red light on Kifissia Avenue. The assassins were believed to be 17 November adherents.

March 6. Gibraltar. British undercover security forces killed three IRA terrorists, including one woman, as they attempted to flee to Spain. The trio had planted a 500-pound car bomb at an area where tourists routinely gathered for an army ceremony. Those killed were Daniel McCann, Sean Savage, and Mairead Farrell. Farrell had served ten years in prison for her part in the 1976 bombing of a hotel outside Belfast.

March 16. Belfast, Northern Ireland. Ten days after the Gibraltar incident (above) at the Milltown Cemetery funeral service for the three IRA Gibraltar terrorists, a Protestant gunman named Michael Stone assaulted the group with a pistol and hand grenades, killing three mourners and injuring as many as fifty others. He evidently intended to kill IRA political leaders in attendance. Arrested, tried, and sent to the Maze prison, Stone gained his release after ten years, in May 1998.

Four days later, two British soldiers

in plain clothes blundered into an Irish Republican Army funeral procession, were dragged from their car, beaten, and then shot to death. Although armed, they had not used their weapons.

March 16. Halabja, Iraq. Dictator Saddam Hussein ordered his forces to use nerve gas to put down a Kurdish revolt against rule from Baghdad, killing about 4,000 civilians.

April 5. Bangkok, Thailand. Nine Shiite gunmen hijacked a Kuwait Airways jumbo jet on the way from Bangkok to Kuwait. Demanding that Kuwait release seventeen pro-Iranian terrorists, the hijackers diverted the plane first to Iran, then Cyprus, and finally to Algeria. During that time they killed two Kuwaiti passengers. On April 20th, the terrorists released the remaining passengers, surrendered to police, and were allowed to leave Algiers.

April 14. Naples, Italy. The Organization of Jihad Brigades exploded a car bomb outside a service recreation club for servicemen, killing one off duty U.S. sailor.

May 1. Sittaru, Sri Lanka. Suspected Tamil Tiger rebels using buried explosives blew up a bus crowded with shoppers, killing at least twenty-six and injuring thirty. It was the second Tamil attack on a passenger bus in two days. On April 30 at Vavuniya in a dense jungle area of the north, gunmen opened fire on a bus from the roadside and killed ten people, five of them civilians, wounding six others.

June 28. Athens, Greece. Terrorists of the left-wing November 17 group set off a car bomb by remote control, killing the defense attaché of the U. S. Embassy, Navy Capt. William E. Nordeen. The group protested the presence in Greece of four U. S. military bases.

Dec. 21. Lockerbie, Scotland. A PanAm Boeing 747 en route from Frankfurt, West Germany, to New York exploded in mid-air at 31,000 feet over Scotland and crashed. All 259 on board and eleven on the ground perished. Forensic specialists found conclusive evidence of a high explosive hidden in a radio believed to have been placed on board in checked luggage by Libyan agents. Washington and London influenced the UN to vote sanctions on Libya and in 1991, Britain issued arrest warrants for two individuals, Abdel Basset Ali Mohmed al-Megrahi and Al Amin Khalifa Fhimah, both men then living in Libya.

After years of legal wrangling, in April 1999, Col. Qadhafi agreed that the two named suspects could be tried under Scottish law in the Netherlands. The trial of the two men before three Scottish Law Lords at a Dutch air base resulted, to the surprise of many, in acquittal for one of the accused, a former airport employee. On January 31, 2001, al-Megrahi, a former intelligence agent, was found guilty; he was immediately sentenced to life in prison; a subsequent appeal by his attorneys was turned down.

Libya long refused to take blame for the act and declined to pay damages claimed on behalf of the victims of the bombing. Eventually, however, by August 2003 the Qadhafi government, in an effort to rehabilitate its international reputation, had set up a $2.7 billion compensation fund and explicitly accepted responsibility.

1989

Feb. 12. Islamabad, Pakistan. Police yesterday fired on hundreds of protesters who stormed a U.S. Information Service office to demand that the United States ban a novel, *The Satanic Verses*, they consider offensive to Muslims. Six persons died in the gunfire and sixty-five were wounded.

Two days later, in Tehran, the Iranian spiritual leader, Ayatollah Ruhollah Khomeini, ordered the killing of the book's author, Salman Rushdie, and of its publishers.

April 12. Quezon City, the Philippines. The Communist Alex Boncayo Brigade (ABB) urban hit squad killed U. S. Army Col. James Rowe, a military adviser to the government, as he was being driven to his office. Following the arrests of several suspects, two individuals were tried, convicted, and sentenced to life imprisonment.

April 15. San Sebastian, Spain. Suspected Basque separatists exploded a car bomb on the docks which was reported to contain 440 pounds of TNT. Later the same day, the same group caused an explosion on a rail line south of Madrid. There were no casualties in either incident.

May 12. Beirut, Lebanon. An elderly British citizen, Jackie Mann, was seized by Iranian-backed terrorists and held until September 23, 1991. Four days later, German aid workers Heinrich Struebig and Thomas Kemptner were kidnapped; they remained in captivity until June 1992. These were the last to be released of some eighty westerners held hostage in Lebanon.

May 17. Beirut, Lebanon. A car bomb exploded by remote control killed Sheikh Hassan Khaled, the spiritual leader of Lebanon's Sunni Moslems, and twenty-one others while wounding 100 or more. Khaled was considered a voice of moderation in the civil strife.

Sep. 12. Madrid, Spain. ETA gunmen killed Carmen Tagle, a government lawyer

who had been involved in prosecuting terrorists. The separatist group asserted she had been given a just reward. A week later in the Basque area town of Renteria, a postman was killed by the explosion of a parcel bomb. According to press reports, over 600 people had died as a result of ETA terrorism since the movement began its campaign twenty-one years earlier.

Sep. 19. Sahara Desert, Niger. Perhaps the most spectacular international terrorist operation in 1989 was the bombing of UTA (*Union Transport Aèrien*) Flight 772 over Niger. That attack accounted for 171 deaths, the greatest number associated with a single attack during the year. French authorities later put six Libyans on trial in absentia, sentencing them to life in prison. The Libyan government eventually acknowledged responsibility and paid compensation to the families of those killed (but less than went to the victims of the Lockerbie crash in 1988).

Sep. 26. Athens, Greece. Three assassins believed to be 17 November members waylaid Deputy Pavlos Bakoyannis of the New Democracy party as he waited for an elevator in his office building. The gunmen shot him in the back five times, killing him almost instantly, and then walked calmly to a waiting get-away car.

Nov. 30. Frankfurt, West Germany. Authorities blamed the Red Army Faction for the assassination of banker Alfred Herrhausen, one of the most influential businessman in the country, as he was driven to work. Their light-activated bomb detonated as his car drove by.

Dec. 7. Lisburn, Northern Ireland. A car bomb planted by the IRA exploded in a shopping center in a Belfast suburbs, injuring twenty-one persons and heavily damaging surrounding stores. Police had managed partially to evacuate the crowded, following a warning telephoned to a radio station. Lisburn was the headquarters for the British army in Northern Ireland.

Notes

1. Halliday, *Two Hours that Shook the World*, p. 77.

2. http://www.atmg.org/ArmenianTerrorism.

1990–1994

*"The actions of terrorist organizations are based on a subjective interpretation of the world rather than objective reality."**

1990

Jan. 15. Lima, Peru. A car bomb exploded at 10:45 p.m. across from the U. S. embassy. At least nine people were killed and thirty wounded. The blast damaged parked cars and nearby buildings, but not the embassy structure itself. It took place three days before the scheduled arrival in Peru of U.S. President George H. W. Bush. A separate explosion early that day damaged the offices of the Spanish-owned telephone company; no one was hurt. The previous night, yet another attack took place when a grenade was tossed from a moving car. No one was hurt in that incident.

Authorities speculated that the attack was the work of the Maoist Shining Path or Tupac Amaru Revolutionary Movement (MRTA) although both had been largely dormant after a relentless government campaign to halt insurgency. Neither group claimed responsibility.

Feb. 4. Egypt. On a desert road near Cairo, unknown terrorists attacked with guns and grenades a bus-load of Israeli tourists. They killed eight and wounded seventeen. An unidentified informant notified a press agency the attack was to protest torture in Egyptian prisons.

Jan. 13. Tripoli (Tarabulus), Lebanon. Three bombs went off in the commercial district of the city, killing one civilian and wounding ten others. The explosion caused panic among early morning commuters. No group laid claim to the deed.

April 11. Bombay, India. Muslim separatists in Kashmir were blamed for a bomb attack that injured thirty-four persons.

April 13. New Delhi, India. A bomb exploded in a crowded bus. At least three people were killed and twenty-four wounded. No group immediately claimed responsibility, but Muslim separatists in Kashmir had acknowledged responsibility in three similar attacks.

April 30. Damascus, Syria. Shiite Moslems, after what was described as extensive talks with Iranian officials, released captive American Frank Reed. He had been held three and one-half years in Lebanon. A previously unheard-of Organization of

Martha Crenshaw, quoted in Hudson, Who Becomes a Terrorist, 62.

Islamic Dawn announced a day beforehand that we would be freed. Reed was the second American freed in a matter of days. American Robert Polhill was released April 22 after 1,182 days in captivity. The gaunt former accounting professor said his anger at his kidnappers had kept him alive.

During 1990 five Westerners held hostage by pro-Iranian extremists in Lebanon were released, but at year's end thirteen remained in captivity.

May 30. Clark Air Force Base, the Philippines. The New People's Army (NPA) murdered two off-duty U. S. airmen near the base.

July 20. London, England. An IRA bomb blew a ten-foot hole in the London Stock Exchange at the beginning of the workday. No one was injured in the blast, due largely to the fact that eight warning calls had been received and the premises evacuated. It was the first time the IRA had given a warning of an attack in England since the December 1983 Harrods bombing (above).

July 30. Eastbourne, England. Conservative Member of Parliament and former Northern Ireland minister Ian Gow died when a bomb exploded under the driver's seat of his Austin automobile. The explosion came as he started the car at his home in East Sussex. Gow was known as an outspoken opponent of the IRA, which claimed responsibility.

Oct. 7. Jerusalem, West Bank. Reacting to a stone-throwing incident, Israeli police opened fire on Palestinian worshipers at al-Aqsa Mosque, killing seventeen and wounding nearly 150.

Dec. 19. Lahore, Pakistan. Iran's cultural center director, Sadiq Ganji, was killed by an activist of the Islamic group

Sipah-i-Sahaba Pakistan (SSP) named Haq Nawaz. The motive was the fact that Ganji was a prominent Shiite leader. Nawaz was hanged more than eight years later, on February 28, 2000.

1991

Jan. 18–19. Djakarta, Indonesia; Manila, the Philippines. At the height of the First Gulf War, an Iraqi, posing as a construction worker at the residence of U. S. Ambassador John Monjo, planted a bomb in a flower pot. It was defused and the government quietly expelled an Iraqi diplomat.

In Manila, an Iraqi embassy car delivered two would-be bombers near the American Cultural Center. As they prepared the bomb it exploded, killing one of them. Iraqi diplomat Muwafak al-Ani was soon deported.

Feb. 12. London, England. The Provisional IRA fired three mortar rounds at No. 10 Downing Street, the official residence of Prime Minister John Major, from a van parked nearby. A cabinet meeting was underway at the time as they debated the Gulf crisis. The first bomb exploded fifty yards away in the Downing Street garden. Most cabinet members ducked: "It seemed to be a good thing to do," said one official. No one was injured and damage was slight.

March 2. Colombo, Sri Lanka. Terrorists set off by remote control a bomb that exploded as the auto of Deputy Defense Minister Ranjan Wijeratne passed by. He died, along with eighteen other persons. About seventy-three people were wounded. Police suspected the separatist Tamil Tiger movement, but Wijeratne also had enemies among Sri Lanka's Sinhalese.

March 9. Beirut, Lebanon. A car bomb exploded in the Christian suburb of Antelias, killing four people and wounding twenty-two. No group claimed responsibility. The assault was seen as a challenge to President Elias Hrawi.

March 26. Istanbul, Turkey. A group described by authorities as leftist claimed to have set the bombs that blasted out windows at the Shell Oil Company near Istanbul and at the U. S. consulate and a bank in the port city of Izmir.

April 1. Dusseldorf, Germany. A Red Army Faction sniper killed industrialist Detlev Rohwedder at his home, shooting through a window. He was responsible for the movement to privatize the East Germany economy. It was one of the group's last reported actions. At least thirty people were killed during the faction's terror campaign that began in the 1960s.

April 19. Athens, Greece. The explosion of a parcel bomb at the British consulate killed seven people and wounded eight others. Greek authorities arrested seven Palestinians and expelled twenty-six diplomats and students.

May 21. Chennai (Madras), India. A Sri Lankan female Tamil Tiger suicide bomber in her twenties called Dhanu (real name — Gayatri Rajaratnam) along with several co-conspirators very recently arrived from Sri Lanka, awaited former prime minister Rajiv Gandhi's arrival under tight security arrangements at a political rally. Mixing with the crowd and watching for an opportunity to approach Gandhi, she found her chance when, upon entering, the political leader paused to hear the recitation of a poem. Forcing her way to the front of the public spectators shortly after 10:00 p.m., she knelt at Gandhi's feet offering a garland of flowers.

Dhanu then set off by battery-operated detonator the plastic explosives strapped around her waist in a denim belt.

Rajiv Gandhi, who while in office had sent Indian troops to help put down a Tamil uprising, died instantly, thus sharing the 1984 fate of his mother, Indira Gandhi (above). Eighteen additional people including the bomber were killed in the blast and thirty-three injured; policemen made up less than half of both totals. Subsequent investigations led eventually to the prosecution of twenty-six individuals belonging to the Liberation Tigers of Tamil Eelam (LTTE); three were found guilty and sentenced to life imprisonment; in January 1998, four received death sentences. The two alleged masterminds of the plot, Sivarasan and Peria Santham, died in India in confrontations with the Indian police later in the year, either in shoot outs or as suicides.

Dec. 22. London, England. The Ulster Freedom Fighters, a Protestant group, planted firebombs in the underground rail system, but police manage to remove them with little damage and few injuries.

1992

Jan. 17, 21. Manila, the Philippines. A group calling itself the Red Scorpions kidnapped an American businessman, Michael Barnes, president of Philippine Geothermal. It was not clear, however, whether the abductors were political extremists or, as some suspected, crooked police officers seeking ransom money.

Jan. 25. Fairfax, VA, USA. A Pakistani national, Amal Khan Kasi, shot to death CIA employees Frank Darling and Lansing Bennett outside the main gate to CIA headquarters. He fled to Pakistan, was arrested there by American FBI agents, and confessed. He was convicted of capital murder in 1997 (below) and executed by lethal injection in Virginia on November 15, 2002.

Feb. 5, Belfast, Northern Ireland. Protestant gunmen burst into a betting shop and shot dead five Catholic civilians.

Feb. 16. Nabi Sheet, Lebanon. Israeli Defense Forces helicopters targeted the automobiles of Hizbollah leader Sheik Abbas Mussawi and aides in southern Lebanon. Firing rockets, the Israelis killed Mussawi, two members of his family, and five body guards. When additional cars came to the scene, Israeli helicopters reportedly returned and fired additional rockets at the new targets.

March 17. Buenos Aires, Argentina. A huge blast set off by a car bomb leveled the five-story Israeli embassy, located in a fashionable area of the capital. The explosion could be heard three miles away and a plume of smoke rose hundreds of feet in the air. The death toll stood at thirty, with as many as 242 injured. The Islamic Hizballah claimed responsibility.

April 10. London, England. An IRA bomb set off at the Baltic Exchange in the City of London, the financial center, killed three and injured ninety-one civilians. Broken glass and debris rained down on people in the crowded area. A second car bomb exploded hours later in northwest London. No fatalities were reported in that incident.

May 2. Eliat, Israel. Islamic Jihad terrorists attacked in the Red Sea resort, killing one tourist. Two Jihad members were capture and one killed by the Israel Defense Force.

June 29. Annaba, Algeria. Mohamed Boudiaf, recently installed president of the High State Committee (head of state) died in an attack by unknown persons with guns and grenades. He was killed while giving a speech at a cultural center in the eastern part of the country. More than forty people were injured. The assassin was immediately arrested, but it was not clear then (or later) whether fundamentalist Muslims or corrupt financial interests were behind the deed.

1993

Jan. 8. Luxor, Egypt. Islamic terrorists attempted to bomb a bus carrying German tourists. No one was injured, however. A day earlier, terrorists had fired on Japanese tourists in southern Egypt.

Jan. 22. Lima, Peru. A bomb planted at a Coca-Cola plant killed at least two people, injured two, and caused substantial damage. Later the same day, a car bomb detonated at another Coca-Cola facility in the city, causing only slight damage.

Six days after that, a car bomb exploded at the IBM headquarters in Lima. Eleven persons were injured; major damage resulted from the blast.

Jan. 24. Ankara, Turkey. Prominent journalist Ungar Muncu, known for his criticism of Muslim extremists, died when a bomb planted under his car exploded.

Feb. 4. Cairo, Egypt. The Islamic terrorist group *Al-Gama'a al-Islamiyya* claimed responsibility for a fire bomb lobbed at a tour bus that South Korean tourists were waiting to board at a hotel outside the city. Note: Indiscriminate bombings in Cairo from February through July killed twenty-two Egyptian nationals and wounded over 100 others.

Feb. 26. Cairo, Egypt. A bomb planted at a downtown café exploded, killing three people and wounding eighteen. Most of those killed and injured were foreign tourists.

Feb. 26. New York, USA. Islamic terrorists carried out the first attack on the World Trade Center by means of a massive truck bomb driven into the building's underground garage. The biggest blast caused by terrorists to that point in recent American history sent shock waves throughout America. It killed six people and injured, largely through smoke inhalation and fire, more than 1,000 others. Hundreds poured out of the towers into the streets of lower Manhattan, gasping, their faces black with soot, after groping their way down from as high as the 105th floor. Eight disabled people were trapped for nine hours on the 94th floor before they were taken to the roof and removed by helicopter, the last people out of the building, The Center suffered major damage.

More than fifty groups and individuals soon claimed responsibility for the attack. Militant Islamist Sheik Omar Abdel Rahman, an Egyptian, and nine others eventually were convicted on conspiracy charges. In April 1995 in the Philippines, six suspects involved in the attack also were convicted of conspiracy and other charges. Three years after that, in the United States, the reputed mastermind of the plot, Ramzi Ahmed Yousef, was tried and convicted for his part in the assault and sentenced to life plus 240 years in prison.

March 3. Belgrade, Yugoslavia. With the Balkan nation disintegrating politically and Serbia trying to maintain its claim to the name of "Yugoslavia," terrorists exploded a hand grenade in front of the U.S. embassy, causing minor damage but no casualties.

March 7. Hamburg, Germany. Suspected Armenian terrorists firebombed the Turkish consulate, causing minor damage but no casualties. Police arrested four suspects.

March 8. San José; Costa Rica. Five masked gunmen took twenty-five hostages in the Nicaraguan Embassy, including the Nicaraguan ambassador, Alfonso Robelo. They initially demanded $6 million in ransom and changes in the Costa Rican government. Later they demanded a freeze on economic aid pending an investigation into President Violeta Chamorro's government. On March 11 they released nine hostages. Ten days later the occupation of the embassy concluded without bloodshed. After the government released the hostages, the terrorists were permitted to leave the country, four going to Nicaragua and their leader, José Urbina Lara, to Nicaragua.

March 20. Warrington, England. Two bombs hidden in trash cans exploded at a crowded market, killing a child and a teenager. Fifty-six civilians were injured. The deed was ascribed to the IRA and was the deadliest such attack in almost a year. Two weeks later, Irish President Mary Robinson joined British Prime Minister John Major at the funeral services.

April 14. Kuwait City, Kuwait. As former U. S. President George H. W. Bush began a visit celebrating victory in the 1990-91 Gulf War, Kuwaiti authorities thwarted a planned terrorist plot against his life. They seized a powerful car bomb and other explosives that had been smuggled into Kuwait the previous night. The attack was to take place during the former president's appearance at Kuwait University. Police, however, arrested sixteen suspects, led by two Iraqi nationals, Ra'ad al-Asadi and Wali al-Ghazali. Evidence indicated that the Iraqi government engineered the plot. In response, in June, U. S. President Bill Clinton launched twenty-three cruise missiles against the Iraqi intelligence headquarters in Baghdad.

April 20. Cairo, Egypt. Terrorists of *Al-Gama'a al-Islamiya* failed in an attempt to assassinate Information Minister Safwat Sharif. Shots fired at his motorcade wounded him slightly; his bodyguard was more seriously wounded.

April 24. London, England. An IRA truck bomb devastated the Bishopsgate area of the capital's financial centre, killing one person and injuring forty-four, as well as causing damage in the hundreds of millions of pounds sterling. St. Ethlburga church dating from 1370 was destroyed by the blast. (It was rebuilt and rededicated in November 2002.)

The attack was adjudged by some as a massive boost to Irish republican morale.

May 1. Colombo, Sri Lanka. While officiating at a May Day parade, President Ranasinghe Premadasa was killed by a suicide bomber. The assassin, believe to be a young teen-aged girl, rammed her explosive-loaded bicycle into the President's motorcade, setting off a bomb that killed Premadasa, herself, and thirty-four other people. The authorities immediately suspected Tamil Tiger (LTTE) complicity and arrested forty people, mostly Tamils. A majority were released, but eighteen of them were indicted. More than four years later, in September 1997, these eighteen were released due to lack of evidence.

May 19. Lima, Peru. At the end of a strike called by the Maoist *Sendero Luminoso* (Shining Path), a car bomb exploded

at the Chilean embassy. The building was damaged, but no one was hurt.

June 8. Cairo, Egypt. Terrorists set off a bomb at an overpass as a bus passed on its way to the pyramids of Giza, across the Nile. Two people were killed and at least twenty-one others (most Middle Easterners) injured. Indications were that it was the work of Islamic extremists who had been carrying on a campaign against foreign tourists for the past year and one-half.

June 27. Antalya, Turkey. Terrorists from the Kurdistan Workers Party (PKK) threw hand grenades at several tourist hotels and restaurants. Twenty-eight persons were injured, including twelve foreigners. PKK leader Abdulla Ocalan earlier had threatened violence against tourism.

July 5. Turkey. Beginning on this date and extending over the next three months, the Kurdistan Peoples Party (PKK) kidnapped nineteen Western tourists in eight separate incidents. All were eventually released unharmed after several weeks in captivity.

On July 25 at Istanbul, two Italian tourists were injured in a bomb blast at a cash-dispensing machine.

July 7. Osaka, Japan. The ultra-leftist *Chukaku-Ha* group claimed responsibility for a bomb exploded at the UN Technology Center. Only minor damage was caused and there were no casualties.

July 27. Lima, Peru. Evidently timed to coincide with a proclaimed *Sendero Luminoso* "armed strike," a car bomb exploded outside the American embassy. One guard was injured and extensive damage was done not only to the embassy facade and perimeter fence, but to the nearby Spanish embassy and a hotel, as well. Three people at the hotel were wounded.

Aug. 18. Cairo, Egypt. Interior Minister Hassan Al-Alfi was slightly wounded in an assassination attempt. A motorcycle bomb killed five persons and wounded some fifteen others. The Islamic extremist group New Jihad claimed responsibility.

Aug. 25. Ankara, Turkey. Two Iranian dissidents, Mohammed Khaderi and Behram Azadfer, were murdered within days of each other. In the first instance, four terrorists disguised as Turkish police abducted and subsequently shot the victim; in the latter incident, Khaderi's body was found on the side of the Kiurschir-Boztepe highway on August 28.

Sep. 8. Johannesburg, South Africa. Pro-Zulu terrorists killed nineteen people and injured twenty-two in a riotous prelude to general elections.

Sep. 11. Port-au-Prince, Haiti. Antoine Izmery, a prominent supporter of exiled President Jean-Bertrand Aristide, died of gunshot wounds suffered outside a church. The UN mission accused leaders of the Haitian armed forces of carrying out state-sponsored terror tactics.

Sep. 20. Oran, Algeria. Terrorists abducted three surveyors, one Algerian and two Frenchmen, driving from Oran to Sidi bel Abbes (the one-time headquarters and principal base of the French foreign legion). The Algerian was released, but the two Frenchmen were murdered.

Oct. 11. Oslo, Norway. William Nygaard, the Norwegian publisher of *Satanic Verses* by Salman Rushdie, was shot and wounded at his home. The book had caused the issuance of a *fatwa* — a decree — in Iran by religious leaders calling for Rushdie's death. The edict caused him to take refuge in Great Britain, where he enjoyed police protection.

Oct. 19. Tiaret, Algeria. Extremists of the Armed Islamic Group kidnapped three foreign construction technicians working for an Italian firm. Two days later they were found dead, their throats cut.

On October 24 in Algiers, the Armed Islamic Group kidnapped three French diplomats, killing a policeman who tried to stop them. Six days later all three diplomats were released unharmed.

Oct. 21. Bujumbura, Burundi. A failed military coup, during which Tutsi tribe soldier murdered the nation's first elected president, Melchior Ndadye, a Hutu, triggered widespread ethnic slaughter. The coup failed when senior officers declined to join in, but horrendous massacres followed. Six years later, in May 1999, five people were sentenced to death for their part in the president's assassination.

Oct 23. Belfast, Northern Ireland. Two IRA terrorists placed a bomb in a busy fish shop in Shankill Road called Frizzell's that exploded on a short-delay timer, killing ten people, including one of the bombers, Thomas Begley, and two children. Fifty-seven people were injured, including the second IRA terrorist. He recovered, only to be tried and receive nine life sentences in prison.

A week later in Greysteel, Ireland, Protestant Ulster Freedom Fighter (UFF) gunmen shot and killed eight people in a place called the Rising Sun bar, evidently as retaliation for the Shankill bombing.

Oct. 25. Lagos, Nigeria. Four dissidents hijacked a Nigerian Airways aircraft bound for Abuja with 149 people aboard shortly after takeoff. After trying without success to land in Chad, the plane was directed by the hijackers to Niamey, Niger Republic. After releasing two groups of passengers and following three days of negotiations that led nowhere, Nigerien paramilitary forces based in Niamey stormed the aircraft, forcing the hijackers to surrender. One crew member died in the encounter. The Movement for the Advancement of Democracy (MAD), headed by Maalam Jerry Yusuf, claimed responsibility.

Oct. 25. Lima, Peru. A large bomb exploded under a minibus near the departure terminal at the international airport. The driver was killed and about twenty other persons injured. The nearby American Airlines cargo office sustained damage. The Shining Path movement was suspected.

Nov. 25. Cairo, Egypt. The Jihad Group set off a car bomb near the passing motorcade of Prime Minister Atif Sedki. He was unhurt, but a young bystander was killed and eighteen persons wounded.

Dec. 2–7. Algeria. In a five-day period, terrorists shot and killed four foreigners—a Spanish businessman driving between Oran and Annaba, a Russian woman in Algiers, a Briton in Arzew, and a locally retired Frenchman in Arba. They also wounded an Italian businessman in Algiers.

Dec. 14. Tamezguida, Algeria. The Armed Islamic Group claimed responsibility for the abduction of fourteen Croatian workers at a hydroelectric project. Twelve of the Croations were killed, their throats cut, and two escaped with injuries. The abductors stated the attack was part of an ongoing campaign to rid Algeria of foreigners and to avenge Muslims killed in Bosnia.

At the end of the month, on December 29, terrorists murdered a Belgian couple resident in Bouira as they slept in their home.

Dec. 27. Cairo, Egypt. A small bomb thrown at a bus, along with gunfire, wounded seven Austrian tourists and eight Egyptians as they traveled in the old district of the city.

1994

Feb. 25. Hebron, West Bank. In what was termed a massacre, right-wing Jewish extremist (and U.S.-born physician) Baruch Goldstein, in his army officer's uniform, opened fire with a submachine gun on Muslim worshipers at a holy site called the Cave of the Patriarchs. The attack took place at early morning prayers during Ramadan. Goldstein killed twenty-nine people and wounded at least 150. Additional worshipers died, trampled in the panic to flee. Goldstein was overpowered and beaten to death on the spot.

March 13. London, England. The IRA carried out a third mortar attack on Heathrow Airport in four days, causing the airport to be closed temporarily. In this attack, as well as on March 9 and 11, terrorists fired mortar shells from a car parked in wooded areas close to the perimeter fence. None of the bombs had exploded, but the capital's main air connection was partially paralyzed.

April 24. Johannesburg, South Africa. Right-wing extremists, trying to disrupt the nation's first democratic elections, bombed the African National Congress offices, killing nine civilians and injuring ninety-two. Three days later, a car bomb blast wounded sixteen at Jan Smuts airport.

June 18. Loughinisland, Northern Ireland. Protestant UVF gunmen killed six Catholics in an attack on a bar. Two days later, IRA gunmen retaliated, gunning down six Protestants, also in a bar.

June 20. Mashhad, Iran. A bomb blast in a crowded mausoleum killed twenty-five people and wounding seventy gathered for prayer. The government blamed the opposition Mujahideen Khalq and Iran's spiritual leader, Ayatollah Ali. The police made a number of arrests.

June 21–22. Fethiye and Marmaris, Turkey. The Kurdish Workers Party (PKK) claimed responsibility (on German television) for three bombs detonated in these two coastal towns. Two tourists died and a total of twenty-two persons were wounded.

June 30. Dhaka, Bangladesh. Muslim extremists demanded the death of an author, Novelist Taslima Nasrin, accused of blasphemy for criticizing Islam. In attacks on her supporters, militants killed one teen-age boy and injured at least 150 people. Militant groups put bounties totaling $5,000 on Nasrin's head.

She fled to Sweden that year, returned in 1998, and again took refuge in Sweden in 1999.

July 18. Buenos Aires, Argentina. In the worst attack on Jews outside of Israel since World War II. a car bomb leveled a Jewish community center in downtown Buenos Aires, killing forty-six people. More than 200 were injured. A Lebanon-based Islamic group claimed responsibility for the act, as well as for the bombing of an airplane in Panama on July 19. The latter attack took twenty-one lives.

In August 2003, Belgian authorities detained an Iranian diplomat, Saied Baghban, for questioning at the behest of Israel, but released him due to his diplomatic status. Argentina ordered the arrest of a total of eight Iranian officials.

July 26. London, England. Fourteen people were hurt in a bomb explosion at the Israeli embassy near Kensington Palace. The blast, at shortly after noon, caused widespread damage and could be heard over a mile away. Twelve hours later, a second bomb struck Balfour House in Finchley, home of an Israeli charity in north London. Four people were injured. Islamic extremists were blamed. The attacks came the day after King Hussein of Jordan and Israeli Prime Minister Yitzhak Rabin met in Washington to declare an end to long-standing hostilities.

Aug. 24. Marrakesh, Morocco. Members of an Islamic radical group assaulted a tourist hotel, killing two Spanish tourists. Part of a wave of violence, including the desecration of a Jewish cemetery in Casablanca, the attack was intended to destabilize the monarchy and lead toward a militant Islamic government. In January 1997, a French court sentenced those involved to up to eight years imprisonment.

Oct. 19. Tel Aviv, Israel. A Hamas suicide bomber killed twenty-two civilians and injured forty-seven when he set off his explosives on a passenger bus in the center of the city.

Dec. 24. Algiers, Algeria. Four terrorists affiliated with the *Groupe Islamique Armée* (GIA) hijacked an Air France flight with 170 persons aboard bound from Algiers for Paris. The terrorists diverted it to Marseille. The two-day incident, staged as a protest against France's support for the Algerian government, ended with French police storming the aircraft. All four terrorists were killed, along with three other persons, and the Airbus' cockpit area was heavily damaged.

1995–1997

*Between 1965 and the end of the twentieth century, the Basque "Homeland and Liberty" ETA reportedly killed more than 800 people, using tactics including bombings, assassinations, extortions and kidnappings.**

1995

Jan. 28. Cairo, Egypt. Police shot and killed fourteen suspected Muslim militants, and radicals killed two policemen and two civilians in one of the bloodiest days in Egypt's Islamic insurgency. In all, eighty-one people were been killed that month.

March 7. Karachi, Pakistan. Two U. S. consulate employees were killed and one wounded when a gunman ambushed them on the way to work in an official car. The assassin emptied the magazine of an automatic rifle into the vehicle before making his escape. The attack possibly was in retaliation for convictions rendered in U. S. courts for the 1993 World Trade Center truck bombing.

March 20. Tokyo and Yokohama, Japan. Nearly simultaneous nerve gas attacks in the subway systems of two Japanese cities resulted in the deaths of twelve people and injury to the astonishing total of 5,700. The doomsday Aum Shinrikyo (Sublime Truth) sect, founded by Shoko Asahara, planted packages that released deadly Sarin gas in crowded subway stations as a means, apparently, to further the apocalyptic quasi-religious views of its founder. The precise reason remains obscure. Three more attacks followed, including in the central Japanese city of Matsumoto, with some 500 persons hospitalized. Authorities quickly rounded up the group's leaders and many members. In May, police stormed the cult's compound at the base of Mt. Fuji and arrested Asahara (real name — Chizuo Matsumoto), along with fourteen of his top aides. The charge: mass murder. The partially blind fanatic Asahara remained in prison undergoing a lengthy trial through the end of 2003.

In April 2003, prosecutors demanded a death sentence for the leader. By the fall of 2003, nine of Asahara's disciples had been sentenced to hanging in connection with the gas attacks, although none of the sentences had yet been carried out. The verdict on Asahara was expected early in 2004.

April 9. Gaza Strip, Palestine. A suicide bomber crashed an explosive-laden van into an Israeli bus, killing eight people.

---

*Yonah Alexander, Michael Swetnam, and Herbert M. Levine, in Cronin, ed., Confronting Fear, 154.

Over fifty other persons were injured. A faction of the Palestine Islamic Jihad claimed responsibility.

April 19. Oklahoma City, USA. Timothy McVeigh, an ex-soldier who had become a militant opponent of the U. S. federal government, stationed a truck loaded with explosives outside a federal office building. When it exploded on a timing device, the entire front of the large building was sheered away, collapsing walls and floors. Those killed numbered 168, including nineteen children. McVeigh and Terry Nichols, who aided in the planning for the lethal attack, undertook the plot mainly in a nihilist effort to avenge a deadly standoff two years earlier between the federal government, especially the Federal Bureau of Investigation, and the Branch Davidian religious cult at Waco, Texas.

It was the deadliest terrorism act ever on U. S. soil to that time. McVeigh, whom the police had happened to detain quickly on a minor infraction of automobile registration laws, confessed to the deed. He was tried, convicted, and sentenced to death. He was executed by lethal injection on June 11, 2001. Nichols received a sentence of life in prison. (In 2003, the state of Oklahoma undertook to try him for murder.) A third conspirator, Michael Fortier, testified against both McVeigh and Nichols and received twelve years in prison.

June 26. Addis Ababa. Ethiopia. An attempt on the life of Egyptian President Hosni Mubarak failed when two vehicles tried to block his motorcade from the airport. Several gunmen fired at his armored limousine, but he was not hurt. Two guards and two gunmen were killed; two other people were injured, including the Palestinian ambassador to Ethiopia. Two gunmen were captured. *Al-Gama'at al-Islamiyya* claimed responsibility.

July 11. Paris, France. Two terrorists assassinated a co-founder of the Algerian Islamic Salvation Front and his bodyguard in a mosque. No one claimed responsibility, but earlier in the year the Armed Islamic Group (GIA) listed the victim as one of their priority targets.

July 25. Paris, France. A bomb went off on a Metro carriage as it arrived at St. Michel station, killing seven commuters and wounding eighty-six. Two and a half weeks later, on August 17, a bomb detonated in a trash bin near a Metro entrance injuring seventeen people. Authorities determined it was a device similar to the one that had been used on July 25. No organization was identified as carrying out the attacks.

Aug. 21. Jerusalem, Israel. A bomb exploded on a bus, killing six persons and wounding over 100 others. The *Izz al-Din al-Qassem* Brigades, the military wing of Hamas (the Islamic Resistance Movement), claimed responsibility.

Aug. 24. Paris, France. A bomb set off at the Etoile in the city's Champs Elysées by the Islamic Armed Group of Algeria wounded seventeen people.

French police authorities at this time listed thirty terrorist groups evidently focused on that country.

Sep. 2. Oran, Algeria. Suspected Armed Islamic Group (GIA) militants shot and killed a foreign national. One day later, a similar incident in the Belcourt district of Algiers resulted in two foreign-national nuns being gunned down..

Sep. 7. Srinagar, India. A woman claiming to be from the militant group *Dukhtaran-e-Millat* delivered a parcel bomb to the office of the BBC in Kashmir. The bomb exploded later, killing one person, injuring two others, and causing major damage. *Dukhtaran-e-Millat* denied responsibility.

Sep. 13. Moscow, Russia. Unknown terrorists fired a rocket-propelled grenade at the U. S. embassy. Although the attack caused only minor damage, security was tightened at American consulates in Vladivostok, St. Petersburg, and Ekaterinburg.

Oct. 9. Hyder, Ariz., USA. A transcontinental train from Miami, Fla., bound for Los Angeles, Cal., was derailed and sent hurtling off a bridge into a dry stream bed, evidently by the removal of track bolts or spikes. One person was killed and eighty-five injured. An unknown group called "The Sons of the Gestapo" claimed responsibility. A letter left at the scene criticized the federal police such as the FBI, reading. in effect, that it is time for an independent federal agency to police the law enforcement agencies.

Oct. 20. Rijeka, Croatia. A car bomb exploded outside the local police headquarters, killing the driver and injuring twenty-nine bystanders. The Egyptian *al-Gama'at al-Islamiyya* claimed responsibility, warning that further attacks would continue unless authorities released one of its imprisoned militants.

Nov. 8. Egypt. Gunmen fired on a train en route from Aswan in the south to Cairo. Three people were injured. *Al-Gama'at al- Islamiyya* (Islamic Group or IG) claimed responsibility for the attack.

Nov. 13. Riyadh, Saudi Arabia. A bomb attack destroyed a U.S.-run three-story military training center, killing seven people. Some sixty persons were injured, half of them Saudis. Perhaps reflecting how the unexpected attack rattled the tightly controlled kingdom, four Saudi dissidents,

possibly connected to the Iranian Party of God, subsequently were beheaded.

Nov. 19. Islamabad, Pakistan. A suicide truck bomber drove into the Egyptian embassy compound and set off an explosion that killed at least sixteen and injured sixty persons. Three separate militant Islamic groups claimed responsibility.

1996

Jan. 8. Irian Jaya Province, Indonesia. Guerrillas of the Free Papua Movement (OPM) abducted twenty-six people in the Lorenta nature preserve. Among various demands, the OPM insisted upon the withdrawal of Indonesian troops from the province. Indonesian special forces troops rescued the nine individuals still being held hostage on May 15.

Jan. 18. Addis Ababa, Ethiopia. A bomb exploded at the Ghion Hotel, killing at least four persons and injuring twenty others. Two months later, *al-Ittihaad al-Islami* (The Islamic Union), an ethnic Somali group, claimed responsibility.

Jan. 31, Colombo, Sri Lanka. A suicide squad of the Liberation Tigers of Tamil Eelam (LTTE — Tamil Tigers) early in the morning drove a truck laden with 400 pounds of explosives into the Central Bank in the heart of the city. The explosion that followed brought down a large section of the bank building and killed approximately ninety civilians, injuring more than 1,400. The explosion was followed by gun battles in the streets between police and the few remaining terrorists.

It was the deadliest such incident in Sri Lankan history. President Chandrika Kumaratunga said, nevertheless, that the tragedy would not halt her efforts to end the country's civil war

Feb. 9. London, England. Shortly after calling an end to a seventeen-month truce, an IRA group set off a very large explosion at South Quay in the Docklands business district. Two people died and scores were injured. Nine days later, on the 18th, IRA member Edward O'Brien was killed by his own bomb when it accidentally detonated and ripped apart the bus on which he was traveling as it passed along Aldwych, central London. The blast injured eight persons.

Feb. 11. Manama, Bahrain. A bomb exploded at the Diplomat Hotel, injuring three people and causing significant damage. The London-based Islamic Front for the Liberation of Bahrain first claimed the bombing, but later denied responsibility.

Feb. 15. Athens, Greece. Unidentified assailants fired an anti-tank rocket at a perimeter wall of the U. S. Embassy, causing minor damage. Police headquarters said that a previously unknown group calling itself "National Struggle" claimed responsibility; other sources indicated it may have been carried out by the 17 November group.

Feb. 20. Istanbul, Turkey. Two member of an Iranian dissident group were shot to death. In April, the authorities arrested several suspects, including Islamic militants, Iranians, and Turks. The Iranians arrested later claimed they received their orders from the Iranian embassy.

Feb. 26. Jerusalem, Israel. A suicide bomber blew up a bus near the Central Station, killing twenty-six persons, most of whom were civilians, and wounding as many as eighty. Hamas was believed to be responsible.

Six days later in Jerusalem, on March 3, another suicide bomber set off an explosive device on a bus, killing nineteen persons and injuring six others. A splinter group of HAMAS claimed responsibility.

March 4. Tel Aviv, Israel. A bombing at a large shopping center claimed twenty lives and injured seventy-five people. Both Hamas and the Palestine Islamic Jihad claimed responsibility.

May 13. Bet El, West Bank. Gunmen opened fire on a bus load of Israeli students, killing one and wounding three others. Hamas was suspected.

March 27. Médéa, Algeria. Armed Islamic Group (GIA) extremists kidnapped seven French Trappist monks from their monastery. They demanded the release of GIA members held in France. On May 21 the group announced that they had executed the monks due to the French government's refusal to negotiate. Paris again advised all French citizens to leave the country.

April 18. Cairo, Egypt. Four *al-Gama-'at al-Islamiyya* (IG) terrorists opened fire on a group of Greek tourists in front of the Europa Hotel, killing eighteen and injuring fourteen. The IG later claimed they mistook their victims for Israelis.

May 28. Athens, Greece. A bomb exploded at the offices of IBM, causing extensive damage but no injuries. An unknown group calling itself the *Fraxia Midheniston* (Nihilist Faction) claimed responsibility.

June 15. Manchester, England. A bomb exploded in a van parked near a shopping center; flying glass and debris injured more than 200 people. The prime ministers of both Britain and Ireland blamed the IRA. The attack came only days after the opening of the latest round of peace talks in Northern Ireland

June 25. Dharan, Saudi Arabia. In a 10:00 p.m. terrorist attack on off-duty military personnel, a devastating truck bomb ripped through Khobar Towers, a U. S. Air Force housing complex, killing nineteen and wounding hundreds more, sixty-four of whom were hospitalized. The bomb virtually destroying an eight-story building. The source of the blast was believed to have been a fuel truck loaded with 4,000 pounds of plastic explosives that was left in a public parking lot in front of building #131. It was the deadliest attack against Americans since 1983, when the bombing of the Marine compound in Beirut cost 241 lives (above).

Early evidence indicated that the act was the work of an Iranian-backed group of Saudi Shiite Muslims, who may have received help from Syria. Five years later, the United States brought formal terrorism charges against thirteen individuals, members of the pro–Iranian Saudi Hezbollah, or "Party of God." U. S. sources described Saudi dissident Osama bin Laden as the mastermind of the plot.

July 8. Addis Ababa, Ethiopia. Two Somali gunmen opened fire on the minister of Transport and Communications as he arrived at his office, wounding him and killing two guards and two passersby. *Al-Ittihaad al-Islami* claimed responsibility for the attack.

July 26. Reus, Spain. Authorities blamed the Basque separatist organization ETA for a bomb set off at the Tarragona International Airport. Thirty-five persons, including British and Irish tourists, were wounded. A day later, police deactivated a bomb after evacuating 500 people from the Hotel Delfin Park in the coastal resort of Salou, adding to concerns that the movement was out to destroy the Spanish tourist industry.

July 27. Atlanta, USA. A large explosion hit Centennial Olympic Park in the downtown part of the city very early in the morning. One person died and at least seventy-five others were injured. The pipe bomb blast at a the social center of the Olympic Games struck near a stage where thousands were attending a rock concert. The attack had overtones of the 1972 Olympic Games violence (see above) and was immediately assumed to be the work of terrorists.

The first suspect, Richard Jewell, a security guard, eventually was fully cleared. Suspicion centered then on a right wing loner named Eric Robert Rudolph, who was wanted for possible involvement in the bombing of an Atlanta abortion clinic and two other attacks. Rudolph disappeared into the North Carolina mountains and was not apprehended until May 30, 2003. In Atlanta in October 2003, he was formally charged with the three crimes.

Aug. 1. Oran, Algeria. A bomb set off at the home of the French archbishop of Oran, Pierre Lucien Claverie, who had just met with the French foreign minister, killed him and his chauffeur. Police suspected the Algerian Armed Islamic Group (GIA).

Aug. 5. Addis Ababa, Ethiopia. A bomb exploded in the lobby of the Wabbe Shebelle Hotel, killing two persons and injuring seventeen others. No group claimed responsibility for the attack.

Aug. 11. Beledweyne, Somalia. Suspected *Al-Ittihaad al-Islami* gunmen killed two Ethiopian businessmen, apparently to protest Ethiopia's two-day military incursion into Somalia earlier in the month.

Aug. 14. Colombo, Sri Lanka. Liberation Tigers of Tamil Eelam (LTTE) rebels bombed the offices and residences of two South Korean companies, causing extensive damage but no injuries. This was the first LTTE attack against foreign investors.

Oct. 1. Vladivostok, Russia. Attackers shot and killed a South Korean consular officer near his apartment. No one claimed responsibility, but South Korean authorities believed that the killers were professional assassins from North Korea. Pyongyang officials denied any involvement in the attack.

Oct. 20. Sanaa, Yemen. Kidnappers took a French diplomat while he was driving in the city. On October 26 they turned him over to local tribe members, who then held him until November 1, when the government negotiated his release.

Nov. 1. Khartoum, Sudan. As just one example of the rash of kidnappings that became more and more prevalent in a number of countries during the 1990's, a faction of the Sudanese People's Liberation Army (SPLA) kidnapped three International Committee of the Red Cross (ICRC) workers, all Westerners. In a complicating factor, five days later, the Khartoum government suspended Red Cross activities, accusing the relief group of allowing rebels to haul fighters and ammunition in one of its planes, a charge the ICRC denied. On December 9 after mediation by U. S. Congressman Bill Richardson, the rebels released the hostages in exchange for Red Cross supplies and a health survey of their camp.

Nov. 15. Bainem Forest, Algeria. Unknown attackers beheaded a Bulgarian businessman, the former Bulgarian defense attaché in Algeria. His body was found at the entrance to the forest west of Algiers. This was only one macabre case of widespread violence in Algeria; a report published four days later noted that during the past six weeks, at least 250 people, most of them civilians with no clear political allegiances, had been killed.

Dec. 2. Ambala, India. A bomb exploded on a crowded passenger train as it left the railway station near the border with Punjab bound for Jammu in Kashmir. At least twelve people died and thirty wounded. No group acknowledged responsibility; Indian officials blamed a Punjab-based militant group without being more specific.

Dec. 3. Paris, France. A rush-hour bombing on a Paris commuter train killed three and wounded dozens of people. The explosion occurred just as the train was pulling into the Port Royal station near the Latin Quarter. Police suspected Islamic militants according to one report; another source blamed Algerian extremists. No one claimed responsibility.

Dec. 11. La Guajira Dept., Colombia. Five armed men, members of the Revolutionary Armed Forces of Colombia, (FARC) kidnapped and later murdered a U.S. geologist at a methane gas exploration site in La Guajira Department on the country's north coast. A week later, at the town of Monteria 300 miles north-west of the capital, a terrorist group police termed "guerrillas" set off a bomb that killed at least four people and injured thirty-four. No one claimed responsibility.

Dec. 17. Lima, Peru. Fourteen armed members of the Tupac Amaru Revolutionary Movement (MRTA) led by a terrorist named Nestor Cerpa took several hundred people hostage at a party given at the Japanese ambassador's residence. Within hours all the women hostages were released. The group demanded the release from prison of all MRTA members and safe passage out of the country for them and the hostage takers. Death threats began, with the first person menaced being the Peruvian foreign minister. The terrorists released most of the hostages by Christmas, but the siege lasted until the following April. They held up to eighty-one Peruvians and Japanese until that time.

In a well-planned, lightning assault on April 22, 1997, Peruvian troops stormed the ambassador's residence and rescued the remaining seventy-one hostages as the unsuspecting terrorists were playing their daily game of soccer. All fourteen of the latter were killed and the bodies of twelve of them interred in unmarked graves scattered around Lima.

Dec. 27. Asmara, Eritrea. Unidentified gunmen opened fire and killed five Belgian tourists and their driver as they returned from a field trip. No one claimed responsibility.

1997

Jan. 2–13. At Washington, New York, London, and Riyadh, Saudi Arabia. Letter bombs with Alexandria, Egypt, postmarks were discovered at *Al-Hayat* newspaper bureaus. Three similar devices, also postmarked in Egypt, were found at a prison facility in Leavenworth, Kan., USA. None exploded.

Jan. 5. Rustenburg, South Africa. The *Boere Aanvals Troepe* claimed responsibility for exploding a bomb at a mosque, injuring two people.

Feb. 4. Cyangugu, Rwanda. Suspected Hutu terrorists killed five human rights team members. They used firearms, grenades, and machetes. The victims include a Briton, a Cambodian, and three Rwandans.

Feb. 4–16. Komsomolabad, Dushanbe and Garm, Tajikistan. In a rash of kidnappings, a paramilitary group headed by Bakhrom Sodirov kidnapped four UN observers and their interpreter, two International Red Cross officials, four Russian journalists and their driver, four UN High Commission for Refugees officials, and the Tajik security minister, Saidamir Zukhorov. Holding their prisoners in the mountains of Central Asia, the kidnappers demanded safe passage for their supporters from Afghanistan to Tajikistan. By February 16, the president of Tajikistan had agreed to meet with Sodirov and the latter had freed five of the hostages.

Sodirov eventually was captured, tried, and sentenced to death in October 1998 for these, as well as other kidnappings two months earlier. The brother of a warlord named Rezvon Sodirov, he was executed in January 1999.

Feb. 11. Harar, Ethiopia. Two unidentified terrorists, although blocked from entering the Belaneh Hotel, threw grenades into the building, killing two people and wounded eight, including five European tourists. The motive for the attack was unclear and no group claimed responsibility.

Feb. 23. New York, USA. A recently arrived visitor named Ali Hassan Abu Kamal opened fire with a semiautomatic pistol on a group of mostly foreign tourists at an observation deck atop the Empire State Building. (He had just bought the weapon in Florida.) The gunman killed one person, a Danish tourist, and wounded six others; he then took his own life. A note carried by the killer, a Palestinian teacher, claimed his action was punishment against the "enemies of Palestine."

March 21. Tel Aviv, Israel. A suicide terrorist killed himself and four other people by setting off a bomb on the terrace of a Tel Aviv cafe. Forty-eight people were injured.

March 30. Phnom Penh, Cambodia. A grenade attack on a rally by the opposition Khmer Nation Party resulted in eleven dead and 112 wounded. Three grenades were thrown from a passing vehicle as party leader Sam Rainsy led the group's demonstration before the National Assembly. Rainsy was among the wounded.

July 12. Havana, Cuba. A bomb exploded at the Hotel Nacional, injuring three people and causing minor damage. It was the first such incident of any note since the early 1960's. A previously unknown group calling itself the Military Liberation Union claimed responsibility.

Two months later, on September 10, Cuban authorities arrested a Salvadorian accused of carrying out bombings at several Havana hotels. Included among the attacks attributed to him were the Hotel Nacional explosion and bombs placed at four hotels on September 4, one of which resulted in the death of an Italian tourist. Eleven people in all were wounded. Havana authorities claimed the terrorist, named Raul Ernesto Cruz Leon, was a mercenary in the pay of a Miami-based exile group, the Cuban-American National Foundation. Tried and convicted, in March 1999 the court sentenced Cruz Leon to death by firing squad.

July 30. Jerusalem, Israel. Two successive suicide bombings in the Mahane Yehuda market resulted in the deaths of sixteen people, with 178 hurt. The armed wing of the militant Islamic organization Hamas claimed responsibility for the attacks.

Sep. 4. Jerusalem, Israel. Three nail-studded bombs carried by suicide terrorists exploded in the crowded Ben Yehuda pedestrian shopping mall, killing eight people including the suicide bombers and wounding 184. Hamas took credit for the attack.

Sep. 18. Cairo, Egypt. Ten people died and nine were injured, nearly all of them German tourists, in a bus at the famed Egyptian National Museum in the city's center. Two terrorists attacked the bus with bombs and guns. Police arrested brothers named Saber Mohamed Farahat and Mahmoud M. Farahat. Tried and convicted, at the end of October they were sentenced to death and hanged in Cairo on May 30, 1998. Six accomplices were convicted of supplying weapons or bombs and were sentenced to between one and ten years at hard labor.

The attackers went to their deaths unrepentant. Earlier, in October 1993 in Cairo, Saber Farahat had gunned down four tourists, killing three of them. Not tried for that crime due to a finding that he was schizophrenic, through bribery he had come and gone from a government mental hospital since then virtually at will—until the attack at the National Museum.

Sep. 22. Algiers, Algeria. Months of deadly civil strife culminated in a four-hour rampage in a suburb of the capital that resulted in approximately 200 people being killed (the official government figure was eighty-five). Nobody claimed responsibility for this and other attacks They authorities blamed them on the Armed Islamic Group, a rival of the Islamic Salvation. Radical members of those organizations sought the establishment of an Islamic fundamentalist government; their membership reportedly included Muslim militants, restless youths, and common bandits.

Sep. 25. Amman, Jordan. Two Israeli agents attempt to assassinate Hamas leader Khalid Mashaal without success.

Oct. 16. Colombo, Sri Lanka. Tamil rebels set off a truck bomb in the parking lot of a five-star hotel in the heart of the city, causing heavy damage to the building, a neighboring hotel, and the twin towers of the thirty-nine-story trade center, only recently opened. Eighteen people were killed by the blast and subsequent gunfire, with more than 100 injured. In the following ten days, authorities rounded up almost 1,000 Tamil Tiger adherents.

Nov. 1. Sanaa, Yemen. Qatar's ambassador to Yemen, Mohamed bin Hamad al-Khalifa, escaped a kidnapping attempt when his driver took evasive action and sped away from an effort to block the embassy vehicle. The incident was believed to be linked to Sanaa's decision to participate in an economic conference in Qatar, a meeting scheduled to be attended by Israel.

Nov. 12. Karachi, Pakistan. Two gunmen assassinated five foreign oil company workers, emptying their automatic rifles into their car in the streets crowded with school busses and then speeding off. The act was believed to be in retaliation for the conviction in the United States of Mir Aimal Kasi, who had murdered two C.I.A. employees in January 1993 (above). Two days after the Karachi murders, an American jury sentence Kasi to the death penalty, carried out in Virginia on November 2002, by lethal injection.

Nov. 17. Luxor, Egypt. Fifty-eight foreign tourists and four Egyptians died at the hands of six gunmen of the Gama'at al-Islamiyya, or Islamic Group (IG), who shot them down and stabbed them to death at the Hatshepsut Temple in the Valley of the Kings, 350 miles south of Cairo. Twenty-six others, most of them foreigners, were wounded. Using machine guns and antique swords, the attackers emerged suddenly from the ruins wielding death and injury right and left. All six were killed by police as they attempted to escape.

No previous incident in the extremist Islamic group's struggle against the presidency of Hosni Mubarak, once led by the now-imprisoned Sheikh Omar Abdel Rahman, had been nearly so bloody. IG claimed it intended to take hostages in exchange for the release of Rahman, a claim that was not widely credited.

Several weeks later two statements— one vowing to halt attacks on foreign tourists and a second denying that such a decision had been made — were issued in the name of the IG. The split in the organization had begun to surface earlier that year, in July.

Dec. 24. Paris, France. After his capture in Sudan and extradition to France, Ilyich Ramirez Sanchez, the notorious "Jackal," was convicted of kidnapping and murder committed in 1979 and sentenced to prison for life.

1998–1999

At the end of the century, kidnapping had become a widespread terrorist activity — sometimes heavily political in nature, sometimes not. According to one authoritative source,[1] in 1999 at least sixty-eight such incidents took place, not including attacks on embassies or aircraft hijackings.

1998

Jan. 25. Wandhama, Kashmir, India. Armed militants attacked Hindu families on the Pakistani side of the Kashmir Line of Control, killing at least twenty-three men, women, and children. A lone survivor described the terrorists as Urdu-speaking foreigners. The terrorists set fire to a Hindu temple and several homes.

Feb. 3. Athens, Greece. Bombs exploded at two McDonald's restaurants in the suburbs, causing extensive damage. Authorities suspected Anarchists carried out the attacks in retaliation for the arrest of a leader of the Fighting Guerrilla Formation (MAS).

Feb. 9. Tbilisi, Georgia. Attackers armed with a grenade launcher machine gunned from ambush a half mile from his residence President Eduard Shevardnadze's motorcade, opening a ten-minute battle.

One attacker and one bodyguard died, but the president escaped unharmed.

Ten days later, the attackers, who were partisans of the late Georgian president Zviad Gamsakhurdia, kidnapped four UN military observers, holding them until the president met with opposition leaders on February 25. Police tracked down and killed a key figure in the attack on March 31.

Feb. 4. Wuhan, China. A bomb detonated on a bus, killing at least sixteen people and wounding scores. Other vehicles were seriously damaged. Police blamed anti-Communist terrorists.

Feb. 14. Coimbatore, India. Thirteen relatively small bombs exploded in several crowded sections of the city prior to a speech by a Hindu political leader, Lal Krishna Advani. Muslim terrorists were blamed.

Feb. 21. Karachi, Pakistan. Gunmen killed two Iranian engineers near the Iranian Cultural Center. No group acknowledged responsibility.

Feb. 23. London, England. Al-Qaeda leader Osama Bin Ladin and five colleagues signed a *fatwah*, a legal opinion issued by an Islamic scholar, that was published in a London-based Arabic-language news weekly on this date. It calls for an all-out war against America. The long document justifying this action reads in a key sentence: "The ruling to kill the Americans and their allies—civilians and military—is an individual duty for every Muslim who can do it in any country in which it is possible."[2]

March 9. Outside Lahore, Pakistan.
A time bomb exploded on the Chilton Express train en route to Quetta, India. Seven people died and thirty-five were injured. The same day, a bomb went off outside a court building in the province of Sind, wounding sixteen persons.

Pakistan later claimed to have "conclusive" proof India masterminded the two bombings, blaming India's security agency, the Research and Analysis Wing. New Delhi denied the charge.

March 23. Bogotá, Colombia.
Rebels of the *Fuerzas Armadas Revolucionarios de Colombia* (FARC) killed three persons, wounded fourteen, and kidnapped at least twenty-seven, including a high election official, at a roadblock near the city. Within days the rebels had released most of the captives. One escaped, and the last of those being held gained their freedom on April 25.

April 4. Kampala, Uganda.
Bombs exploded at two restaurants, the Nile Grill and the Speke Hotel cafe, killing five persons and wounding at least six others. A government official claimed an organization called the Allied Democratic Forces was responsible.

April 6. Riga, Latvia.
Suspected far right terrorists set off an antipersonnel mine outside the Russian embassy. There were no casualties.

April 10. Istanbul, Turkey.
Two Kurdistan Workers' Party (PKK) terrorists on a motorcycle threw a bomb into a park near the Blue Mosque. Nine persons were injured. Two days later, the police arrested two PKK suspects.

April 18. Udhampur, Kashmir, India.
Muslim extremists attacked villagers, killing twenty-nine persons. A group called *Lashkar-i-Taiba* took responsibility for the massacre.

April 24. Sanaa, Yemen.
A bomb explosion in the courtyard of the *Al-Kheir* mosque after midday prayers killed two persons and wounded twenty-six others.

May 1. Shupiyan, India.
A bomb exploded under a crowded bus, injuring six persons. Muslim militants were suspected in this and three other instances of violence in the following few days. In Kashmir, a total of eighteen Hindus, all but one civilians, were killed by terrorists in the period May 4–6.

May 23. Srinagar, India.
A provincial legislator and five others were injured when a bomb detonated on the outskirts of town. The legislator's armored car was totally destroyed. Pakistani-supported Muslim extremists were suspected.

June 21. Beirut, Lebanon.
PFLP terrorists launched four rocket propelled grenades against the U. S. embassy. No casualties resulted in that attack, but two days earlier, two people died in a car bombing attributed to the PFLP.

June 23. Kashmir, India.
Police indicated that Muslim extremists set off a remote-controlled bomb under the Delhi-bound Shalimar Express train, derailing seven cars and injuring at least thirty-five passengers. Five days later, at Anantnag in Kashmir, a bomb detonated in a park, killing two persons and injuring fifteen or more.

A month afterward, on July 24, a bomb narrowly missed derailing the same express train. It exploded prematurely, not affecting the train's passage but still injuring three people.

July 20. Tavildara, Tajikistan. Unidentified gunmen ambushed and killed three UN observers and their Tajikistani interpreter.

July 26. New Delhi, India. A bomb exploded at the interstate bus terminal, killing two persons and injuring at least eight. The bomb destroyed one bus and caused major damage to six others.

July 28. Doda, Kashmir, India. Suspected Muslim terrorists killed at least eight members of two Hindu families and wounded three others. Eyewitnesses reported that the gunmen lined up the victims and shot them at point blank range.

Aug. 1. Banbridge, Northern Ireland. A 500-pound car bomb exploded outside a shoe store, injuring thirty-five persons and damaging a large number of homes. Authorities, having received a warning telephone call, were evacuating the area when the bomb went off. A splinter group called the Real IRA claimed responsibility.

Aug. 7. Nairobi, Kenya, and Dar es Salaam, Tanzania. Truck bombs exploded almost simultaneously outside two U.S. embassies 400 miles apart, killing at least 300 people. More than 290 persons (the great majority of them Kenyans) died in Nairobi, where the explosion took place virtually in the rear entrance to the embassy, which is located in a crowded part of the city. That blast blew out windows ten blocks away with a force equal to that of over 500 pounds of TNT. As of a week later, more than 300 persons were still hospitalized and about 4,300 had been treated

for injuries. At Dar es Salaam, the death toll came to eleven, with eight-five people wounded. There the suicide bomb truck was unable to penetrate the embassy perimeter because a large water truck blocked the gate.

The two morning attacks caused more casualties than any other terrorist action during the year. They occurred despite a number of security measures in place and caused massive property damage. Two weeks after the bombings, the U. S. government launched cruise missiles against what were described as a terrorist training camp in Afghanistan and what was thought (erroneously) to be a terrorist-sponsored chemical plant in the Sudan.

A U.S. federal grand jury later indicted twenty-two men in connection with the attacks, including Saudi dissident and al-Qaeda leader Osama bin Laden. In October 2001 in New York, four men — a Tanzanian, a Jordanian, a Saudi Arabian, and an American born in Lebanon, Wahid El-Haje — were convicted of complicity in the killings and sentenced to life in prison. Thirteen others, including bin Laden, remained on the U.S. "most wanted" list of terrorists.

Aug. 14. Sri Lanka. The Liberation Tigers of Tamil Eelam (LTTE) hijacked a Dubai-owned cargo ship with twenty-one crew members, including seventeen Indians. The LTTE evacuated the crew before the Sri Lankan Air Force bombed and destroyed the ship. The Indian hostages were released to the International Red Cross on August 19.

Aug. 15. Omagh, Northern Ireland. A large car bomb destroyed the center of the city, leaving at least twenty-eight dead and 300 injured. It was the deadliest attack in Ireland in thirty years. The Real IRA, headed by Michael McKevitt, claimed responsibility. In March 2001, McKevitt was arrested and jailed in Dublin.

Aug. 25. Uganda. Grenades or bombs exploded on three buses in Uganda, killing at least twenty-one people. No one claimed responsibility for any of the blasts. The explosions— two in southern Uganda and one in the north — appeared to have been caused by explosives hidden in stowed luggage.

Aug. 25. Capetown, South Africa. A bomb exploded in the Planet Hollywood restaurant, killing one person and injuring at least twenty-four others; it caused major damage. A group called Muslims Against Global Oppression (MAGO) claimed responsibility, stating that the bomb was in retaliation for the recent U.S. missile attacks on terrorist facilities in Sudan and Afghanistan (above).

Sep. 21. Sukhumi, Georgia. Unknown assailants fired on a bus, wounding four UN military observers.

Oct. 6. Kashmir, India. In Tral, terrorists believed to be Muslim extremists threw a bomb at a vehicle carrying a former political activist, killing him and ten others. Two days later in Srinagar, a grenade attack on a police post resulted in injuries to thirteen people, five of them civilians.

Oct. 18. Machuca, Colombia. The *Ejercito de Liberación National* (ELN) claimed responsibility for a bomb that exploded at the Ocensa pipeline in Antioquia Department. As many as seventy-one people died, with at least 100 others injured. The explosion caused major damage when the spilled oil caught fire and burned nearby houses. The pipeline is jointly owned by the Colombia State Oil Company Ecopetrol and a consortium including U.S., French, British, and Canadian companies.

Nov. 8. Lunda Norte Province, Angola. Fifty or more armed men attacked a Canadian-owned diamond mine, killing six people and wounding eighteen. The assailants also took four foreign workers hostage. UNITA claimed responsibility for the attack, but denied taking hostages.

Nov. 17. Surankot, Kashmir, India. An explosion near the Madana bridge killed four persons and injured several others. Muslim militants were suspected.

The same day at Anantnag, also in Kashmir, a bomb detonated near a crowded bus stand. Three people died and thirty-eight were wounded.

Nov. 24. Sanaa, Yemen. A car bomb exploded near the German embassy, killing two persons and injuring several others.

Dec. 7, Italy. During the week, the Arab Liberation Front (ALF) in Italy sent cakes laced with rat poison to two branches of the Italian news agency ANSA. Two Italian subsidiaries of Swiss Nestle were forced to halt production, costing the company $30 million. According to the ALF, the poisoned cakes were sent to protest Nestle's genetic manipulation of food.

Dec. 28. Habban, Yemen. Armed men kidnapped a group of foreign tourists traveling on the main road from Habban to Aden. The following day, Yemeni security forces undertook a rescue attempt, during which four tourists were killed, and one injured seriously. Yemeni officials reported that the kidnappers belong to the Islamic Jihad.

1999

Jan. 12. Peshawar, Pakistan. Gunmen attacked the home of well-known Afghan moderate Abdul Haq and murdered his wife, young son, and a guard. Haq was not at home. No group claimed responsibility.

The number of people who died from terrorist actions in 1999 declined from 744 the previous year to 233. No one attack causing large-scale casualties took place.[3]

Jan. 17. Sanaa, Yemen. Armed men kidnapped six foreigners, including two children. They demanded the freedom of an imprisoned tribesman. On 2 February the hostages were released unharmed.

The same day, gunmen tried to kidnap two U.S. embassy employees as they drove to work. They managed to escape, however.

In 1999, kidnappings of individuals took place most frequently in Colombia, Nigeria, and Yemen.[3]

Jan. 18. Bangladesh. Two men attempted to assassinate poet Samsur Rahman, an outspoken opponent of Islamic extremism. He was unharmed, but his wife suffered knife wounds. The assailants, a Pakistani and a South African, told police they received financial support from Osama bin Ladin for terrorist training. Police arrested at least forty-seven members of the *Harakat ul-Jihad Islami* (HUJI).

Feb. 8. Komotini, Greece. A bomb exploded near the Turkish Consulate, wounding a member of the police bomb squad. A telephone caller claimed responsibility on behalf of a group called the "Support to Ocalan—The Hawks of Thrace."

Feb. 14. Eastern Nigeria. In a puzzling incident typical of the many kidnappings in various countries during this era, three armed men took captive a Shell Oil employee and his young son, releasing them a day later. No ransom was paid and no one claimed responsibility.

Feb. 14. Kampala, Uganda. On that same day, a pipe bomb exploded at a bar that killed five persons and injured thirty-five others. Most of the casualties were Ugandan nationals. Authorities blamed the attack on an organization called the Allied Democratic Forces (ADF).

Feb. 15. Srinagar, India. In a day filled with violence, suspected Muslim extremists exploded a bomb in a market place, wounding six people, and shot and wounded four other individuals, including three television technicians. The latter, shot in the legs, were warned to broadcast only news—no commentary.

Feb. 16. Western Europe. The Turkish government's announcement that its agents had captured Kurdistan Workers' Party (PKK) leader Abdullah Ocalan in Kenya, where he had thought to find asylum with Greek support. Hundreds if Kurdish protesters erupted in anger, occupying temporarily the Greek embassies or consular offices in Vienna, Leipzig, Bonn, the Hague, Zurich, and London. In addition, they displayed their anger at Kenya by according the same treatment to Kenyan embassies in Paris and Bonn, and to the Kenyan tourist office in Frankfurt. Within hours the protesters released their hostages and left the offices they had occupied. No casualties resulted. The following day, however, when some 200 Kurds broke into the Israeli consulate in Berlin armed with clubs, guards shot and killed three of the protesters and wounded another fifteen.

Ocalan had been on the run since the 1980's. In June, a Turkish court sentenced him to death by hanging for treason and other crimes.

Feb. 28. Lusaka, Zambia. Sixteen bombs exploded in and around the city. One at the Angolan embassy killed one person and damaged the building. Others detonated near water mains and power lines, injuring two persons and causing major damage. Bomb experts detonated five more bombs and defused two others. No one claimed responsibility.

March 25. Skopje, Macedonia. About 200 protesters occupied the U.S. embassy compound. Armed with rocks and Molotov cocktails, they set fire to several vehicles and caused major damage to the exterior of the building. The protesters did not gain entry into the embassy, and police eventually dispersed them.

March 26. Athens, Greece. Several hundred Greek and Serbian protesters broke into the British embassy and entered the ambassador's residence, injuring three guards and causing property damage.

March 27. Peshawar, Pakistan. Unidentified gunmen assassinated Mohammed Jehanzeb, secretary to Taliban opponent Haji Qadir. Qadir was the brother of Afghan moderate Abdul Haq, whose wife and son were murdered in Peshawar in January (above).

March 28. Anantnag, Kashmir, India. Police reported suspected Muslim extremists threw a grenade into a crowd, injuring at least twenty-eight persons.

April 12. Bucaramanga, Colombia. Armed men of the National Liberation Army (ELN) hijacked an Avianca Airlines Fokker 50 flight en route to Bogotá, forcing it to land at a remote northern airstrip on the Magdalena River. All of the passengers were herded into jungle. The following day six hostages were released, three more in mid-April, and an additional seven on May 7. The ELN released eight more hostages in June, seven in September, and the lone American on October 2, nearly six months after his capture.

As government and guerrilla leaders were to begin talks on ending the civil war, the hijacking and kidnapping was seen possibly as a means to strengthen the rebels hand at the bargaining table. It was the third such incident in Colombia, other hijackings (to Cuba) coming in 1980 and 1982, and a military cargo plane was hijacked in 1992.

April 20. Rajauri, Kashmir, India. A bomb exploded in a goldsmith shop, killing five people and injuring forty-seven. No one claimed responsibility.

April 21. Voinjama, Liberia. Unidentified gunmen crossed the border from Guinea and kidnapped the visiting Dutch ambassador, first secretary of Norway, European Union representative, and from Guinea seventeen aid workers. The hostages were released later that day. Eyewitnesses said the assailants were members of the militia groups.

April 27. Athens, Greece. A bomb exploded at the Intercontinental Hotel, killing one person and injuring another. The beginning of NATO air strikes in Serbia set off almost daily anti-U.S. demonstrations, some of which were violent.

June 7. Burgos and Barcelona, Spain. Authorities safely defused a letter bomb sent to an Italian diplomat in Burgos and another sent to the Italian consulate in Barcelona. The following day, in Zaragoza, yet another letter bomb sent to the Italian consulate was disarmed. The police suspected the Italian Red Brigades (BR).

June 9. Baghdad, Iraq. A car bomb exploded next to a bus carrying members of the exiled Iranian opposition group *Mujahedin-e-Khalq* (MEK). It killed seven members and injured twenty-three others, including Iraqi civilians. Officials of the MEK, itself a practitioner of terrorist tactics, suspected the Iranian government was responsible.

June 22. Julpaiguri, India. The United Liberation Front of Assam, supposedly with the backing of Pakistan's intelligence service, claimed responsibility for a bomb set off at the railroad station that killed ten people and injured eighty.

June 29. East Timor, Indonesia. Unidentified armed militants attacked an outlying UN mission. Twelve persons were injured.

July 9. Sukhumi, Georgia. A bomb exploded outside the UN observer mission in Georgia, causing minor damage. Authorities discovered and defused a second bomb nearby. No one claimed responsibility.

July 23. Munich, Germany. An unidentified terrorist threw a bomb into a Turkish travel agency, injuring two persons and causing minor damage. Police authorities suspected the attack was connected with the June conviction in a Turkish court of PKK terrorist leader Abdullah Ocalan (above).

Aug. 4. Occra Hills, Sierra Leone. In the midst of deadly civil strife, an Armed Forces Revolutionary Council (AFRC) faction kidnapped a group of thirty-three people, many of them UN representatives from several different countries. The group also included a local bishop, two journalists, and sixteen Sierra Leoneans. The rebels demanded the release of their leader

Johnny Paul Koroma, who was briefly head of state from 1997 to February 1998. The AFRC faction released two of their captives the following day and the rest on August 10. Also released at that time, Koroma had been imprisoned in eastern Sierra Leone by the succeeding military regime.

Aug. 14. Dina, Pakistan. A bomb exploded in a van, killing six persons and injuring fourteen others. No group claimed responsibility.

Aug. 21. Dire Dawa, Ethiopia. Suspected *al-Ittihaad al-Islami* operatives detonated a mine beneath a train carrying 400 Djiboutian nationals. The explosion severely wounded two Ethiopian conductors, destroyed one locomotive, and caused extensive damage to the railway line, shutting it down for four days. No one claimed responsibility.

Aug. 23. Caracas, Venezuela. A small bomb exploded outside the Colombian consulate, causing minor damage, but no injuries. Security men defused a second explosive device at the consulate. Police located and safely defused a bomb found on the first floor of Credival Tower, the building housing the Colombian embassy. The Tupamaros claimed responsibility.

Sep. 29. Srinagar, India. Unidentified terrorists threw grenades at a government building, killing one police officer and causing undetermined damage. The *Harakat ul-Mujahidin* (HUM) claimed responsibility.

Oct. 1. Bangkok, Thailand. Five Burmese students armed with AK-47 automatic rifles stormed the Burmese embassy, taking eighty-nine persons hostage. The group — the "Vigorous Burmese Student Warriors" — demanded the release of all political prisoners held in Burma. The following day the hostages were released unharmed and the terrorists were flown to the Burmese border. (Their lot was to land up eventually in the Htam Hin refugee camp in Burma.)

Nov. 11. Pathancot, India. A bomb exploded in a third class carriage of the Punjab Express bound for New Delhi, killing thirteen persons and injuring some fifty others. No one claimed responsibility, but groups seeking independence for Kashmir had bombed trains in the area in the past.

This was noted as the eighteenth time in 1999 that Indian Railways has been subjected to terrorist attack.

Dec. 18. Colombo, Sri Lanka. President Chandrika Kumaratunga was wounded in the eye and thirty-eight people were killed in a suicide bombers attack at an election rally. (See following for an account of another suicide attack, in January 2000.)

Dec. 24. Cali, Colombia. A bomb exploded outside the Colombo-American cultural center, causing a number of minor injuries and damage to the building. A group calling itself the Colombian Patriotic Resistance claimed responsibility; police indicated, however, that the National Liberation Army (ELN) carried out the attack.

Dec. 24. Kathmandu, Nepal. Five heavily armed Islamic terrorists reportedly seeking independence for Kashmir hijacked an Indian Airlines Airbus carrying 189 passengers and eleven crew members en route from Kathmandu to New Delhi. After refueling in Pakistan, the plane was diverted to Dubai, United Arab Emirates. There the hijackers released twenty-seven hostages, along with the body of one hostage they had murdered. They then forced the plane to fly to Kandahar, Afghanistan. There they made a series of shifting demands, including the release of thirty-six terrorists imprisoned in India. On the last day of the year, the Indian Government agreed to release three prisoners, including the centerpiece of the hijackers demands, a Muslim cleric named Maulana Masood Azharin. In exchange, the plane and remaining hostages were released later that day.

On January 7, 2000, Indian authorities announced that the hijackers were Pakistanis and arrested four Pakistanis in Bombay as accomplices. Pakistan, in turn, denied the charge, claiming that India was trying to depict Pakistan in world eyes as a terrorist state.

Notes

1. US Dept. of State, *Patterns of Global Terrorism, 1999.* Apr. 2000,1.

2. Full text in http://www.ict.org.il/articles/fatwah.htm.

3. US Dept. of State, *Patterns of Global Terrorism, 1999,* Apr. 2000, 1.

2000–2001

"Yesterday we worried about retail acts of terror — assassinations, bombings, and hijackings.... Tomorrow we may be faced with terrorist mass weapons — nuclear, chemical, and biological — capable of destroying entire cities and more."[1]

2000

Jan. 5. Colombo, Sri Lanka. At least eleven people died and twenty-nine were wounded when a suicide bomber set off an explosion near the office of Prime Minister Sirimavo Bandaranaike. She was not in her office at the time. No one claimed responsibility for the blast. Officials said the bomber, whom they believed to be a woman, was walking past the prime minister's office. When guards stopped her for questioning, she touched off the blast.

Two weeks earlier, on December 18, 1999, a suicide bomber from the separatist Liberation Tigers of Tamil Eelam blew herself up at a campaign rally for President Chandrika Kumaratunga (Mrs. Bandaranaike's daughter). At least thirty-eight people were killed and as many as 100 wounded, including Mrs. Kumaratunga.

Jan. 27. Iturreta, Spain. Unidentified terrorists set fire to a Citroen car dealership, destroying twelve vehicles and causing damage to the building. Police said the attack bore the hallmark of the Basque separatist ETA.

On February 8, a similar attack was carried out by suspected ETA members on a Citroen dealership in Amorebieta. The business was destroyed by fire.

Jan. 29. Araquita, Colombia. Suspected Revolutionary Armed Forces of Colombia (FARC) or National Liberation Army (ELN) rebels bombed a section of the Cano-Limon pipeline, causing major damage and suspending oil production for three days.

Five days later, on February 3, terrorists bombed a section of the Cano-Limon pipeline, causing major damage, including an oil spill, and halting production temporarily.

On February 8 at Campo Hermoso, suspected ELN guerrillas bombed an oil pipeline owned by Canadian, British, and Colombian interests. The attack caused extensive damage, an oil spill, and a forest fire.

The largest number of terrorist incidents during the year 2000 came, somewhat surprisingly, in Colombia, mainly associated with attacks on pipe lines (186 total) and India, beset with the Kashmir question (63).[2]

Feb. 27. New Delhi, India. A bomb exploded at a railroad station, injuring eight persons and causing major damage.

Indian authorities suspected Kashmiri or Sikh terrorists.

May 1. Makeni, Sierra Leone. Revolutionary United Front (RUF) terrorists attacked a UN mission, killing five UN peacekeepers and took captive more than 300 UN personnel throughout the country. On May 15, the RUF militants released 139 hostages at Foya, and thirteen days later, at the Liberian border, the freed the remaining captives.

The RUF's attacks continued. On May 25, a car bomb in Freetown blamed on the RUF killed two people. On June 6, additional UN peacekeeping troops were taken in Freetown and held prisoner temporarily.

May 15. Chabran, India. A land mine exploded, killing Kashmir's power minister and four other government employees. Their vehicle was destroyed. No one claimed responsibility.

May 23. Kashmir, India. Militants fired six grenades at the civil secretariat building, killing one civilian and injuring three others. No group acknowledged responsibility.

June 8. Athens, Greece. Two gunmen ambushed and killed the British embassy defense attaché, Brigadier Stephen Saunders. The leftist 17 November group acknowledged responsibility. It was the twenty-third assassination attributed to that organization, which emerged in December 1975 with the slaying of Richard Welch, the U.S. CIA head in Athens (above). No member of November 17 had ever been arrested.

June 8. Colombo, Sri Lanka. A suicide bomber assassinated Industry Minister C. V. Gooneratne, himself, and twenty-four others, including the minister's wife.

The attack took place near the capital city as the nation marked its first War Heroes Day. Dozens were wounded. The bomber, believed to be a Tamil Tiger separatist, walked up to the minister, embraced him, and set off the bomb. Police arrested four suspects.

Aug. 10. Srinagar, India. A remote-controlled car bomb exploded, killing nine persons and injuring twenty-five. Four cars were damaged. Eight police officers were killed and five journalists were among the wounded. The group *Hizbul Mujahedeen* claimed responsibility.

Aug. 14. Pulwama, India. Terrorists threw a grenade at a bus; the explosion injured fourteen passengers. No one claimed responsibility.

Sep. 7. Pamlap, Guinea. Suspected Revolutionary United Front terrorists kidnapped three Catholic missionaries, all foreigners. Two of the three captives escaped three months later.

Sep. 15. Colombo, Sri Lanka. A suicide bomber, thought to be a Tamil Tiger, killed himself and six others in an apparent effort to disrupt campaigning for the following month's elections. At least twenty-five people were injured. The bomb blast came at the entrance to Colombo's main eye hospital as a security guard was performing a routine check.

Following this attack, government spokesmen announced that more than 60,000 people had died in Sri Lanka's seventeen-year ethnic conflict.

Sep. 17. Macenta, Guinea. Unidentified rebels attacked and killed a UN refugee agency employee and kidnapped another person. No one immediately claimed responsibility, but the RUF was suspected.

Oct. 1. Dushanbe, Tajikistan. Unidentified terrorists detonated two bombs in a Christian church, killing seven persons and injuring seventy. The church was founded by a Korean-born U.S. citizen; most of those killed and wounded were Korean nationals. No group claimed responsibility.

Oct. 2. Kitgum, Uganda. Lord's Resistance Army terrorists shot and killed an Italian priest as he drove to church. No one else was injured.

Oct. 3. Muttur, Sri Lanka. A Tamil Tiger suicide bomber killed a Muslim parliamentary candidate, Mohammed Baithullah, who was departing a campaign stop. Nineteen others died. The dozens of wounded were taken to local hospitals. Baithullah had been a high-ranking police official and had previously been the target of assassins.

Oct. 12. Aden, Yemen. In what might best be characterized as an act of war rather than a terrorist attack, the U.S. Navy destroyer USS *Cole* was heavily damaged when a small boat loaded with explosives blew up alongside it in port. Seventeen sailors were killed and thirty-nine injured in a suicide assault that set the stage for the attack on the United States proper eleven months later. Osama bin Laden and members of his al-Qaeda terrorist network were believed responsible.

Oct. 13. Lombok, Indonesia. A powerful bomb damaged the offices of the PT Newmont Nusa Tenggara Mining Company, an international firm registered in Indonesia and jointly owned by Indonesian, U. S,, and Japanese interests. No one claimed responsibility.

Oct. 13. Sanaa, Yemen. A small bomb explosion in the compound of the British Embassy caused no injuries.

Oct. 19. Colombo, Sri Lanka. A suicide bomber detonated the explosives he was wearing near the town hall, killing four persons and wounding twenty-three others. The Liberation Tigers of Tamil Eelam (LTTE) were thought to be responsible.

Nov. 19. Amman, Jordan. Israeli Vice Consul Yoram Havivian was wounded but survived a drive-by shooting as he entered his automobile early on a Sunday morning. Two different terrorist groups claimed responsibility for the attempted assassination.

Nov. 27. Barcelona, Spain. Basque separatist ETA terrorists shot to death former Socialist health minister Ernest Lluch as he returned to his home late in the evening and stepped from his automobile. Almost immediately thereafter, a car bomb exploded 300 meters from the scene, designed apparently as a diversion.

According to government sources, ETA had killed forty-eight people in Barcelona and its province, including Lluch, since June 1975, when they committed their first attack.[2]

Nov. 27. Santiago, Chile. A bomb exploded in front of the Colombian Embassy, causing property damage. No one was injured. No group claimed responsibility.

Dec. 1. India. In separate incidents that took place in Pattan and Srinagar, grenades thrown in the street at security vehicles resulted in fifteen bystanders being wounded. The same day, in Udhampur terrorists broke into the home of a village defense committee member and murdered four children, injuring two others. No group claimed responsibility for any of the attacks.

Dec. 5. Amman, Jordan. In the second attack in two weeks, armed assailants shot and wounded an official of the Israeli embassy — Shlomo Razabi, an administrative employee. He, his wife, and an embassy security officer were leaving a supermarket when the drive-by shooting occurred. An Amman group called The Movement for the Struggle of the Jordanian Islamic Resistance claimed responsibility. (It was also one of the two organizations claiming to have made the attempt in November on the Israeli vice consul. See above.)

Dec. 7. India. In Kupwara, armed militants threw a grenade at a bus stop, injuring twenty-four people. The same day, a bomb exploded near a mosque in Shopian, injuring thirty-one persons, and a bomb blast at Gohlan killed one and wounded one. Two days later, a bomb exploded in Neelum Valley, killing three persons. In none of these incidents did a person or organization claim responsibility.

Dec. 12. India. Two assaults, mostly on civilians, were ascribed to the Pakistani *Jaish-e-Mohammed* (JEM). A grenade thrown at an outdoor marketplace in Chadoura resulted in injury to sixteen people, including four police officers. In Qamarwari, a police vehicle was destroyed by a remote-controlled bomb, killing five policemen and injuring five civilians. The JEM, or Army of Mohammed, claimed responsibility.

Dec. 25. Srinagar, India. A car bomb exploded at the main gate of a military base, killing nine persons, including three civilians, and injuring twenty-three civilians. The JEM and Kashmir-based *Jamiat-ul-Mujahedin* claimed responsibility.

Dec. 30. Manila, Philippines. A bomb, likely planted by the Moro Islamic Liberation Front, exploded in a plaza across the street from the U.S. embassy. Nine persons were injured.

2001

"On September 11, 2001, the United States suffered its bloodiest day on American soil since the American Civil War [1861-65], and the world experienced the most devastating international terrorist attack in recorded history."[3]

Jan. 5. Srinagar, India. A hand grenade thrown at a police post fell short but still caused injury to four policemen and twenty-three other persons. No group claimed responsibility for the attack.

Jan. 17. Srinagar, India. Six members of the *Lashkar-i-Taiba* (LT) militant Pakistani group were killed by police when they tried to take control of the airport.

Jan. 21. Kashmir, India. In the town of Rajpura, the explosion of a thrown grenade killed three people and injured twenty others. At Jammu, a bomb exploded near the headquarters of the National Conference Party, wounding six people. No one claimed responsibility in either instance.

The following day, in Kareri, a public bus ran over a land mine. Six people were killed and twenty-four were injured, all but ten of the casualties were civilians.

Jan. 29. Lombok, Indonesia. A bomb exploded at the office of the American firm Newmont Mining Corporation, causing damage but no casualties. No group claimed responsibility.

Feb. 2. Cesar and Auraca, Colombia. A bomb explosion at Cesar caused major damage to the railroad tracks supplying coal to the U. S. multinational firm Drummond. In Auraca the same day, six bombs exploded along the Cano Limon-Covenas pipeline. The blasts derailed a train and brought a halt to the pumping of crude oil. In both instances, the FARC was believed to be responsible.

Feb. 9. Rajauri, India. Unknown terrorists set fire to several homes, killing a reported fifteen people.

March 4. London, England. A car bomb exploded at midnight outside the British Broadcasting Corporation's main production studios. No injuries were reported.

March 28. Kefar Sava, Israel. A suicide bomber from a wing of Hamas set off a bomb at a bus stop, killing two people and wounding four others.

April 6. Kholargas, Greece. Members of the previously unheard-of Anarchic Attack Group claimed responsibility for setting on fire the offices of two foreign bank branches.

April 13. Baramula, India. A grenade thrown in the direction of a police vehicle missed and exploded in a crowded bazaar, wounding sixteen people. Elsewhere in Kashmir state that day, armed terrorists assassinated a local political leader as he returned home from the mosque. No organization claimed responsibility for either action.

April 22. Kfar Sava, Israel. A Hamas suicide bomber detonated explosives near a bus stop, killing one person and injuring sixty.

April 22. Sopur, India. A bomb exploded in a vegetable cart in a crowded marketplace, injuring a policeman and nine civilians. The blast caused considerable damage. The following day, at Kishtwar, a bomb blast at a bus stop wounded five persons. In neither case did anyone claim responsibility.

May 2. Dharan, Saudi Arabia. At the Saad Medical Center, a letter bomb opened by a foreign doctor, an American, exploded causing severe injury. No group claimed responsibility.

May 5. Herat, Afghanistan. A bomb blast near a mosque killed twelve people and injured twenty-eight. The nearby Iranian consulate was damaged, as were twelve parked cars. There was no claim to responsibility for the action.

May 26. Palawan, Philippines. The Abu Sayyaf Group (ASG) kidnapped twenty people, including three foreigners, at a beach resort and took them to the Sulu Archipelago. At month's end, three captives were released, but on June 2 the ASG raided a hospital and took some 200 more prisoners. As the weeks went by, a few were released from time to time. During that month the terrorists beheaded an American prisoner. At year's end, two of the original twenty captives still remained in the hands of the ASG.

May 29. Newe Daniyyel, West Bank. Members of the al-Aqsa Martyrs Brigade attacked an Israel settlement, killing two people and wounding four others.

June 1. Tel Aviv, Israel. Hamas claimed responsibility for an explosion in the evening in front of a popular nightclub that caused heavy casualties. A suicide bomber approached the establishment and abruptly set off a blast that resulted in the deaths of twenty people and injury to well over 100.

June 2. Kupwara and Tsrar Sharif, India. In the first town, a bomb exploded at a crowded bus stop; two people died and thirty-two others suffered injuries. Six days later, on June 8 at Tsrar Sharif, an explosion set off near a mosque killed four persons and wounded fifty-four others. In neither case did any group claim responsibility.

June 22. Ruvumu, Burundi. Armed terrorists seized a van belonging to a British relief organization, killing one person and kidnapping three. A search effort located the three captives unharmed. No organization claimed responsibility for the attack.

July 21. Sheshang, India. A bomb explosion killed eight people, including two police officers, and wounded fifteen civilians. The following day at Chirji, terrorists shot and killed fifteen people; at Chatroo, another group kidnapped five people. Unknown assailants carried out all of the acts.

July 24. Colombo, Sri Lanka. A devastating Tamil Tiger — the Liberation Tigers of Tamil Eelam — suicide attack on the international civil airport and the military air base shocked the Sri Lankan government. Twelve people were killed and nine wounded. The terrorists destroyed thirteen aircraft, ammunition dumps, and oil storage depots.

Aug. 9. Jerusalem, Israel. A Hamas suicide bomber walked into a busy restaurant and set off his ten-pound explosive device, killing fifteen people and wounding more 130 others.

Aug. 10. Kashmir, India. A cycle of localized but extreme violence began that lasted several days. At Narbal, a bomb explosion killed one person and wounded five; at Srinagar, a bomb blast claimed the same casualty totals — one dead and five injured; elsewhere in Kashmir, an explosion at a Muslim shrine claimed six lives, with twenty-four other persons wounded.

Three days later at Damhalhanjipora, terrorists fired on the Kashmir tourism minister's home, using rifle grenades in addition to other firearms. They killed four security guards. The following day, August 14, at Riasi, terrorists used a particularly diabolical method of attack: They shot and killed three people and then placed armed hand grenades under their bodies before fleeing. Two more people died when they sought to examine the victims.

In none of these incidents did a group admit responsibility.

Sep. 1. Nimule, Uganda. Terrorists waylaid a vehicle belonging to the Catholic Relief Services and killed five people, wounding two others. Authorities believed the Lords' Resistance Army was responsible.

Sep. 11. New York, Washington, and Pennsylvania, USA. In one of the worst days of international terrorist attacks seen over the past century anywhere in the world, four separate but coordinated airplane hijackings resulted in the deaths of approximately 2,800 people and massive destruction of property, especially in New York. Al-Qaeda operatives, numbering nineteen in all, on a suicide mission crashed two fully fueled jetliners — huge flying incendiary bombs, in effect — into the Twin Towers of New York's World Trade Center; another jetliner crashed into the Pentagon in Washington, headquarters and nerve center of U. S. military forces. Only the terrorists in the fourth jetliner were unsuccessful. They were prevented almost certainly by the passengers from crashing that aircraft in Washington, likely on the White House.

As noted by the observer quoted

Top: Washington, DC, USA. Aerial view of the Pentagon following the terrorist attack on September 11, 2001, using American Airlines Flight no. 77. Library of Congress LC-DIG-ppmsca-02093. *Bottom:* New York City, Manhattan skyline, September 11, 2001, the terrorist attack on the Twin Towers underway. Library of Congress LC-A05-A01.

above at the beginning of this section, it was the bloodiest single day on American soil since the devastating Civil War that had ended 136 years previously. In New York, where the death toll was the highest, citizens of seventy-eight different countries died in the Twin Towers crashes, explosions, and final collapse of the two buildings.

The tragic drama began with the early morning hijacking of American Airlines flight #11 from Boston, bound for Los Angeles. Five al-Qaeda terrorists took over the aircraft, using box cutters and knives as weapons. One or more of them (a number had been partially trained earlier in American commercial flight schools) at 8:45 am flew the plane directly into the upper floors of the North Tower of the World Trade Center.

Five al-Qaeda terrorists commandeered United Airlines flight #175, also leaving from Boston with Los Angeles as its destination. Eighteen minutes after the first plane crashed into its target, this aircraft was flown straight into the South Tower. Both tower structures soon completel'v — and unexpectedly—collapsed in upon themselves, trapping or crushing large numbers of people, including fire and police department rescuers. A count in 2003 set the Twin Towers death total a 2,792; thousands more suffered injuries. The twin skyscrapers were utterly destroyed.

Shortly after 9:30 am that same morning, another hijacked flight, American Airlines flight #77, just departed from Washington's Dulles airport, headed for Los Angeles. Soon after takeoff, al-Qaeda operatives took control, using box cutters and knives, and flew the airplane into the Pentagon in Washington. The aircraft impacted at close to 9:40 am. The death toll there came to 189, with scores injured; considerable damage resulted, as well.

The fourth airplane-cum-bomb involved, United Airlines flight #93, scheduled for the trip from Newark, NJ, to Los Angeles, did not make it to Washington. There quite possibly the White House was the al-Qaeda target, although no one knows for sure. After the hijacking had taken place, passengers contested control of the aircraft with the four terrorists aboard. The plane evidently then went out of control, crashing at 10:10 am at Stony Creek township, Pennsylvania, many miles from its target. Forty-four passengers died.

High U. S. government officials almost immediately indicated that Osama Bin Laden and his al-Qaeda network were the prime suspects and that they considered the United States from that point on in a state of war against international terrorism. By October 7, U. S. attacks on al-Qaeda training camps in Afghanistan had begun.

Thus ends in 2001 this account of almost exactly 100 years of terror worldwide— September 1901 to September 2001. These pages begin and end, it happens, in the United States, from the McKinley assassination to 9/11, and cover much — but nowhere near everything— that occurred on the international terrorism front in between.

Notes

1. Dershowitz, *Why Terrorism Works*, 9-10.

2. U. S. Department of State, *Patterns of Global Terrorism*— App. F: International Terrorist Incidents, 2000.

3. U.S. Amb. Francis X. Taylor, *Patterns of Global Terrorism: 2001*, v. Note that 2,343 American servicemen died in the Japanese attack December 7, 1941, on Hawaii, then a U.S territory.

Terrorism Examined

"The brutality of the recent assassinations... fills every sound mind with a sense of horror and repulsion. But their utter futility is not so often mentioned."
New York Times, June 22, 1922

During the century only recently concluded, the world experienced mayhem and destruction on an enormous, unprecedented scale: Two World Wars were fought, one of which was truly almost global in scope; nations engaged in the contest of a long, danger-filled Cold War between two superpowers with nuclear arsenals; innumerable comparatively small "brushfire" regional wars and localized clashes took place. It was a blood-soaked globe over much of its surface, both land and sea. To put casualty figures in a twentieth century frame, in the World Wars the death toll ran to the millions of men. About 420,000 French and German troops died in the single (if prolonged) 1916 Battle of Verdun in France. The 1945 fight for the Pacific island of Okinawa cost the lives of more than 100,000 Japanese troops. Over 50,000 American soldiers died in each of the undeclared Korean War, 1950 to 1953, and the extended U. S. intervention in Vietnam that ended in 1972. As tragic as these figures are, the politically aware public of all nations recognized such statistics for what they represent: lamentable human losses on a grand scale, but losses of life incurred while countries fought conflicts between armed forces in wars as defined historically — armed men against armed men, not armed terrorists against unarmed, innocent civilians.

Even with the widespread carnage and ruin those major wars and the many other conflicts the century brought, individual acts of terrorism frequently captured the headlines and caught the close attention of opinion leaders, as well as the general public. This was increasingly the case over the last third of the 1900's, in part due to spectacular advances in mass communications. Overnight (or even more promptly) news stories reporting outrage after outrage came to suggest strongly that many individual terrorist movements were powerful, pervasive dangers. The popular impact of terrorism over time heightened additionally with advances in weaponry, explosives, and transportation, plus the increased use of suicide tactics in the delivery of lethal vehicular bombs, especially as the century drew to a close. Terrorists deliberately perpetrated violence on civilian targets on as large a scale and in as spectacular a fashion as could be contrived.

Terrorist movements thus were able more and more to attract public attention, often beyond what might have been expected, given the usually small scale of the violence they wrought in comparison with the century's many wars and insurrections.

In 1901, the educated, concerned public was shocked by the fatal wounding of an American president, obviously a high government official, in New York state. That public was horrified three generations later by the use, again in the United States, of loaded airliners as suicide flying bombs against randomly chosen civilians in New York City, Washington, D.C., and rural Pennsylvania, resulting in close to 3,000 deaths in one morning. Individual acts of terrorism became increasingly baneful and spectacular. Terrorists were able to grab print and electronic headlines with even greater frequency.

Virtually all active terrorists are highly motivated; they generally dedicate themselves to a cause (usually political) to the point of fanaticism and beyond. As seen by one scholar,[1] the motives of practitioners of terror, especially recently, include a feeling of alienation, a sense of humiliation, and dedication to a struggle for ethno-religious supremacy. These impulsions—and likely others difficult to identify or for most to identify with—have brought on the spread of violence directed often randomly and usually against defenseless civilians.

Even noting the presence and granting the validity of these various factors, questions arise, questions reflected in the 1922 editorial comment quoted at the beginning of this chapter about the "utter futility" of the assassinations cited.[2] What did twentieth century terrorism accomplish? What did it avail politically oriented organizations to use terrorist tactics? To what extent, that is, did terrorist campaigns succeed in general in their practitioners' aims over the century beginning in 1901?

The question invites debate and engenders disagreement. Central to any discussion of terrorism in this context especially is the complicated matter of definitions (see Chapter 1). First and foremost, terrorism should be viewed, at least for the sake of discussion on this point, as *not* equating with guerrilla warfare. The special case of officially sponsored state terrorism might be considered in that same light. Those two areas of conflict are no less worthy of study and consideration, but they involve irregular forces opposing military and police establishments in the case of guerrilla action, and in the second instance, a ruling political group's police forces and military being employed ruthlessly against actual or potential rivals to an established regime. Twentieth century success eventually attended the guerrilla efforts of, among others, Mao Zedong in China, Fidel Castro in Cuba, and Ho Chi Minh in Vietnam. Nationalist movements, especially, often enough during the century demonstrated the willingness to exercise the requisite patience to wait until an opportune moment came for a guerrilla group to face the regular military in direct engagements of arms. They thereby in numerous instances achieved success. State terrorism as practiced by Tsarist and Stalinist Russia and Nazi Germany, as prime examples, indeed achieved the regime's aim -- promoting the political interests of given iron-fisted ruler -- for varying but substantial periods of time. A substantial number of established twentieth century governments, backed by the control mechanisms and power of a nation state, utilized terror tactics quite deliberately, often in dreadfully efficient ways, to stamp out political opposition.

Guerrilla warfare and state-sponsored repression thus were exercised successfully during the period 1901–2001.

Armed action such as conventional or guerrilla warfare or state-sponsored repression was not, however, available to small bands of aggrieved or visionary revolutionaries during the past century. Their tactics necessarily centered on hit-and-run or suicidal violence, occasionally on a large

scale, directed mainly and quite deliberately at civilian targets. Such practitioners
of terror in the past 100 years viewed their
efforts (realistically) as the only means of
an asymmetric warlike conflict open to
them and (unrealistically) as a path to success in reaching their goals or in satisfying
their demands. The world recognized terrorists as assemblages of radicals, often
small in numbers, bent upon overthrowing
the society in which they operated. Such
groups intended to destabilize and eventually supplant existing institutions,
whether coming at the task from the political left or right — or essentially from
nowhere politically in the case of the Anarchists.

Terrorism in this sense of murderous
attacks on civilians further was used in
anti-colonial struggles, engendering
thereby opposing state terrorism, with
most international notice accorded the terrorist attacks. Twentieth century examples
of terroristic struggles in the colonial field
include the Kenyan Mau Mau revolt
against the United Kingdom and Algerian
terrorists pitted against France. Terrorists
tactics also loomed large in disputes between different ethnic groups over contested homelands, including the Armenians in Turkey, but with the Palestinians
and Israelis the clearest illustration of such
a drawn-out conflict. The long campaign
of terror waged by the IRA against Great
Britain, while a contest for political control, had as well overtones of a religious
conflict, as is notably the case in the Middle East.

How much did the twentieth century's various terrorist movements accomplish? What were their chances for
long-term success? In few instances since
1901 can a case be made for terrorism's
achievement of its various goals, as great a
problem and difficulty as the phenomenon
has been — and remains—for the world at
large. Ultimately terrorists fail. One obvi-

ous reasons for this lack of success centers
on their removal from mainstream politics
and their isolation from the vast majority
of the populace. Many terrorist groups —
importantly excluding those originating in
the Middle East — could trace their roots
back to the Anarchists and Social Revolutionaries of the late nineteenth and early
twentieth centuries. Lacking as they did
any kind of a base of popular support, due
in large measure to the unrealistic and un-
workable nature of their proposals, both
Anarchists and Social Revolutionaries re-
sorted to horrendous acts of violence to
attract attention to and thus somehow
promote their ideas. Their bombings and
assassinations, however, met with general
public abhorrence and frequently brought
severe retaliation from the national authorities such as Tsarist Russia's large,
sometimes efficient police apparatus.

Those movements failed — and in
fairly short order in historical terms. The
employment of tactics of violence without
limits alienated the very segment of the
population in which terrorists thought to
build support or to find justification for
their deeds. Groups resorting to violence
against civilians, far from calling favorable
attention to their cause, engaged in a self-
defeating tactic by killing, maiming, and
destroying, often aimlessly. This has taken
place, perversely almost, frequently in the
segment of society that could be of most
assistance over time in advancing the cause
being proposed. Fundamentally, terrorism's underlying conviction that great
power can be achieved through great violence has fallen flat: The one does not follow the other.

To a considerable extent, the imped-
iment of scant public support also hin-
dered the nationalist movements that came
to the fore. A particular case is that of Ireland, where major acts of violence against
Britain occurred at least as early as the
Easter Rising of 1916. The IRA pursued its

course over decades, with more popular backing than, say, Russia's pre-Marxist Social Revolutionaries had; nevertheless, the IRA likely never commanded popular majorities, especially with respect to the Northern Ireland question, an area that remains politically separate from Eire. In such countries as Algeria and South Africa, the aims of terrorist organizations had most of the adult population, if not a majority of the electorate, behind them as to ultimate goals. Members of these and other national liberation groups came to believe that, in light of official opposition, they had no option but to resort to violence. This course of action in turn led in many instances to state terrorism, as well as the rise of far-right terroristic opponents such as France's unofficial OAS.

In the Middle East, terrorist tactics contributed to London's decision to wash its hands of the region's problems following World War II. How much the Stern Gang and the Irgun and the Muslim Brotherhood forced that move, however, or even influenced the timing thereof, is uncertain. The most important factor in the mix undoubtedly was the weakening effect on Britain of its all-out effort to win the 1939–1945 war, this following upon the sacrifices required for victory in the First World War. Palestinian terrorist groups failed to head off the establishment of the Israeli state. Arab armies in turn proved unable to dislodge Israel, once established, in conventional warfare. Following the Arab nations' defeats, the Palestinian pursuit of terrorist tactics equally failed to erase that nation from the map. Even more importantly, those tactics thus far virtually have precluded a peaceful two-nation Israel-Palestinian State solution to the nagging, dangerous problem.

The result globally during the twentieth century therefore has not been success wherever terrorism fiercely reared its ugly head. The convictions have changed that drove — and continue to drive — adherents of given causes to kill and maim and destroy, and to give up their lives for that cause. A number of ideologies and organizations have simply faded away over time. The once-dreaded Anarchists and Russia's Social Revolutionaries and their programs have been relegated to the dusty archives of history, as have the feared state terror organizations of the Soviet Union, Germany of the 1930's and '40's, Iran under the Shah, and a number of other comparable regimes. Those non-state groups were replaced as time marched on during the century by other fanatics espousing nationalist and separatist and ethnic ambitions, as well as by other repressive religious-based national governments. All relied on terror tactics no less than their forerunners in the century. Various violent bands operating in the 1970s and '80s in Europe and Japan are no more, however. New crops of extremists from both ends of the political spectrum, as well as those espousing secular hatred tinged heavily with religion, have made their appearances. Some have come on the scene only briefly; others not. During the latter part of the century, Muslim extremist groups in particular, often well financed and imbued with religious fervor combined with political ambitions, emerged as deadly opponents of world peace except on their own somewhat unclear terms. Al Qaeda's suicide aircraft attack in the United States on September 11, 2001, demonstrated these terrorists' capacity for inflicting grievous harm, whatever their prospects for eventual success on the world scene.

The perpetrators of postmodern terrorism[3] — to a large extent Muslim fanatics acting out their resentment and hatred of the West — have taken the leading place in the world's concern. The danger can indeed exist and preoccupy much of the literate world during a given period of time, notwithstanding the point made many years ago by the *New York Times* editorialist cited above. In the end, however, violence intentionally directed against random civilian targets as a means to influence policies and even, in the instance of recent attacks, to change the basic world view of major nations—to change the course of history, that is—will prove futile. Terrorist assaults are death-dealing and damaging, with tragic results in human terms for many. But with the benefit of historical perspective, practitioners of terrorism can be shown almost never to have accomplished what the fanatics in leadership positions set out to do. By destroying and killing, they antagonized and sickened and angered; they did not persuade; they did not manage often to coerce policy changes. If partially successful in some few cases, typically years of struggle and hardship went by before the practitioners of terror achieved to some extent their aims. Even then, other political, social or economic factors more often than not were crucial in effecting such shifts in policy. Terrorism historically has failed to force the changes its adherents seek.

Notes

1. See Stern, *Terror in the Name of God*, passim. The author also cites a less defined and less convincing factor of messianic history.

2. The "recent assassinations" phrase refers to the shooting by IRA gunmen of retired Field Marshall Henry Wilson in London on June 22 and the murder by right-wing extremists of the former Weimar foreign minister, Walther Rathenau, in Berlin on June 24. See Chapter 4 above.

3. The apt phrase is from Walter Lacquer, "Postmodern Terrorism: New Rules for the Old Game," *Foreign Affairs*, September/October 1996.

Appendix I

Notable Terrorist Organizations

Name	Organized	Country/Area
Abdalla [Note: anti-Castro]	1970s	New York City
*Abu Nidal Organization	1974	Middle East, Int'l
**Abu Sayyaf* Group (ASG)	early 1990s	Philippines
Ação Libertadora Nacional	1967	Brazil
Action Directe (AD)	1979	France. Europe
Action Organization for the Liberation of Palestine	1970	W. Germany
Action pour la Renaissance de la Corse Corsican Resistance Action (ARC)	1967	Corsica
African National Congress (ANC)	1912	South Africa
Afro-American Liberation Army	1970s	Calif., USA
**Al-Aqsa* Martyrs Brigade	1999	W. Bank, Gaza
Al-Asifa	1970s	Europe
Ak-Ittahad al-Islami (AIAI)	early 1990s	Somalia
Alex Boncayao Brigade (ABB)	mid-1980s	Philippines
Alianza Anticomunista Argentina	1970s	Argentina (AAA)
Allied Democratic Forces (ADF)	1995	Congo
Anarchism (not organized formally, by definition)	pre-1901	United States, W. Europe
The Angry Brigade	1976	England
Animal Rights Militia	1980s	United Kingdom
Anti-Imperialist Territorial Nuclei	1995	Italy
Arab Liberation Front	1968	Iraq
Arab Revolutionary Council (see Abu Nidal Organization)		
Argentine Anticommunist Alliance	1974	Argentina
Argentinian Revolutionary (ERP) Workers' Party	1970s	Argentina, Paraguay
Armed Commandos of Liberation	1970s	Puerto Rico
Armed Forces of National Resistance (FARN)	1970s	El Salvador
*Armed Islamic Group (GIA)	1992	Algeria
Armed Vanguard of the Proletariat	1980s	Mexico
Armed Revolution Squads	1980s	Italy
Armée de Liberation Quebecois (ALQ) Quebec Liberation Army	1964	Canada
Armenian Secret Army for the Liberation of Armenia (ASALA)	1975	Lebanon, W. Europe
Army for the Liberation of Rwanda (ALIR)	1994	Congo & Rwanda
**'Asbut al-Ansar* Band of Partisans	1990s	Lebanon
*Aum Supreme Truth (AUM),	1987	Japan

Name	*Organized*	*Country/Area*
Aum Shinriko, Aleph		
Baader-Meinhof Gang (See *Rote Armee Fraktion*)		
Basque Fatherland and Liberty (ETA)	1959	Spain
Euzkadi Ta Askatasuna		
Black Dragon Society	1890s	Japan
Black Hand Society	1908	Serbia, Europe
Black Liberation Army (BLA)	1971	United States
Black Panther Party (BPP)	1966	United States
Black September (BSO	1970	Mid East, Europe
(See also Abu Nidal Organization)		
Boxers	ca. 1900	China
Brigate Rosse, Red Brigades	1968	Italy
[Note: One of 150 Italian terror groups		
at the height of violence.]		
Cambodian Freedom Fighters (CFF)	1998	Cambodia
Carlos group (see *Mohamed Boudia Commando*)		
Cellules Communistes Combattantes	1984	Belgium
Communist Combatant Groups (CCC)		
Comandos Armados de Liberación	(CAL) 1968	Puerto Rico
*Communist Party of Philippines/	1969	Philippines
New People's Army (CPP/NPA)		
Community Irish Republican Army (CIRA)	1994	Ireland
Croation Revolut. Brotherhood (HRB)	1930s	Croatia, Int'l
Hrvatsko Revolucionarno (Ustashi)		
Crypto	1980s	Malaysia
Cuban Action Commandos	late 1960s	United States
Emiliano Zapata Unit	1975	United States
Eritrean Liberation Front (ELF)	1980s	Eritrea
Ejercito de Liberación National (ELN)	1963	Peru, Colombia, Bolivia
National Liberation Army		
Ethniki Organosis Kypriakou Agoniston	1955	Cyprus
(EOKA) Nat. Organiz. of Cypriot Fighters		
Ejercito Popular de Liberación (EPL)	1980	Peru
Ejercito Revolucionario del Pueblo (ERP)	1968	Argentina, El
People's Revolut. Army		Salvador
Farabundo Marti National Liberation Front	1980s	El Salvador
Al-Fatah (The Victory)	1957	Mid East, Int'l
[Note: Merged with PLO in 1968]		
Fatah Revolutionary Council	1974	International
(see Abu Nidal Organization)		
Forces Populares 25 de Abril (FP-25)	1974	Portugal
Free Corps	1920s	Germany
Frente Revolucionario Anti-Fascista	1971	Spain
y Patriota (FRAP)		
Frente Sandinista de Liberación Nacional (FSLN)	1961	Nicaragua
Frente Urbano Zapatista (FUZ)	1970s	Mexico
Front de Liberation de la Bretagne	1980s	France
Armee Revolutionnaire Breton (FLB/ARB0		
Front de Libeation d'Algerie (FLN)	1980s	Algeria
Front de Liberation du Quebec (FLQ)	early 1960s	Canada
Fuerzas Armadas de Liberación Nacional (FALN)	1974	Venezuela
Fuerzas Armadas Revolucionarias de Colombia (FARC)	1966	Colombia
Fuerzas Revolucionarias Armadas	early 1970s	Mexico
del Pueblo (FRAP)		
Al-Gama'a al-Islamiyya (IG) Islamic Group	1970's	Egypt

Name	Organized	Country/Area
Grey Wolves (see *Milliyetci Hareket Partisi*)		
Groupe de Liberation de la Marti- *nique* Martinique Liberation Group	ca.1980	France
Grupo de Resistencia Antifascista Primero de Octubre (GRAPO), First of October Anti-Fascist Group	1975	Spain
Guatemalan Committee of Patriotic Unity	1982	Guatemala
*HAMAS (Islamic Resistance Movement)	1987	West Bank, Israel
Harakat ul-Jihad-I-Isalami (HUJI) Movement of Islamic Holy War	1980	Pakistan, Kashmir
Harakat ul-Jihad-I-Islami/Bangladesh	ca. 1999	Bangladesh
Harakat ul-Mujahidin (HUM) Movement of Holy Warriors)	ca. 1994	Pakistan
Hizballah (Party of God)	1982	Lebanon, Int'l.
Hizbul Mujahedeen (HM)	1989	Kashmir
Industrial Workers of the World (IWW)	ca. 1900	United States
Inner Macedonian Revolutionary Organization (IMRO)	1893	Greece, Balkans
Irgun Zvai Luemi (Irgun, IZL)	????	Palestine
Irish Republican Army (IRA)	1916	Ireland, United Kingdom
Iron Guard	1920s	Romania
Islamic Army of Aden (IAA)	1998	Yemen
*Islamic Movement of Uzbekistan (IMU)	1999	Uzbekistan
Jaish-e-Mohammed (JEM) Army of Mohammed	1994	Pakistan, India
Al-Jihad (Egyptian Islamic Jihad)	1970's	Egypt
Al-Jama'a al-Islamiyyah al-Muqatilah al-Libya (Libyan Islamic Fighting Group)	1995	Libya, Mid East
Japanese Red Army (JRA)	1969	Asia, Lebanon
Jemaah Islamiya (JI)	1997	S.E. Asia
Jewish Defense League (JDL)	1968	New York, Middle East
Justice Commandos of the (JCAG) Armenian Genocide	1975	International
Kahane Chai (Kach), "Kahane Lives"	ca.1991	Israel
Kumpulan Muhahidin Malaysia (KMM)	1995	Malaysia
*Kurdistan Workers' Party (PKK)	1978	Turkey, W. Europe
Lashkar-e-Tayyiba (LT), Army of the Righteous	1989	Pakistan
Lashkar I Jhangvi (LIJ)	1996	Pakistan
*Liberation Tigers of Tamil Eelam (LTTE or Tamil Tigers)	1976	Sri Lanka, India
Lohame Herut Israel (Stern Gang) Fighter for the Freedom of Israel	1940	Palestine
Lord's Resistance Army (LRA)	1989	Uganda, Sudan
Los Macheteros	1976	Puerto Rico
Mau Mau	1950	Kenya
Milliyetci Hareket Partisi Nationalist Action Party (Grey Wolves)	1960s	Turkey, Europe
Mohamed Boudia Commando (Carlos group)	1973	International
Monteneros	early 1970's	Argentina
Moro Islamic Liberation Front (MILF)	1977	Philippines
Movimiento de la Ezquierda *Revolucionaria* (MIR)	1965	Venezuela, Chile, Peru
Movimiento de Liberación Nacional (MLN)—*Tupamaros*	1965	Uruguay

Name	Organized	Country/Area
Movimiento Independencia Revolucionario Armada (MIRA)	1970s	Puerto Rico
Movimiento Revolucionario de Octobre 8 (MR-8)	1960s	Brazil
Movement for the Struggle of the Jordanian Islamic Resistance	1990s	Jordan
Mujahedin-e-Khalk Organization (MEK or MKO)	1960	Iran
Muslim Brotherhood	1928	Egypt, Mid East
National Algerian Movement MNA) *Mouvement National Algérien*	1950s	Algeria
*National Liberation Army (ELN)	1965	Colombia
National Liberation Front (FLN)		Algeria
National Union for the Total Independence of Angola (UNITA0	1966	Angola
New People's Army (NPA)	1969	Philippines
9 June Group [Note: Armenian]	1991	Switzerland
Nippon Sekigun (see JRA)		
November 17 (see Revolutionary Organization 17 November)		
Orange Volunteers (OV)	1998	N. Ireland
Organisation de l'Armée Secrète (OAS)	1961	France, Algeria
*Palestine Islamic Jihad (PIJ)	1970's	Gaza, Syria
*Palestine Liberation Front (PLF)	1970's	Syria
Palestine Liberation Organization (PLO)	1964	Middle East
People Against Gangsterism and Drugs (PAGAD)	1996	South Africa
People's Liberation Army of Kurdistan (ARGK)	early 1990s	Turkey
Popular Democratic Front for the Liberation of Palestine (PDFLP)	1969	Middle East
*Popular Front for the Liberation of Palestine (PFLP — Habash)	1967	Mid East & Int'l
*Popular Front for the Liberation of Palestine — General Command (PFLP -GC)	1968	Middle East & Europe
Proletarian Action Group (GAP)	1960's	Italy
Provisional Irish Republican Army Provos, PIRA	1969	Ireland, United Kingdom
*Al-Qaida, The Base	ca.1988	Middle East, Int'l.
*Real IRA (RIRA)	1998	N. Ireland
Red Hand Defenders (RHD)	1998	N. Ireland
*Revolutionary Armed Forces of Colombia (FARC)	1964	Colombia
*Revolutionary Nuclei (Successor to Revolutionary People's Struggle — ELA) Revolutionary Organization of Socialist Muslims (see Abu Nidal Organiz.)	1995-98	Greece
*Revolutionary Organization 17 November	1975	Greece
*Revolutionary People's Liberation Party/Front (DHKP/C)	1978	Turkey
Revolutionary Proletarian Initiative Nuclei (NIPR)	2000	Italy
Revolutionary United Front (RUF) Guinea	1990s	Sierra Leone, Liberia,
Rote Armee Fraktion (RAF) Red Army Faction (Baader-Meinhof gang)	1967	W. Europe
As Saiqa The Thunderbolt	1966	Syria
*Salafist Group for Call and Combat (GSPC)	1996	Algeria
Sendero Luminoso, Shining Path (SL)	late 1960's	Peru

Name	*Organized*	*Country/Area*
Siahkal	1961	Iran
Stern Gang—See *Lohame Herut Israel.*		
Socialist Revolutionary Party (SR)	1901	Russia
Symbionese Liberation Army (SLA)	1973	United States
Tamil Tigers (see Liberation Tigers of		
Tamil Eelam)		
The Tunisian Combatant Group (TCG)	2000	Tunisia
Tupac Amaru Revolutionary Movement (MRTA)	1983	Peru
Tupamaros—See *Movimiento de Liberación Nacional*		
Turkish Hizballah	late 1980s	Turkey
Turkish People's Liberation Army (TPLA)	????	Turkey
Ulster Defense Association/Ulster	1971	N. Ireland
Freedom Fighters (UDA/UFF)		
*United Self-Defense Forces/Group	1997	Colombia
of Colombia (AUC)		
Ustashi (see Croation Revolutionary Brotherhood)		
Vanguardia Popular Revolucionaria	1960s	Brazil
Weathermen (Weather Underground Orgaznization)	1969	United States
Zapata (see *Frente Urbano Zapatista*)		
Al-Zulfikar	1980s	Pakistan

* Asterisk denotes organizations designated as of 2003 by the U. S. Secretary of State as "Foreign Terrorists Organizations" pursuant to U. S. law.

Note: The above, compiled from various sources, necessarily presents a selected, abbreviated listing of twentieth century terrorist organizations—other than those on the U. S. government's roster of such organizations as defined by law. A selection must be made due to the large numbers that existed, past and present, and their often fleeting organizational life. In France alone toward the latter part of the century, as one example, about thirty groups for a brief time at least were considered active problems; of these, only four warrant inclusion above.

Appendix II

International Conventions on Terrorism

Twelve major multilateral conventions (below) relate to states' responsibilities for combating terrorism. In addition to these conventions, other instruments may be relevant to particular circumstances, such as bilateral extradition treaties, the 1961 Vienna Convention on Diplomatic Relations, and the 1963 Vienna Convention on Consular Relations. Moreover, there are now a number of important United Nations Security Council and General Assembly Resolutions on international terrorism, including three important Security Council resolutions dealing with Libya's conduct in connection with the 1988 sabotage of Pan Am 103. This latter set includes UN Security Council Resolutions 731 (January 21, 1992); 748 (March 31, 1992) and 883 (November 11, 1993).

The following list identifies the major terrorism conventions and provides a brief summary of some of the major terms of each instrument. In addition to the provisions summarized below, most of these conventions provide that parties must establish criminal jurisdiction over offenders (e.g., the state or states where the offense takes place, or in some cases the state of nationality of the perpetrator or victim).

1. *Convention on Offenses and Certain Other Acts Committed On Board Aircraft*

(*Tokyo Convention*, agreed September 1963):

* Applies to acts affecting in-flight safety.

* Authorizes the aircraft commander to impose reasonable measures, including restraint, on any person he or she has reason to believe has committed or is about to commit such an act, when necessary to protect the safety of the aircraft and for related reasons.

* Requires contracting states to take custody of offenders and to return control of the aircraft to the lawful commander.

2. *Convention for the Suppression of Unlawful Seizure of Aircraft* (*Hague Convention*, agreed December 1970):

* Makes it an offense for any person on board an aircraft in flight [to] "unlawfully, by force or threat thereof, or any other form of intimidation, [to] seize or exercise control of that aircraft" or to attempt to do so.

* Requires parties to the convention to make hijackings punishable by "severe penalties."

* Requires parties that have custody of offenders to either extradite the offender or submit the case for prosecution.

* Requires parties to assist each other in connection with criminal proceedings brought under the convention.

3. *Convention for the Suppression of Unlawful Acts Against the Safety of Civil Aviation (Montreal Convention, agreed September 1971— Acts of aviation sabotage such as bombings aboard aircraft in flight):*

* Makes it an offense for any person unlawfully and intentionally to perform an act of violence against a person on board an aircraft in flight, if that act is likely to endanger the safety of that aircraft; to place an explosive device on an aircraft; and to attempt such acts or be an accomplice of a person who performs or attempts to perform such acts.

* Requires parties to the convention to make offenses punishable by "severe penalties."

* Requires parties that have custody of offenders to either extradite the offender or submit the case for prosecution.

* Requires parties to assist each other in connection with criminal proceedings brought under the convention.

4. *Convention on the Prevention and Punishment of Crimes Against Internationally Protected Persons (agreed December 1973 — protects senior government officials and diplomats):*

* Defines internationally protected person as a Head of State, a Minister for Foreign Affairs, a representative or official of a state or of an international organization who is entitled to special protection from attack under international law.

* Requires each party to criminalize and make punishable "by appropriate penalties which take into account their grave nature," the intentional murder, kidnapping, or other attack upon the person or liberty of an internationally protected person, a violent attack upon the official premises, the private accommodations, or the means of transport of such person; a threat or attempt to commit such an attack; and an act "constituting participation as an accomplice."

* Requires parties that have custody of offenders to either extradite the offender or submit the case for prosecution.

* Requires parties to assist each other in connection with criminal proceedings brought under the convention.

5. *Convention on the Physical Protection of Nuclear Material (Nuclear Materials Convention, agreed October 1979):*

* Criminalizes the unlawful possession, use, transfer, etc., of nuclear material, the theft of nuclear material, and threats to use nuclear material to cause death or serious injury to any person or substantial property damage.

* Requires parties that have custody of offenders to either extradite the offender or submit the case for prosecution.

* Requires parties to assist each other in connection with criminal proceedings brought under the convention.

6. *International Convention Against the Taking of Hostages (Hostages Convention, agreed 12/79):*

* Provides that "any person who seizes or detains and threatens to kill, to injure, or to continue to detain another person in order to compel a third party, namely, a State, an international intergovernmental organization, a natural or juridical person, or a group of persons, to do or abstain from doing any act as an explicit or implicit condition for the release of the hostage commits the offense of taking of hostages within the meaning of this Convention."

* Requires parties that have custody of offenders to either extradite the offender or submit the case for prosecution.

* Requires parties to assist each other in connection with criminal proceedings brought under the convention.

7. *Protocol for the Suppression of Unlawful Acts of Violence at Airports Serving International Civil Aviation (agreed February*

1988 — extends and supplements Montreal Convention):

  * Extends the provisions of the Montreal Convention (see above) to encompass terrorist acts at airports serving international civil aviation.

8. *Convention for the Suppression of Unlawful Acts Against the Safety of Maritime Navigation, (agreed March 1988):*

  * Establishes a legal regime applicable to acts against international maritime navigation that is similar to the regimes established against international aviation.

  * Makes it an offense for a person unlawfully and intentionally to seize or exercise control over a ship by force, threat, or intimidation; to perform an act of violence against a person on board a ship if that act is likely to endanger the safe navigation of the ship; to place a destructive device or substance aboard a ship; and other acts against the safety of ships.

  * Requires parties that have custody of offenders to either extradite the offender or submit the case for prosecution.

  * Requires parties to assist each other in connection with criminal proceedings brought under the convention.

9. *Protocol for the Suppression of Unlawful Acts Against the Safety of Fixed Platforms Located on the Continental Shelf (agreed March 1988):*

  * Establishes a legal regime applicable to acts against fixed platforms on the continental shelf that is similar to the regimes established against international aviation.

  * Requires parties that have custody of offenders to either extradite the offender or submit the case for prosecution.

  * Requires parties to assist each other in connection with criminal proceedings brought under the protocol.

10. *Convention on the Marking of Plastic Explosives for the Purpose of Identification*

(agreed March 1991 — provides for chemical marking to facilitate detection of plastic explosives, e.g., to combat aircraft sabotage). Consists of two parts: the Convention itself, and a Technical Annex which is an integral part of the Convention.

  * Designed to control and limit the used of unmarked and undetectable plastic explosives (negotiated in the aftermath of the Pan Am 103 bombing).

  * Parties are obligated in their respective territories to ensure effective control over "unmarked" plastic explosive, i.e., those that do not contain one of the detection agents described in the Technical Annex.

  * Generally speaking, each party must, among other things: take necessary and effective measures to prohibit and prevent the manufacture of unmarked plastic explosives; take necessary and effective measures to prevent the movement of unmarked plastic explosives into or out of its territory; take necessary measures to exercise strict and effective control over possession and transfer of unmarked explosives made or imported prior to the entry-into-force of the convention; take necessary measures to ensure that all stocks of such unmarked explosives not held by the military or police are destroyed or consumed, marked, or rendered permanently ineffective within three years; take necessary measures to ensure that unmarked plastic explosives held by the military or police, are destroyed or consumed, marked, or rendered permanently ineffective within fifteen years; and, take necessary measures to ensure the destruction, as soon as possible, of any unmarked explosives manufactured after the date-of-entry into force of the convention for that state.

  * Does not itself create new offenses that would be subject to a prosecution or extradition regime, although all states are required to ensure that provisions are complied within their territories.

11. *International Convention for the Suppression of Terrorist Bombing (agreed December 1997 — expands the legal framework for international cooperation in the investigation, prosecution, and extradition of persons who engage in terrorist bombings):*

* Creates a regime of universal jurisdiction over the unlawful and intentional use of explosives and other lethal devices in, into, or against various defined public places with intent to kill or cause serious bodily injury, or with intent to cause extensive destruction of the public place.

* Like earlier conventions on protected persons and hostage taking, requires parties to criminalize, under their domestic laws, certain types of criminal offenses, and also requires parties to extradite or submit for prosecution persons accused of committing or aiding in the commission of such offenses.

12. *International Convention for the Suppression of the Financing of Terrorism (agreed 1999):*

* Requires parties to take steps to prevent and counteract the financing of terrorists, whether direct or indirect, though groups claiming to have charitable, social or cultural goals or which also engage in such illicit activities as drug trafficking or gun running.

* Commits states to hold those who finance terrorism criminally, civilly or administratively liable for such acts.

* Provides for the identification, freezing and seizure of funds allocated for terrorist activities, as well as for the sharing of the forfeited funds with other states on a case-by-case basis. Bank secrecy will no longer be justification for refusing to cooperate.

Note: During the negotiations on the Rome Statute of the International Criminal Court, many states supported adding terrorism to the list of crimes over which the court would have jurisdiction. This proposal was not adopted; however the Statute provides for a review conference to be held seven years after the entry into force of the Statute, which will consider (among other things) an extension of the court's jurisdiction to include terrorism.

Sources: www.wujuoedua.org/wiki/terrorism; UNODC.

Appendix III

United Nations Security Council Resolution 1373 (2001)

28 September 2001

"The Security Council,

"Reaffirming its resolutions 1269 (1999) of 19 October 1999 and 1368 (2001) of 12 September 2001,

"Reaffirming also its unequivocal condemnation of the terrorist attacks which took place in New York, Washington, D.C., and Pennsylvania on 11 September 2001, and expressing its determination to prevent all such acts,

"Reaffirming further that such acts, like any act of international terrorism, constitute a threat to international peace and security,

"Reaffirming the inherent right of individual or collective self-defense as recognized by the Charter of the United Nations as reiterated in resolution 1368 (2001),

"Reaffirming the need to combat by all means, in accordance with the Charter of the United Nations, threats to international peace and security caused by terrorist acts,

"Deeply concerned by the increase, in various regions of the world, of acts of terrorism motivated by intolerance or extremism,

"Calling on States to work together urgently to prevent and suppress terrorist acts, including through increased cooperation and full implementation of the relevant international conventions relating to terrorism,

"Recognizing the need for States to complement international cooperation by taking additional measures to prevent and suppress, in their territories through all lawful means, the financing and preparation of any acts of terrorism,

"Reaffirming the principle established by the General Assembly in its declaration of October 1970 (resolution 2625 (XXV)) and reiterated by the Security Council in its resolution 1189 (1998) of 13 August 1998, namely that every State has the duty to refrain from organizing, instigating, assisting or participating in terrorist acts in another State or acquiescing in organized activities within its territory directed towards the commission of such acts,

"Acting under Chapter VII of the Charter of the United Nations,

"1. Decides that all States shall:

"(a) Prevent and suppress the financing of terrorist acts;

"(b) Criminalize the willful provision or collection, by any means, directly or indirectly, of funds by their nationals or in their territories with the intention that the funds should be used, or in the knowledge that they are to be used, in order to carry out terrorist acts;

"(c) Freeze without delay funds and other financial assets or economic resources of persons who commit, or attempt to commit, terrorist acts or participate in or facilitate the commission of terrorist acts; of entities owned or controlled directly or indirectly by such persons; and of persons and entities acting on behalf of, or at the direction of such persons and entities, including funds derived or generated from property owned or controlled directly or indirectly by such persons and associated persons and entities;

"(d) Prohibit their nationals or any persons and entities within their territories from making any funds, financial assets or economic resources or financial or other related services available, directly or indirectly, for the benefit of persons who commit or attempt to commit or facilitate or participate in the commission of terrorist acts, of entities owned or controlled, directly or indirectly, by such persons and of persons and entities acting on behalf of or at the direction of such persons;

"2. Decides also that all States shall:

"(a) Refrain from providing any form of support, active or passive, to entities or persons involved in terrorist acts, including by suppressing recruitment of members of terrorist groups and eliminating the supply of weapons to terrorists;

"(b) Take the necessary steps to prevent the commission of terrorist acts, including by provision of early warning to other States by exchange of information;

"(c) Deny safe haven to those who finance, plan, support, or commit terrorist acts, or provide safe havens;

"(d) Prevent those who finance, plan, facilitate or commit terrorist acts from using

their respective territories for those purposes against other States or their citizens;

"(e) Ensure that any person who participates in the financing, planning, preparation or perpetration of terrorist acts or in supporting terrorist acts is brought to justice and ensure that, in addition to any other measures against them, such terrorist acts are established as serious criminal offences in domestic laws and regulations and that the punishment duly reflects the seriousness of such terrorist acts;

"(f) Afford one another the greatest measure of assistance in connection with criminal investigations or criminal proceedings relating to the financing or support of terrorist acts, including assistance in obtaining evidence in their possession necessary for the proceedings;

"(g) Prevent the movement of terrorists or terrorist groups by effective border controls and controls on issuance of identity papers and travel documents, and through measures for preventing counterfeiting, forgery or fraudulent use of identity papers and travel documents;

"3. Calls upon all States to:

"(a) Find ways of intensifying and accelerating the exchange of operational information, especially regarding actions or movements of terrorist persons or networks; forged or falsified travel documents; traffic in arms, explosives or sensitive materials; use of communications technologies by terrorist groups; and the threat posed by the possession of weapons of mass destruction by terrorist groups;

"(b) Exchange information in accordance with international and domestic law and cooperate on administrative and judicial matters to prevent the commission of terrorist acts;

"(c) Cooperate, particularly through bilateral and multilateral arrangements and agreements, to prevent and suppress terrorist attacks and take action against perpetrators of such acts;

"(d) Become parties as soon as possible to the relevant international conventions and protocols relating to terrorism, including the International Convention for the Suppression of the Financing of Terrorism of 9 December 1999;

"(e) Increase cooperation and fully implement the relevant international conventions and protocols relating to terrorism and Security Council resolutions 1269 (1999) and 1368 (2001);

"(f) Take appropriate measures in conformity with the relevant provisions of national and international law, including international standards of human rights, before granting refugee status, for the purpose of ensuring that the asylum seeker has not planned, facilitated or participated in the commission of terrorist acts;

"(g) Ensure, in conformity with international law, that refugee status is not abused by the perpetrators, organizers or facilitators of terrorist acts, and that claims of political motivation are not recognized as grounds for refusing requests for the extradition of alleged terrorists;

"4. Notes with concern the close connection between international terrorism and transnational organized crime, illicit drugs, money-laundering, illegal arms-trafficking, and illegal movement of nuclear, chemical, biological and other potentially deadly materials, and in this regard emphasizes the need to enhance coordination of efforts on national, subregional, regional and international levels in order to strengthen a global response to this serious challenge and threat to international security;

"5. Declares that acts, methods, and practices of terrorism are contrary to the purposes and principles of the United Nations and that knowingly financing, planning and inciting terrorist acts are also contrary to the purposes and principles of the United Nations;

"6. Decides to establish, in accordance with rule 28 of its provisional rules of procedure, a Committee of the Security Council, consisting of all the members of the Council, to monitor implementation of this resolution, with the assistance of appropriate expertise, and calls upon all States to report to the Committee, no later than 90 days from the date of adoption of this resolution and thereafter according to a timetable to be proposed by the Committee, on the steps they have taken to implement this resolution;

"7. Directs the Committee to delineate its tasks, submit a work programme within 30 days of the adoption of this resolution, and to consider the support it requires, in consultation with the Secretary-General;

"8. Expresses its determination to take all necessary steps in order to ensure the full implementation of this resolution, in accordance with its responsibilities under the Charter;

"9. Decides to remain seized of this matter."

Selected Bibliography

The published literature on terrorism is extensive, even if a listing is restricted to the English language. At the end of 2003, the small but excellent Ralph J. Bunche Library at the U. S. Department of State in Washington, D.C., for example, held more than 320 tiles relating directly to "terrorism," seventy-five relating to "Anarchism" and "nihilism," twenty to "Al Qaeda" and "Islam and terrorism," sixteen to aircraft hijacking, and no less than 113 titles in the collection relating to September 11, 2001. The list of publications on the subject continues to grow apace.

A comprehensive listing of books published in the field of terrorism as of its publication date (1988) is that in Schmid and Jongman, *Political Terrorism*. Walter Laqueur's 2001 study, *The New Terrorism*, includes an informative bibliographic essay. See below for citations to both of those publications. The following compilation of book-length studies draws selectively from, among other sources, the inquiries of those authors and it benefits from their scholarship. The listing is restricted to those in English, the language of the present study.

I. Books

Alexander, Yonah, ed. *International Terrorism: National, Regional, and Global Perspectives.* New York: Praeger, 1976.

_____, and Kenneth A. Myers. *Terrorism in Europe.* New York: St. Martin's, 1982.

_____, and Alan O'Day, eds. *Terrorism in Ireland.* London: Croom Helm, 1984.

Anderson, Sean. *Historical Dictionary of Terrorism*, 2d ed. Lanham, MD: Scarecrow, 2002.

Anzovin, Steven, ed. *Terrorism.* New York: H. W. Wilson, 1986.

Atkins, Stephen E. *Terrorism: A Reference Handbook.* Santa Barbara, CA: ABC-CLIO, 1992.

Baumann, Carol Edler. *The Diplomatic Kidnappings: A Revolutionary Tactic of Urban Terrorism.* The Hague: Nijhoff, 1973.

Becker, Jillian. *Hitler's Children: The Story of the Baader-Meinhof Gang.* London: Granada, 1977.

Benjamin, Daniel, and Steven Simon. *The Age of Sacred Terror.* New York: Random House, 2002.

Bethell, Nicholas. *The Palestine Triangle: The Struggle between the British, the Jews and the Arabs, 1935-48.* London: Deutsch, 1979.

Brogan, Patrick. *World Conflicts.* London: Bloomsbury, 1989.

Brown, G., and M. Wallace, eds. *Terrorism.* New York: NY Times, 1979.

Carr, Caleb. *The Lessons of Terror: a History of Warfare Against Civilians.* New York: Random House, 2002.

Chapman, Robert D., and M. Lester Chapman. *The Crimson Web of Terror.* Boulder, CO: Paladin, 1980.

Clarke, James W. *American Assassins: The Darker Side of Politics.* Princeton, NJ: Princeton, 1982.

Cline, Ray S., and Yonah Alexander. *Terrorism: the Soviet Connection.* New York: Crane, Russak, 1984.

Clutterbuck, Richard. *Guerrillas and Terrorists.* Athens: Ohio U., 1980.

_____. *The Media and Political Violence.* London: Macmillan, 1981.

_____. *Kidnap, Hijack and Extortion: The Response.* New York: St. Martin's, 1987.

_____. *Terrorism, Drugs and Crime in Europe After*

1992. New York: Routledge, Chapman & Hall, 1990.

Combs, Cindy C. *Terrorism in the Twenty-First Century,* 2d ed. Upper Saddle River, NJ: Prentice Hall, 2000.

Coogan, Tim Pat. *The IRA: A History.* Niwot, CO: Roberts Rinehart, 1993.

Courtois, Stéphan, et al. T*he Black Book of Communism: Crimes, Terror, Repression.* Cambridge, MA: Harvard, 1999. (Translated from the French by Jonathan Murphy & Mark Karmer.)

Crenshaw, M., ed. *Terrorism, Legitimacy, and Power: the Consequences of Political Violence.* Middletown, CT: Wesleyan U, 1983.

_____, and John Pimlott, eds. *International Encyclopedia of Terrorism.* Chicago: Fitzroy Dearborn, 1998.

Cronin, Isaac, ed. *Confronting Fear: A History of Terrorism.* New York: Thunder's Mouth, 2002.

Daniel, Clifton, ed. *Chronicle of the 20th Century.* London: DK, 1995.

Davis, Joyce M. *Martyrs: Innocence, Vengeance and Despair in the Middle East.* London: Palgrave Macmillan, 2003.

Davis, Lee. *Man-Made Catastrophes: From the Burning of Rome to the Lockerbie Crash.* New York: Facts on File, 1993.

Dershowitz, Alan M. *Why Terrorism Works.* New Haven: Yale, 2002.

Dobson, Christopher, and Ronald Payne. *The Terrorists: Their Weapons, Leaders, and Tactics.* New York: Facts on File, 1982.

_____ and _____. *War Without End. The Terrorists: An Intelligence Dossier.* Bury St. Edmonds, Suffolk: Sphere, 1987.

Elliott, Paul. *Assassin! The Bloody History of Political Murder.* London: Blandford, 1999.

_____. *Brotherhoods of Fear: A History of Violent Organizations.* London: Blandford, 1998.

_____. *Warrior Cults.* London: Blandford, 1995.

Esposito, John L. *Islam and Politics.* 4th ed. Syracuse: Syracuse Univ., 1998.

_____. *The Islamic Threat: Myth or Reality?* 3d ed. New York: Oxford, 1999.

_____. *Unholy War: Terror in the Name of Islam.* New York: Oxford, 2002.

Evron, Y. *International Violence: Terrorism, Surprise and Control.* Jerusalem: Hebrew U., 1979.

Featherling, George. *The Book of Assassins: A Biographical Dictionary from Ancient Times to the Present.* New York: John Wiley & Sons, 2001.

Figes, Orlando. *A People's Tragedy: A History of the Russian Revolution, 1891-1924.* New York: Penguin, 1998.

Ford, Franklin L. *Political Murder: From Tryrannicide to Terrorism.* Cambridge: Harvard, 1985.

Gökay, Bülent and R. J. B. Walker, eds. *11 September 2001: War, Terror, and Judgment.* London: Frank Cass, 2003.

Gordon, Lois, and Alan Gordon. *American Chronicle: Year by Year through the Twentieth Century.* New Haven: Yale, 1999.

Grover, Verinder, ed. *Encyclopaedia of International Terrorism.* New Delhi: Deep & Deep, 2002.

Grun, Bernard. *The Timetables of History: A Horizontal Linkage of People and Events.* New York: Touchstone, 1991.

Gunter, Michael M. *"Pursuing the Just Cause of the People"— A Study of Contemporary American Terrorism.* New York: Greenwood, 1985.

Gutteridge, William, ed. *Contemporary Terrorism.* New York: Facts on File, 1986.

Hacker, Frederick J. *Crusaders, Criminals, Crazies: Terror and Terrorism in our Time.* New York: Norton, 1996.

Halliday, Fred. *Islam and the Myth of Confrontation: Religion and Politics in the Middle East.* London: Tauris, 1996.

_____. *Two Hours That Shook the World September 11, 2001: Causes & Consequences.* London: Saqi Books, 2002.

Han, Henry H. *Terrorism, Political Violence, and World Order.* Lanham, MD: Univ. Press of Amer., 1984.

Hanle, Donald. *Terrorism: The Newest Face of Warfare.* Washington: Pergamon-Brasseys, 1989.

Hayes, David. *Terrorists and Freedom Fighters.* Watton, Norfolk, England: Wayland, 1980.

Heaps, Willard A. *Assassination: A Special Kind of Murder.* New York: Meredith, 1969.

Hildermeier, Manfred. *The Russian Socialist Revolutionary Party Before the First World War.* New York: St. Martin's, 2000.

Hoffman, Bruce. *Inside Terrorism.* New York: Columbia, 1998.

Hudson, Miles. *Assassination.* Phenix Mill, Glostershire, England: Sutton, 2000.

Hudson, Rex A., et al. *Who Becomes a Terrorist and Why: The 1999 Government Report on Profiling Terrorists.* Guilford, CT: Lyons, 1999.

Jane's World Insurgency and Terrorism. Alexandria, VA: Jane's Information Group, 1999.

Jentleson, Bruce W., and Thomas G. Paterson, sr. eds. *Encyclopedia of U. S. Foreign Relations.* Vol. 4. New York: Oxford, 1997.

Juergensmeyer, Mark. *Terror in the Mind of God: The Global Rise of Religious Violence.* Los Angeles: University of California Press, 2000.

Kedward, Roderick. *The Anarchists.* London: Macdonald, 1971.

Kelley, Kevin. *The Longest War: Northern Ireland and the IRA.* New York: Brandon, Lawrence Hill, 1982.

Korn, David A. *Assassination in Khartoum.* Bloomington: Indiana U., 1993.

Laqueur, Walter. *The Age of Terrorism.* Boston: Little, Brown, 1987.

_____. *A History of Terrorism.* New Brunswick, NJ: Transaction, 2001.

_____. *The New Terrorism: Fanaticism and the Arms of Mass Destruction.* New York: Oxford, 1999.

Lentz III, Harris M. *Assassinations and Executions: An Encyclopedia of Political Violence 1865-1986.* Jefferson, NC: McFarland, 1986.

Lesberg, Sandy. *Assassination in Our Time.* London: Preebles, 1976.

Liston, Robert A. *Terrorism.* Nashville: Thomas Nelson, 1979.

Lodge, Juliet. *Terrorism: A Challenge to the State.* New York: St. Martin's, 1981.

Long, David E. *The Anatomy of Terrorism.* New York: Free Press, 1990.

MacKinley, James. *Assassination in America.* New York: Harper & Row, 1977.

Merkl, Peter H., ed. *Political Violence and Terror: Motifs and Motivations.* Berkeley: U. of Cal., 1986.

Metlzer, Milton. *The Terrorists.* New York: Harper & Row, 1983.

Mickolus, Edward F. *International Terrorism: Attributes of Terrorist Events, 1968-1977.* Ann Arbor, MI: Inter-university Consortium for Political and Social Research, 1982.

_____. *International Terrorism: A Chronology of Events, 1968 — 1979.* Westport, CT: Greenwood, 1980.

_____. *International Terrorism in the 1980's: A Chronology of Events.* Ames: Iowa State, 1989.

_____. *The Literature of Terrorism: A Selectively Annotated Bibliography.* New York: Greenwood, 1988.

_____. *Terrorism, 1980–1987: A Selectively Annotated Bibliography.* New York: Greenwood, 1988.

_____. *Terrorism, 1992-1995: A Chronology of Events and a Selectively Annotated Bibliography.* Westport, CT: Greenwood, 1997.

Mommsen, Wolfgang J., and Gerhard Hirschfeld, eds. *Social Protest, Violence and Terror in Nineteenth- and Twentieth-Century Europe.* London: Berg, 1982.

Moss, R. *Urban Guerrillas: The New Face of Political Violence.* London: Temple Smith, 1972.

Moxon-Browne, Edward. *Spain and the ETA: The Bid for Basque Autonomy.* London: Center for Security and Conflict Studies, 1989.

O'Ballance, Edgar. *Islamic Fundamentalist Terrorism, 1979-95: The Iranian Connection.* New York: New York U., 1997.

_____. *The Palestinian Infitada.* New York: St. Martin's, 1998.

_____. *Terror in Ireland: The Heritage of Hate.* Novato, CA: Presidio, 1981.

Nash, Jay Robert. *Encyclopedia of World Crime: Criminal Jurisdiction, Criminals, and Law Enforcement.* 4 Vols. Wilmette, IL: CrimeBooks, 1990.

_____. *Terrorism in the 20th Century: A Narrative Encyclopedia from the Anarchists, through the Weathermen, to the Unabomber.* New York: M. Evans, 1998.

O'Kane, Rosemary H. T. *The Revolutionary Reign of Terror: The Role of Violence in Political Change.* Aldershot, England: Edw. Elgar, 1991.

O'Sullivan, Noel, ed. *Terrorism, Ideology, and Revolution.* Boulder: Westview, 1986.

Parry, Albert. *Terrorism from Robespierre to Arafat.* New York: Vanguard, 1976.

Pilar, Paul R. *Terrorism and U. S. Foreign Policy.* Washington: Brookings, 2001.

Rapoport, David C., and Yonah Alexander, eds. *The Rationalization of Terrorism.* Frederick, MD: Univ. Publ. of Amer., 1982.

Raynor, Thomas. *Terrorism: Past, Present, Future.* New York: Watts, 1982.

Rubenstein, Richard E. *Alchemist of Revolution: Terrorism in the Modern World.* New York: Basic Books, 1987.

Rubin, Barry, ed. *The Politics of Terrorism: Terror as a State and Revolutionary Strategy.* Washington: Johns Hopkins, 1989.

Schmid, Alex P. and Albert J. Jongman, *Political Terrorism: A New Guide to Actors, Authors, Concepts, Data Bases, Theories and Literature.* Amsterdam: North Holland, 1983, rev. 1988.

_____, and Janny de Graaf. *Violence as Communication: Insurgent Terrorism and the Western News Media.* London: Sage, 1982.

Schwarz, Fred. *The Three Faces of Revolution.* Washington: Capitol Hill, 1972.

Segaller, Stephen, *Terrorism into the 1990s.* London: Sphere Books, 1987.

Sobel, Lester A. *Political Terrorism.* New York: Facts on File, 1975.

Sterling, Claire. *The Terror Network: The Secret War of International Terrorism.* New York: Holt, Rinehart and Winston, 1981.

Stern, Jessica. *Terror in the Name of God.* New York: HarperCollins, 2003.

Stohl, Michael. *The Politics of Terrorism.* New York: Dekker, 1983.

Taheri, Amir. *Holy Terror: Inside the World of Islamic Terrorism.* Bethesda, MD: Adler & Adler, 1987.

Tanter, Raymond. *Rogue Regimes: Terrorism and Proliferation.* New York: St. Martin's, 1998.

Taylor, Maxwell. *The Terrorists.* London: Brassey's, 1988.

Trayer, James. *The People's Chronology: A Year-by-Year Record of Human Events from Prehistory to the Present.* New York: Henry Holt, 1992.

Ulam, Adam B. *The Bolsheviks*. New York: Collier, 1976.

Wardlaw, Grant. *Political Terrorism: Theory, Tactics, and Counter-Measures*. 2d. ed. Cambridge: Cambridge U., 1989.

Warner, Martin, and Roger Crips, eds. *Terrorism, Protest and Power*. Aldershot, England: Elgar, 1990.

Whittaker, David J., ed. *Terrorism: Understanding the Global Threat*. London: Longman, 2002.

_____. *The Terrorism Reader*. New York: Routledge, 2001.

Wolfgang, Marvin E. *International Terrorism*. Beverly Hills: Sage, 1982.

II. Encyclopedias

Crenshaw, Martha and John Pimlott, eds. *Encyclopedia of World Terrorism*. Armonk, NY: Sharpe Reference, 1997.

Kushner, Harvey W. *Encyclopedia of Terrorism*. Thousand Oaks, CA: Sage Publications, 2003.

Sifakis, Carl. *Encyclopedia of Assassinations*. London: Headline, 1993.

Thackrah, John Richard. *Encyclopedia of Terrorism and Political Violence*. London and New York: Routledge & Kegan Paul, 1987.

III. Government Publications

U. S. Department of State. *Patterns of Global Terrorism*. Publication 10535, Annual Report to Congress, 1990 — 2002.

IV. Newspapers

Boston Globe online news archives, 1979-2001. http://www.boston.com/globe/search.

New York Times Historical Newspaper, 1901-1999, online

IV. Worldwide Web Sites

http://avpv.tripod.com/AmericanVictims.html
http://cain.ulst.ac.uk/1
http://globalspecops.com/terchron.html
http://lexicorient.com/e.o/index.htm
http://middleeastreference.org.uk/
http://1920s.net
http://onwar.com
http://www.afa.org/magazine/Feb2002/0202terror
http://www.armscontrolcenter.org/terrorism/101/timeline.html
http://www.atmg.org/ArmenianTerrorism.html
http://baader-meinhof.com/timeline
http://www.din-timelines.com
http://www.emergency-management.net/airterror_acts.htm
http://www.fortunecity.com/bally/sligo/93/past/troubles/
http://www.frankcass.com/jnls/tpv.htm
http://www.israel.org/mfa/go
http://www.marxists.org
http://www.mediasnews.com/chrono
http://www.multied.com
http://www.specialoperations.com/Terrorism/
http://www.state,gov/
http://www.terrorism.com/
http://www.terrorismanswers.com/
http://www.turkishforum.com/
http://www.wikipdia.org/wiki/terrorism

Index